Financial Management

For the US CPA Exam

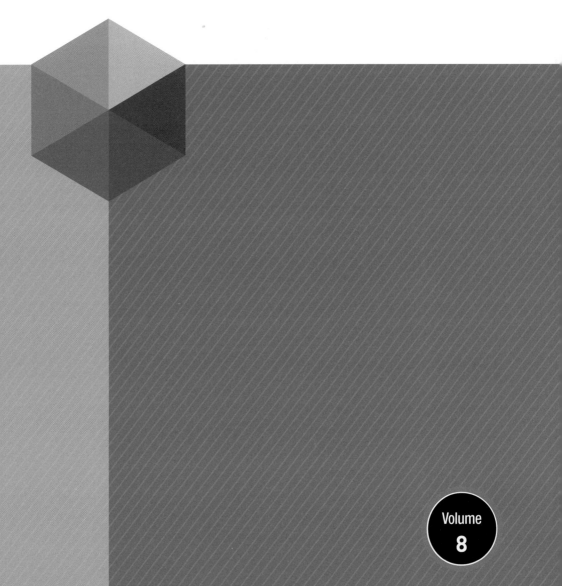

Volume
8

목 차

Chapter 04 | Interest Rate and Risk

Chapter 05 | Capital Structure

Chapter 06 | Capital Budgeting

Chapter 10 | Market Influences on Business

Chapter 11 | Enterprise Risk Management Frameworks

부록

서문 · Preface

Financial Management for the US CPA Exam 의 특징입니다.

● WHO?

미국 공인회계사 시험을 응시하는 수험생을 대상으로 한 교재이다. 미국 공인회계사 시험 4과목 중 하나인 'Business Analysis and Reporting (BAR)' 과목에서 중요한 부분을 차지하고 있는 'Business Analysis' 영역을 대비하기 위한 교재이다.

● WHAT?

미국공인회계사 시험의 추세 및 난이도에 맞게 구성된 내용으로 장마다 미국 공인회계사 시험에 출제되는 'Task-Based Simulation' 유형의 문제를 대비하기 위한 문제를 수록하였다. 또한 미국 관리회계사 자격증인 CMA(certified management accountant)의 MCQ(multiple choice questions) 기출문제를 포함하였다. 시험에서 사용하고 있는 엑셀(Excel)기능을 대비하도록 Excel을 이용한 풀이도 설명하였다.

● HOW?

미국공인회계사 오랜 강의 경력의 경험과 노하우를 압축한 교재이다. 'Business Analysis and Reporting (BAR)' 과목은 Discipline exam의 과목이므로 Core exam보다 난이도가 높다.
따라서 Financial Management에서 높은 점수를 획득하여야 하므로 이 교재와 강의로 스마트한 합격을 기원한다.

● CHAPTER

본서의 구성은 다음과 같다. 1장~4장은 재무관리의 기초개념의 내용이며, 5장~9장은 재무관리의 의사결정에 대한 내용이다. 10장은 시험에서 출제되는 경제학의 내용이며, 11장은 기업의 위험관리 규정에 대한 내용이다.

A house of cards

"기초가 약하면 오래가지 못한다."

이 책은 관리회계 공부를 시작하는 학습자들에게 반석처럼 튼튼한 기초를 만들어 줄 것이다.

공인회계사 / 미국공인회계사 / 미국재무분석사(**CFA**)

김용석.

⊚ CBT Introduction ● ● ● ● ● ● ● ● ● ●

Ⅰ. CBT 과목구성

미국 공인회계사 시험은 2004년도에 PBT에서 CBT로 변경이 되었으며, 2017년에는 TBS(Task-Based Simulation)의 비중을 높인 새로운 방식으로 변경되었다. 2023년에 시험제도는 새롭게 변경이 되어 2024년 1월 1일 이후의 시험은 아래의 표와 같다.

Section	Section time	MCQ	TBS
AUD-Core	4 hours	50%(78)	50%(7)
FAR-Core	4 hours	50%(50)	50%(7)
REG-Core	4 hours	50%(72)	50%(8)
BAR-Discipline	4 hours	50%(50)	50%(7)
ISC-Discipline	4 hours	60%(82)	40%(6)
TCP-Discipline	4 hours	50%(68)	50%(7)

MCQ : Multiple Choices Questions
TBS: Task-Based Simulation

The CPA licensure model requires all candidates to pass three Core exam sections and one Discipline exam section of a candidate's choosing.

The Core exam sections assess the knowledge and skills that all newly licensed CPAs (nlCPAs) need in their role to protect the public interest. The three Core exam sections, each four hours long, are: Auditing and Attestation(AUD), Financial Accounting and Reporting (FAR) and Taxation and Regulation(REG).

The Discipline exam sections assess the knowledge and skills in the respective Discipline domain applicable to nlCPAs in their role to protect the public interest.The three Discipline exam sections, each four hours long, are: Business Analysis and Reporting (BAR), Information Systems and Controls (ISC) and Tax Compliance and Planning (TCP).

II. Business Analysis and Reporting (BAR)

The Business Analysis and Reporting section of the Uniform CPA Examination assesses the knowledge and skills nlCPAs must demonstrate with respect to:

- Financial statement and financial information analysis with a focus on an nlCPA's role in comparing historical results to budgets and forecasts, deriving the impact of transactions, events (actual and proposed) and market conditions on financial and nonfinancial performance measures and comparing investment alternatives.

- Select technical accounting and reporting requirements under the Financial Accounting Standards Board (FASB) Accounting Standards Codification and the U.S. Securities and Exchange Commission (SEC) that are applicable to for-profit business entities and employee benefit plans.

- Financial accounting and reporting requirements under the Governmental Accounting Standards Board (GASB) that are applicable to state and local government entities.

The following table summarizes the content areas and the allocation of content tested in the BAR section of the Exam:

	Content area	Allocation
Area I	Business Analysis	40~50%
Area II	Technical Accounting and Reporting	35~45%
Area III	State and Local Governments	10~20%

(1) Area I : Business Analysis

- Financial statement analysis, including comparison of current period financial statements to prior period or budget and interpretation of financial statement fluctuations and ratios.

- Non-financial and non-GAAP measures of performance, including use of the balanced scorecard approach and interpretation of non-financial and non-GAAP measures to assess an entity's performance and risk profile.

- Managerial and cost accounting concepts and the use of variance analysis techniques.

- Budgeting, forecasting and projection techniques.

- Factors that influence an entity's capital structure, such as leverage, cost of capital, liquidity and loan covenants.

- Financial valuation decision models used to compare investment alternatives.

- The Committee of Sponsoring Organizations of the Treadway Commission (COSO) Enterprise Risk Management framework, including how it applies to environmental, social and governance (ESG) related risks.

- The effect of changes in economic conditions and market influences on an entity's business.

(2) Area II : Technical Accounting and Reporting

- Indefinite-lived intangible assets, including goodwill.

- Internally developed software.

- Revenue recognition, specifically focusing on the analysis and interpretation of agreements, contracts and other supporting documentation to determine whether revenue was appropriately recognized.

- Stock compensation.

- Research and development costs.

- Business combinations.

- Consolidated financial statements, specifically focusing on topics including variable interest entities, noncontrolling interests, functional currency and foreign currency translation adjustments.

- Derivatives and hedge accounting.

- Leases, specifically focusing on recalling and applying lessor accounting requirements and analyzing the provisions of a lease agreement to determine

- whether a lessee appropriately accounted for the lease.

- Public company reporting topics, specifically focusing on Regulation S-X, Regulation S-K and segment reporting.

- Financial statements of employee benefit plans.

(3) Area III : State and Local Governments

- Basic concepts and principles of the government-wide, governmental funds, proprietary funds and fiduciary funds financial statements.

- Preparing government-wide, governmental funds, proprietary funds and fiduciary funds financial statements and other components of the financial section of the annual comprehensive financial report.

- Deriving the government-wide financial statements and reconciliation requirements.

- Accounting for specific types of transactions such as net position, fund balances, capital assets, long-term liabilities, interfund activity, nonexchange revenue, expenditures and expenses and budgetary accounting within the governmental entity financial statements.

Financial Management For the **US CPA** Exam

Chapter 01

Financial Management

Volume
8

Financial Management

01 The Functions of Financial Management

재무관리는 자본조달과 투자결정에 관한 의사결정을 공부하는 학문이다. 재무관리는 크게 기업 재무(corporate finance)와 투자론(investments)으로 분류할 수 있다.

기업재무(corporate finance)는 주로 기업의 관점에서 자금을 조달하고 운용하는 문제를 다루는 영역으로서, 좁은 의미의 재무관리라고 하면 기업재무를 일컫는다. 구체적으로는 주식이나 부채 로 자금을 조달하고 이렇게 조달한 자금을 생산설비를 구입하는 등 실물투자와 관련된 의사결정을 연구대상으로 한다. 미국 공인회계사 시험목적으로의 재무관리는 주로 기업재무를 말하며, 이 책 은 대부분 기업재무를 주로 다룬다.

투자론(investments)은 투자자의 관점에서 주식 또는 채권 등 증권투자와 관련된 문제를 다루는 영역이다. 구체적으로는 증권의 균형가격을 도출하고 이를 이용하여 시장가격의 과소평가 또는 과 대평가의 판단을 한다.

재무관리의 기능은 일반적으로 재무상태표를 중심으로 설명된다. 재무상태표의 부채와 자본은 자금조달의 형태를 나타내고, 자산은 조달한 자금을 운용한 상황을 나타낸다.

자산 측면에서 볼 때 재무관리의 중요한 기능은 투자결정(investment decision)기능이다. 구체적 으로는 건물, 기계설비 등 고정자산에 대한 투자결정을 하는 자본예산(capital budgeting)과 유동자 산과 관련된 운전자본관리(working capital management)이다.

부채와 자본은 자산투자를 위해서 기업이 조달한 자금의 형태를 나타내는 것인데, 이와 관련된 재무관리 기능은 자본조달결정(financing decision)기능이다. 구체적으로는 자본을 조달하면서 부 담하게 되는 자본비용을 최소화시키는 문제를 다루는 자본구조이론(capital structure)과 기업의 이익을 배당과 유보이익으로 결정하는 배당이론(dividend theory)이다.

　재무관리의 기능 중 하나는 위험관리이다. 위험관리(risk management)란 투자자가 적절한 기법을 이용해서 자신의 투자목적에 따라서 미래현금흐름의 변동가능성을 관리하는 것을 말한다. 위험관리를 통해서 얻을 수 있는 효과는 헤지(hedge)효과로서, 헤지란 위험을 감소하거나 제거하는 효과를 말하며, 이러한 효과에 유용한 수단이 파생금융상품(financial derivatives)으로서 이를 이용하여 불확실한 투자환경에서 안정적인 수익을 확보할 수 있다. 재무관리의 기능을 요약하면 다음과 같다.

Investment decision	Capital budgeting	Decision for long-term assets
	Working capital management	Decision for current assets & current liabilities
Financing decision	Capital structure	Decision for minimization of cost of capital
	Dividend theory	Decision for dividend & retained earnings
Risk management	Derivative instruments Hedge	

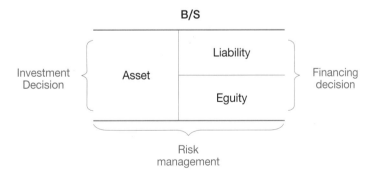

02 ▷▷ The Organizational Structure of the Firm

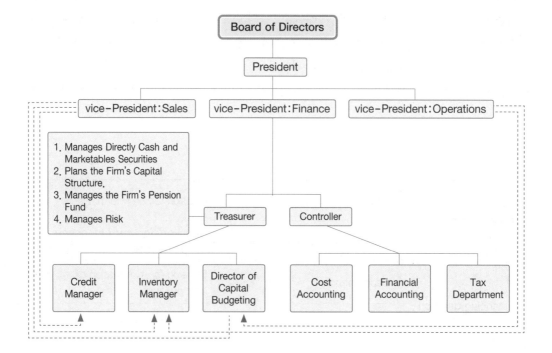

- Chief Executive Officer (CEO)

  heads the management team, and ideally is separate from chairman of the board.

- Chief Operating Officer (COO)

  In charge of the firm's actual operations.

- Chief information officer (CIO)

  the most senior executive in an enterprise who works for the traditional information technology and computer systems that support enterprise goals.

- Chief Financial Officer (CFO)

  responsible for the accounting system, raising capital, and evaluating major investment decisions and the effectiveness of operations.

- Controller

  a senior position who oversees the quality of accounting and financial reporting of an organization, implements and monitors internal controls and reports to the CFO.

- Treasurer

  the person responsible for running the treasury of an organization (including cash and liquidity management, risk management, and corporate finance) and reporting to the CFO.

- Audit committee

  an operating committee of the board of directors charged with oversight of financial reporting and disclosure.

  - Overseeing the financial reporting and disclosure process.
  - Monitoring choice of accounting policies and principles.
  - Overseeing hiring, performance and independence of the external auditors.
  - Oversight of regulatory compliance and ethics.
  - Monitoring the internal control process.
  - Overseeing the performance of the internal audit function.
  - Discussing risk management policies and practices with management.

03 ▶ The Goals of Financial Management

1 Firm value maximization

재무관리의 목표는 기업의 가치를 극대화시키는 데에 있다. 여기서 기업가치란 재무상태표의 기업의 총자산가치를 의미하는 것으로, 기업의 소유주를 채권자와 주주로 보고 계산한 미래현금흐름의 현재가치이다. 기업 가치를 계산하기 위한 현금흐름은 기업잉여현금흐름(FCFF : free cash flows to firm)이며, 할인율은 가중평균자본비용(WACC : weighted average cost of capital)이다. 이에 대한 자세한 내용은 5장과 6장에서 설명한다.

$$V = \sum_{t=1}^{n} \frac{CF_t}{(1+R)^t} = \sum_{t=1}^{n} \frac{FCFF_t}{(1+k)^t}$$

FCFF : Free cash flows to firm (기업잉여현금흐름)
k : Cost of capital (자본비용)

2 Shareholders wealth maximization

기업가치의 극대화 목표는 채권자와 주주의 몫을 합한 것을 최대로 한다는 것이다. 하지만 채권자의 몫은 기업가치에 관계없이 일정하나, 주주의 몫은 기업가치에 비례하여 변화하기 때문에 기업의 미래성과에 대한 위험을 궁극적으로 부담하는 자본제공자인 주주를 진정한 기업의 소유주로 보는 관점이 자기자본가치의 극대화 목표이다.

자기자본이 가지고 있는 권리는 주식의 형태로 거래되므로 자기자본가치의 극대화는 곧 주식가치의 극대화(maximization of stock price)이다.

대체로 타인자본의 가치가 일정하므로 기업가치의 극대화 목표는 자기자본의 가치를 극대화 하는 목표와 일치한다.

3 Profit maximization

주당이익(EPS)를 가장 높일 수 있는 방안을 기업의 목표로 세우는 것을 말한다.

그러나 이익 극대화는 단기적인 안목에 치울 칠 가능성이 높고, 다음과 같은 요소들을 간과하기 때문에 재무관리의 목표로는 적합하지 않다.

- 이익개념의 모호성

- 시간성의 무시

- 이익실현의 불확실성 무시

- 자기자본비용의 무시

회계이익의 크기는 회계처리방법에 따라 크게 달라질 수 있다. 예를 들어 재고자산을 평가하는 방법이나 유형자산의 감가상각방법을 어떻게 적용하는지에 따라 회계이익은 달라진다.

선입선출 (FIFO) 평가방법은 기말재고를 최근에 구입한 재고로 평가하므로, 물가 상승 시에 기말재고를 크게 평가하여 매출원가를 줄여서 이익을 극대화 한다. 하지만 이익이 커져 법인세를 빨리 납부하여야 하므로 세후 현금흐름의 현재가치가 감소하기 때문에 이 방법은 다른 방법과 비교할 때 기업 가치를 감소시킨다.

04 ▷ Financial Statements for Finance

1 Financial Position (Balance Sheet)

기업가치 평가를 위하여 회계기준(GAAP)의 재무제표는 재구성하여야 한다. 회계기준의 재무제표는 기업의 소유주를 주주로 보는 것이라면, 재구성한 재무제표는 기업의 소유주를 채권자와 주주로 보는 것이 때문이다.

재무상태표를 재구성하면 다음과 같다.

GAAP	Finance
Asset = Liability + Equity	Capital(총자본) = Debt(타인자본) + Equity (자기자본)

회계기준에서 보고하는 부채를 실물시장에서 발생하여 이자비용이 지급되지 않는 영업부채(Operating Liability)와 금융시장에서 발생하여 이자비용이 지급되는 타인자본(Debt)으로 구분한다.

$$Liability = Operating\ Liability + Debt$$

$$Debt = Liability - Operating\ Liability$$

총자본(Capital)은 타인자본과 자기자본의 합이며, 총자산은 부채와 자기자본의 합이므로 이를 정리하면 다음과 같다.

$$Capital = Asset - Operating\ Liability$$

2 Income Statement

기업가치 평가를 위하여 회계기준(GAAP)의 손익계산서는 재구성하여야 한다. 회계기준의 재무
제표는 주주에게 귀속하는 이익을 측정하지만, 가치평가를 위한 손익계산서는 주주와 채권자 모두
에게 귀속하는 이익을 측정한다.

Financial Accounting		Managerial Accounting		Finance	
(1) Sales	xxx	(1) Sales	xxx	(1) Sales	xxx
(2) COGS	(xxx)	(2) VC	(xxx)	(2) CO	(xxx)
(3) GP	xxx	(3) CM	xxx	(3) EBITDA	xxx
(4) S&A	(xxx)	(4) FC	(xxx)	(4) D&A	(xxx)
(5) EBIT	xxx	(5) EBIT	xxx	(5) EBIT	xxx
(6) I	(xxx)			(6) T	(xxx)
(7) EBT	xxx			(7) NOPAT	xxx
(8) T	(xxx)				
(9) NI	xxx				

COGS : Cost of goods sold

GP : Gross profit

S&A : Selling and administrative expenses

EBIT : Earnings before interest and taxes

I : Interest expense

T : Income tax expense

NI : Net income

VC : Variable cost

CM : Contribution margin

FC : Fixed cost

CO : Cash operating cost

D&A : Depreciation & amortization expense

EBITDA : Earning before interest, Taxes, depreciation & amortization

NOPAT : Net operating profit after tax

t : income tax rate

회계기준의 이익과 기업가치 평가를 위한 이익간의 관계를 정리하면 다음과 같다.

$$NI = (EBIT - I) \times (1 - t)$$
$$= EBIT \times (1 - t) - I \times (1 - t) \leftarrow NOPAT = EBIT \times (1 - t)$$
$$= NOPAT - I \times (1 - t)$$

$$NOPAT = NI + I \times (1 - t)$$
$$EBIT = NI + T + I$$

Comprehensive example

Balance sheet			
Cash & cash equivalents	400	Account payables	400
Marketable securities	200	Note payables	500
Account receivables	900	Long-term debt	600
Inventories	200	Common stock	1000
Property, plant & equipment	1200	Retained earnings	400
Total assets	2900	Total liabilities & equity	2900

Operating liability = Account payables = 400
Debt = Note payables + Long − term debt = 500 + 600 = 1100
Equity = Common stock + Retained earnings = 1000 + 400 = 1400
Capital = 2900 − 400 = 1100 + 1400 = 2500

Income statement	
Sales	4000
Cost of goods sold	3000
Gross profit	1000
Operating expenses (S&A)	650
Operating income	350
Interest expense	50
Earning before tax	300
Income taxes(20%)	60
Net income	240

$$NOPAT = NI + I \times (1-t) = 240 + 50 \times (1-0.2) = 280$$
$$EBIT = NI + I + T = 240 + 60 + 50 = 350$$

3 The flows of financial management

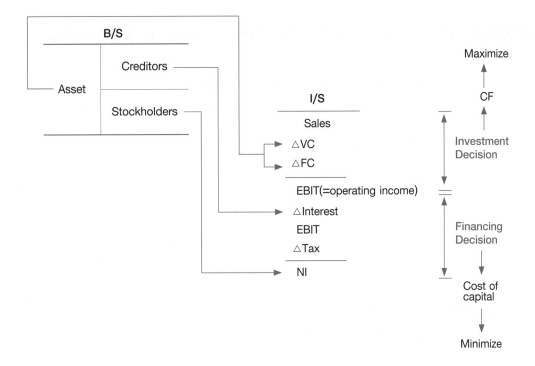

05 ▶ Agency Problems

1 A conflict of interests between the principal and the agent

대리관계란 위임자(principal)가 의사결정권한을 대리인(agent)에게 위임한 계약관계를 말하는데, 재무관리에서는 기업을 직접 경영하는 경영자는 주주의 자본을 제공받아 의사결정을 하므로, 주주는 위임자가 되고 경영자는 대리인이 된다.

대리인이 전적으로 위임자의 효용을 극대화하도록 의사결정을 한다면 가장 바람직한 의사결정이 되겠지만 현실적으로는 그렇지 못하다. 왜냐하면 대리인과 위임자는 목표가 서로 다르고, 또한 서로 보유한 정보가 똑같이 않기 때문이다. 이러한 목표불일치(goal incongruency)와 정보비대칭성(information asymmetry)으로 인해서 나타나는 부의 손실을 대리 비용(agency cost)이라고 하며 다음과 같이 분류된다.

(1) Monitoring cost (감시비용)

대리인의 행위가 위임자의 이익으로부터 이탈하는 것을 감시하는 비용

(2) Bonding cost (확증비용)

대리인이 위임자에 해가 되가 되는 행위를 하고 있지 않음을 확정하는 과정에서 발생하는 비용

(3) Residual loss (잔여손실)

대리인의 의사결정과 위임자의 입장에서 본 최적의사결정 사이에 존재하는 괴리로 말미암아 감수하게 되는 위임자의 부(wealth)의 감소

2 Motivations for managers to act in shareholder's best interests

기업의 주주와 경영자 간에 발생하는 이해다툼을 줄이려는 노력은 기업지배구조(corporate governance structure)의 핵심사항으로, 주주의 대리인인 경영자의 이해관계를 주주의 이해관례와 일치될 수 있도록 유인을 제공하고 경영자가 주주의 이해관계와 어긋나는 행동을 하는 경우 그에 대한 벌칙을 마련하여야 한다.

(1) Corporate Governance

기업지배구조란 주주, 채권자, 경영자 기타 이해관계자들 간의 상호작용 관계를 규정하는 메커니즘을 의미한다. 주주의 권리를 보호하기 위한 여러 가지 법적 및 제도적 장치들이 실효성을 가질 수 있도록 세밀하게 설계되고 운영될 필요가 있다.

- Board of Directors (이사회)

- Audit Committee (감사위원회)

- Minority Shareholder Protection (소액주주권 보호제도)

- Insider Trading Regulations (내부자 거래금지제도)

(2) Managerial compensation (stock option, stock appreciation right)

경영자의 보상을 고정급으로 지급하지 않고 기업성과의 시장가치(주가 또는 회계이익)와 연계시키는 보상계약을 설계하여 경영자에게 대리비용절감유인을 제공한다.

(3) Competitive managerial labor market

어느 경영자가 기업경영을 방만하게 하여 대리비용이 많아진다면, 그 경영자는 노동시장에서 가치가 하락하게 된다. 경영자는 다른 주주에게 최대한 이익을 가져다 줄 때 노동시장에서 자신의 가치를 높일 수 있다. 따라서 경쟁적인 노동시장은 대리비용을 감소시키는 역할을 한다.

(4) Hostile M&A

경영자가 주주의 이익을 위하여 노력을 하지 않는다면 기업의 주식가격은 하락할 것이며, 이 때 자본시장을 통하여 그 기업을 인수하려는 시도가 나타날 수 있다. 그 결과 경영자는 기업의 지배권을 상실함은 물론 자신의 지위에서 쫓겨나는 경우가 생긴다.

(5) Direct intervention of institutional investors

기관투자자의 기업에 대한 영향력의 증가는 대주주의 감시기능의 강화를 통하여 주주와 경영자 간의 대리문제로 인한 대리비용의 발생을 억제한다.

(6) Debt covenant

주주와 채권자 사이에 의견이 일치되지 않을 소지가 있는 여러 문제들에 대하여 양자의 합의가 이루어진다면 대리비용을 줄일 수 있으며, 이에 따라 주주가 부담해야 할 이자비용도 낮출 수 있다.

06 ▶ Finance's Law

1 현재가치와 미래가치의 현금흐름

> 현재가치의 현금흐름과 미래가치의 현금흐름은 반대흐름이어야 한다.

현재시점의 현금흐름이 유출이면 미래시점의 현금흐름은 유입이 되어야 하며 그 크기에 따라 투자수익률이 결정된다. 예를 들면 현재시점에서 100이 유출되고 1년 후에 110이 유입된다면 투자수익률은 10%이다.

현재시점의 현금흐름이 유입이면 미래시점의 현금흐름은 유출이 되어야 하며 그 크기에 따라 자본비용이 결정된다. 예를 들면 현재시점에서 100이 유입되고 1년 후에 110이 유출된다면 자본비용은 10%이다.

2 Zero-Sum Game

> 금융시장의 투자수익률 = 기업의 자본비용

현재시점에서 투자자가 기업에게 100을 투자하고 1년 후에 110을 받는다면

	현재시점	1년 후
투자자의 현금흐름	−100	+110
기업의 현금흐름	+100	−110

투자자의 투자수익률 =10% = 기업의 자본비용

이를 응용하면 다음과 같다.

주식 투자자의 투자수익률 = 기업의 자기자본비용(k_e)

채권 투자자의 투자수익률 = 기업의 타인자본비용(k_d)

k_e : cost of equity (the rate of return a shareholder requires for investing in a business)

k_d : cost of debt (the effective rate a company pays on its current debt)

3 High Risk High Return

위험이 큰 증권일수록 투자수익률이 더 크다. 따라서 투자자의 입장에서 주식 투자수익이 채권 투자수익보다 불확실성이 더 커서 위험이 더 크기 때문에 주식의 투자수익률은 채권의 투자수익률보다 커야 한다. 또한 법칙3와 법칙2를 응용하면 자기자본비용은 타인자본비용보다 더 커야 한다.

> 주식 투자자의 투자수익률 〉 채권 투자자의 투자수익률
>
> 기업의 자기자본비용(k_e) 〉 기업의 타인자본비용(k_d)

01. Which of the following is not a function of financial management?

    a. Financing

    b. Risk management

    c. Internal control

    d. Capital budgeting

02. Which of the following statements is not a mechanism to reduce the agency problem and motivate managers?

    a. Poison pill

    b. Threat of firing

    c. Threat of takeover

    d. Managerial compensation

03. With respect to the shareholder/manager relationship, which of the following statements is false?

    a. Performance shares can be used to align manager/shareholder interests.

    b. Executive stock options do not have expiration date and are held in perpetuity.

    c. Executive stock options tend to be issued out-of-the-money.

    d. The managerial salary package should include an incentive component.

04. For which two of a company's stakeholders does information asymmetry most likely make monitoring more difficult?

    a. Suppliers and employees.

    b. Employees and managers.

    c. Managers and shareholders.

    d. Managers and directors.

Items through 5 and 6

Eastman Kodak Co. reported these data at year-end :

Current assets	4,000,000
Long-term assets	16,000,000
Operating liabilities	2,000,000
Long-term debt	5,000,000

The long-term debt's fair value equaled its book value at year-end. The fair value of the equity capital is $6 million greater than its book value.

05. What is the firm's capital?

    a. $13,000,000   b. $15,000,000

    c. $18,000,000   d. $20,000,000

06. What is the firm's value?

    a. $13,000,000   b. $19,000,000

    c. $20,000,000   d. $24,000,000

07. The interest expense for a company is equal to its earnings before taxes. The company's tax rate is 40% and its net income is $30,000. The company's earnings before interest and taxes is equal to ?

a. $50,000

b. $75,000

c. $100,000

d. $150,000

Solution

1	2	3	4	5	6	7
C	A	B	C	C	D	C

1. 재무관리의 주요 분야는 자본예산, 자본구조, 순운전자본관리 및 위험관리이다.

2. Poison pill은 기업의 경영권 방어수단의 하나로, 적대적 M&A나 경영권 침해 시도가 발생하는 경우에 기존 주주들에게 시가보다 훨씬 싼 가격에 지분을 매입할 수 있도록 미리 권리를 부여하는 것으로 대리비용 감소요인은 아니다.

3. Stock option은 종업원에게 부여한 옵션계약으로 만기가 존재한다.

4. 내부자인 경영자가 자신의 기업에 대해 외부 투자자들이 보유하고 있지 않은 정보를 가지고 있는 경우가 비대칭 정보(asymmetric information)상황의 하나이며, 비대칭 정보는 '도덕적 해이' 현상을 야기할 수 있다.

5. Equity = 4,000,000 + 16,000,000 − 2,000,000 − 5,000,000 = 13,000,000
   Capital = 5,000,000 + 13,000,000 = 18,000,000

6. Market value of debt = 5,000,000
   Market value of equity = 13,000,000 + 6,000,000 = 19,000,000
   Firm value = 5,000,000 + 19,000,000 = 24,000,000

7. EBT = $30,000 ÷ (1 − 0.4) = $50,000
   EBT = I 이므로 EBIT 50,000 = 50,000 → EBIT = 100,000

Financial Management For the **US CPA** Exam

Chapter 02

Time Value of Money

Volume
8

Chapter

2 Time Value of Money

01 Future Value

미래가치는 이자의 재투자를 전제로 계산하기 때문에 이를 복리계산(compound)한다고 하며 이때에 사용되는 이자율은 수익률이다. 복리계산은 만기가 될 때까지 중간에 이자를 찾지 않고 재투자한다는 전제하에 계산하는 과정으로서, 임의의 n시점까지 이자율이 일정하다고 가정하면 현재 투자금액(PV)의 n시점의 미래가치(FV)는 다음과 같다.

$$FV = PV \times (1+R)^n$$

그리고 이때에 $(1+R)^n$은 현재 1원의 n시점에서의 미래가치를 나타내는데 이를 복리이자요소(FVIF : Future Value of Interest Factor)라고 하며 계산의 편의를 위하여 이자율과 기간별로 구분하여 미리 산출해 놓은 표를 이용한다. (부록 참조)

$$FV = PV \times FVIF_{R,n}$$

Excel Spreadsheet를 이용하여 미래가치를 구하면 다음과 같다.

[EXCEL] 함수선택 FV

Rate, Nper, Pmt, Pv, Type

Rate : 기간별 이자율
Nper : 총 납입 기간 수
Pmt : 총 기간 동안 일정한 각 기간의 납입액(생략 또는 0)
Pv : 현재가치
Type : 납입시점 (0 또는 1이며. 생략하면 0으로 간주)
※ PV는 투자금액이므로 마이너스(−)로 입력, FV는 투자회수금액이므로 플러스(+)로 계산

이자의 재투자를 가정하기 않는 계산방법을 단리계산(simple interest)한다고 하며, 단리계산방법에 의한 미래가치는 다음과 같이 계산한다.

$$FV = PV \times (1 + R \times n)$$

이자계산이 1기간에 m회 행해질 때 미래가치는 다음과 같이 계산한다.

$$FV = PV \times (1 + \frac{R}{m})^{n \times m}$$

총 이자수익 (투자수익)은 미래가치에서 현재가치를 차감하여 계산한다.

$$총투자수익 = FV - PV$$

$FV = PV \times (1 + R)^n$ 의 공식에서 미래가치의 결정요인은 다음과 같다.

다른 조건이 일정하면(Ceteris paribus : all other things being equal),

✔ 현재가치(PV)가 증가하면 미래가치는 증가

✔ 수익률(R)이 증가하면 미래가치는 증가

✔ 기간(n)이 증가하면 미래가치는 증가

Example 2-1

If you deposit $10,000 in a bank account under each of the following conditions, how much would be in your account after 5 years?

(1) 8% compounded annually.
(2) 8% compounded semi-annually.

Solution

(1) Annually compounding
   1) Numerical Solution : $FV = \$10,000 \times (1+0.08)^5 = \$14,693$
   2) Tabular Solution : $FV = \$10,000 \times FVIF_{8\%,5} = 10,000 \times 1.4693 = \$14,693$
   3) Spreadsheet Solution : [EXCEL] 함수선택 FV

$$Rate = 8\%, \ Nper = 5, \ Pv = -10,000$$
$$\rightarrow FV = 14,693$$

Total interest revenue = $14,693 - 10,000 = \$4,693$

(2) Semi-annually compounding
   1) Numerical Solution : $FV = \$10,000 \ (1+0.04)^{10} = \$14,802$
   2) Tabular Solution : $FV = \$10,000 \times FVIF_{4\%,10} = 10,000 \times 1.4802 = \$14,802$
   3) Spreadsheet Solution : [EXCEL] 함수선택 FV

$$Rate = 4\%, \ Nper = 10, \ Pv = -10,000$$
$$\rightarrow FV = 14,802$$

Total interest revenue = $14,802 - 10,000 = \$4,802$

Economic Thinking

※ 오늘의 1원이 내일의 1원보다 더 가치가 있는 이유는?

(1) 시차선호 : 미래의 소비보다도 현재의 소비를 더 선호

(2) 자본의 생산성 : 현재의 현금을 가지고 생산기회를 이용가능

(3) 미래의 불확실성 : 사람들은 위험을 싫어함

※ Rule of 72

By dividing 72 by the annual rate of return, investors obtain a rough estimate of how many years it will take for the initial investment to duplicate itself.

Q) 현금 1,000만원을 연리 10%로 매년 복리계산 몇 년 후에 2,000만원이 될까?

기간= 72 ÷ 이자율 = 72 ÷ 10 = 7.2년

Q) 10만원을 5년 후에 2배로 만들고 싶다면 몇 % 상품에 투자해야 할까요?

5 = 72 ÷ R → R = 14.4%

※ Albert Einstein

"The most powerful force in the world is compound interest"

※ Warren Buffett's Snowball Effect

"My wealth has come from a combination of living in America, some lucky genes and compound interest. All there is to investing is picking good stocks at good times and staying with them as long as they remain good companies."

※ Peter Lynch (Fidelity Magellan Fund)

"Consider the Indians of Manhattan, who in 1625 sold all their real estate to a group of immigrants for $24 in trinkets and beads. For 362 years, the Indians have been the subjects of cruel jokes because of it. But it turns out that they may have made a better deal than the buyers who got the island. At 8% interest on $24 compounded over all those years, the Indians would have built up a net worth just short $30 trillion."

02 ▶ Present Value

미래의 현금흐름에 대해서 그 현재가치를 구하는 과정을 할인(discount)한다고 하며 이때에 사용되는 이자율을 할인율(discount rate)라고 한다. 이자율이 일정하다고 가정하면 임의의 n시점 후의 금액(FV)이 현재가치(PV)는 다음과 같다.

$$PV = \frac{FV_n}{(1+R)^n}$$

그리고 이때에 $\frac{1}{(1+R)^n}$ 은 n시점에서의 1원의 현재가치를 나타내는데 이를 현재가치요소(PVIF : Present Value of Interest Factor)라고 하며 계산의 편의를 위하여 이자율과 기간별로 구분하여 미리 산출해 놓은 표를 이용한다. (부록 참조)

$$PV = FV_n \times PVIF_{R,n}$$

Excel Spreadsheet를 이용하여 현재가치를 구하면 다음과 같다.

[EXCEL] 함수선택 PV

Rate, Nper, Pmt, Fv, Type

Rate : 기간별 이자율
Nper : 총 납입 기간 수
Pmt : 총 기간 동안 일정한 각 기간의 납입액(생략 또는 0)
Fv : 미래가치
Type : 납입시점 (0 또는 1이며. 생략하면 0으로 간주)
※ FV는 투자회수금액이므로 플러스(+)로 입력, PV는 투자금액이므로 마이너스(−)로 표시

이자계산이 1기간에 m회 행해질 때 현재가치는 다음과 같이 계산한다.

$$PV = FV_{nm} \div (1 + \frac{R}{m})^{nm}$$

현재가치의 공식에서 현재가치의 결정요인은 다음과 같다.

다른 조건이 일정하면(all other things being equal),

✔ 미래가치(FV)가 증가하면 현재가치는 증가

✔ 할인률(R)이 증가하면 현재가치는 감소

✔ 기간(n)이 증가하면 현재가치는 감소

Example 2-2

What is the present value of a security that will pay \$10,000 in 5 years

(1) if securities of equal risk pay 8 percent annually?
(2) if securities of equal risk pay 8 percent semi-annually?

Solution

(1) Annually compounding

    1) Numerical Solution : $PV = \dfrac{10,000}{(1+0.08)^5} = \$6,806$

    2) Tabular Solution : $PV = \$300 \times PVIFA_{8\%,5} = 10,000 \times 0.6806 = \$6,806$

    3) Spreadsheet Solution : [EXCEL] 함수선택 PV

                Rate=8%, Nper=5, Fv=10,000

                → PV = −6,806

Total interest revenue = $10,000 - 6,806 = 3,194$

(2) Semi−annually compounding

    1) Numerical Solution : $PV = \dfrac{10,000}{(1+0.04)^{10}} = \$6,756$

    2) Tabular Solution : $PV = \$10,000 \times PVIFA_{4\%,10} = 10,000 \times 0.6756 = \$6,756$

    3) Spreadsheet Solution : [EXCEL] 함수선택 PV

                Rate=4%, Nper=10, Fv=10,000

                → PV = −6,756

Total interest revenue = $10,000 - 6,756 = 3,244$

Example 2-3

(1) Your parents will retire in 25 years. They currently have $350,000, and they think they will need $1,000,000 at retirement. What annual interest rate must they earn to reach their goal, assuming they don' save any additional funds?

(2) If you deposit money today in an account that pays 5 percent annual interest, how long will it take to double your money?

Solution

(1) Finding the required interest rate

1) Numerical Solution : $350,000 = \dfrac{1,000,000}{(1+R)^{25}} \rightarrow R = 0.0429$

2) Spreadsheet Solution : [EXCEL] 함수선택 RATE

$$\text{Nper} = 25, \ \text{Pv} = -350,000, \ \text{Fv} = 1,000,000$$

$$\rightarrow \text{RATE} = 4.29\%$$

(2) Time for a lump sum to double

1) Numerical Solution : $1 = \dfrac{2}{(1+0.05)^{n}} \rightarrow n = 14.2067$

2) Spreadsheet Solution : [EXCEL] 함수선택 NPER

$$\text{Rate} = 5\%, \ \text{Pv} = -1, \ \text{Fv} = 2$$

$$\rightarrow \text{NPER} = 14.2067$$

03 Annuity

1 Terminology

(1) Annuity

A series of payments of an equal amount at fixed intervals.

(2) Ordinary annuity (Annuity in arrear, 정상연금)

An annuity whose payments occur at the end of each period.

(3) Annuity due (Annuity in advance, 선불연금)

An annuity whose payments occur at the beginning of each period.

2 Future value

(1) Ordinary annuity (정상연금)

매기 말 1원씩 수령하는 연금의 n시점에서의 미래가치를 나타내는 것을 연금의 복리이자요소 (FVIFA : Future Value of Interest Factor for Annuity)라고 하며 계산의 편의를 위하여 이자율과 기간별로 구분하여 미리 산출해 놓은 표를 이용한다. (부록 참조)

매년 말에 동일한 금액(PMT)을 수령하는 현금흐름의 미래가치는 다음과 같다.

$$FV = \sum_{t=1}^{n} PMT \times (1+R)^{n-t} = PMT \times FVIFA_{R,n}$$

Excel Spreadsheet를 이용하여 미래가치를 구하면 다음과 같다.

[EXCEL] 함수선택 FV

Rate, Nper, Pmt, Pv, Type

Rate : 기간별 이자율
Nper : 총 납입 기간 수
Pmt : 총 기간 동안 일정한 각 기간의 납입액
Pv : 현재가치 (생략 또는 0)
Type : 납입시점 (0 또는 생략)

(2) Annuity due (선불연금)

매년 초에 동일한 금액(PMT)을 수령하는 현금흐름의 n시점에서의 미래가치는 다음과 같다.

$$FV^D = \sum_{t=1}^{n} PMT \times (1+R)^{n-t+1} = PMT \times FVIFA_{R,n} \times (1+R)$$

$$FV^D = FV^O \times (1+R)^1$$

Excel Spreadsheet를 이용하여 미래가치를 구하면 다음과 같다.

[EXCEL] 함수선택 FV

Rate, Nper, Pmt, Pv, Type

Rate : 기간별 이자율
Nper : 총 납입 기간 수
Pmt : 총 기간 동안 일정한 각 기간의 납입액
Pv : 현재가치 (생략 또는 0)
Type : 납입시점 (1)

3 Present value

(1) Ordinary annuity (정상연금)

매기 말 1원씩 수령하는 연금의 n시점에서의 현재가치를 나타내는 것을 연금의 현가이자요소 (PVIFA : Present Value of Interest Factor for Annuity)라고 하며 계산의 편의를 위하여 이자율과 기간별로 구분하여 미리 산출해 놓은 표를 이용한다. (부록 참조)

매년 말에 동일한 금액(PMT)을 수령하는 현금흐름의 현재가치는 다음과 같다.

$$PV = \sum_{t=1}^{n} \frac{PMT}{(1+R)^t} = PMT \times PVIFA_{R,n}$$

Excel Spreadsheet를 이용하여 현재가치를 구하면 다음과 같다.

[EXCEL] 함수선택 PV

Rate, Nper, Pmt, Fv, Type

Rate : 기간별 이자율
Nper : 총 납입 기간 수
Pmt : 총 기간 동안 일정한 각 기간의 납입액
Fv : 미래가치 (생략 또는 0)
Type : 납입시점 (0 또는 생략)

(2) Annuity due (선불연금)

매년 초에 동일한 금액(PMT)을 n회 수령하는 현금흐름의 현재가치는 다음과 같다.

$$PV^D = \sum_{t=1}^{n} \frac{PMT}{(1+R)^{t-1}} = PMT \times PVIFA_{R,n} \times (1+R)$$

$$PV^D = PV^O \times (1+R)^1$$

Excel Spreadsheet를 이용하여 현재가치를 구하면 다음과 같다.

[EXCEL] 함수선택 PV

Rate, Nper, Pmt, Fv, Type

Rate : 기간별 이자율
Nper : 총 납입 기간 수
Pmt : 총 기간 동안 일정한 각 기간의 납입액
Fv : 미래가치 (생략 또는 0)
Type : 납입시점 (1)

Example 2-4

(1) What's the future value of a 7 percent, 5-year ordinary annuity that pays $300 each year? If this were an annuity due, what would its future value be?

(2) What's the present value of a 7 percent, 5-year ordinary annuity that pays $300 each year? If this were an annuity due, what would its present value be?

Solution

(1) Future value: ordinary annuity

   1) Tabular Solution : $FV^O = \$300 \times FVIFA_{7\%,5} = 300 \times 5.7507 = \$1,725$

   2) Spreadsheet Solution : [EXCEL] 함수선택 FV

$$\text{Rate} = 7\%, \ \text{Nper} = 5, \ \text{Pmt} = -300 \rightarrow \text{FV} = 1,725$$

   Total interest revenue $= 1,725 - 300 \times 5 = \$225$

(1) Future value: annuity due

   1) Numerical Solution : $FV^D = FV^O \times (1+R) = 1,725 \times 1.07 = 1,846$

   2) Spreadsheet Solution : [EXCEL] 함수선택 FV

$$\text{Rate} = 7\%, \ \text{Nper} = 5, \ \text{Pmt} = -300, \ \text{Type} = 1 \rightarrow \text{FV} = 1,846$$

   Total interest revenue $= 1,846 - 300 \times 5 = \$346$

(2) Present value: ordinary annuity

   1) Tabular Solution : $PV^O = \$300 \times PVIFA_{7\%,5} = 300 \times 4.1002 = \$1,230$

   2) Spreadsheet Solution : [EXCEL] 함수선택 PV

$$\text{Rate} = 7\%, \ \text{Nper} = 5, \ \text{Pmt} = 300 \rightarrow \text{PV} = -1,230$$

   Total interest revenue $= 300 \times 5 - 1,230 = \$270$

(2) Present value: annuity due

   1) Numerical Solution : $PV^D = PV^O \times (1+R) = 1,230 \times 1.07 = 1,316$

   2) Spreadsheet Solution : [EXCEL] 함수선택 PV

$$\text{Rate} = 7\%, \ \text{Nper} = 5, \ \text{Pmt} = 300, \ \text{Type} = 1 \rightarrow \text{PV} = -1,316$$

   Total interest revenue $= 300 \times 5 - 1,316 = \$184$

4 Amortized loan

A loan that is repaid in equal payments over the life.

원리금균등분할상환은 매 지급시마다 원금과 이자의 합계가 일정한 금액이 되는 방식으로서 원금상환액은 체증, 이자는 체감하면서 원리금합계가 동일한 금액을 유지한다. 그러나 원금균등분할상환은 원금을 균등하게 나누어 상환하면서 이자는 점차 감소하게 하는 방식으로 매 지급금액이 감소한다.

Example 2-5

Exxon Mobil Corporation borrows $10,000 and the loan is to be repaid in five equal payments at the end of each of the next five years. The lender charges a 6% interest rate on the loan balance that is outstanding at the beginning of each year. Prepare the amortization table.

Solution

(1) Calculate PMT

   1) Tabular Solution : $10,000 = PMT×4.21236 → PMT = $2,374

   2) Spreadsheet Solution : [EXCEL] 함수선택 PMT

$$Rate = 6\%, Nper = 5, Pv = 10,000 → PMT = -2,374$$

(2) Prepare loan amortization schedule

Year	A Beginning Balance	B PMT	C Interest	D Payment of Principal	E Remaining Balance
1	10,000	2,374	600	1,774	8,226
2	8,226	2,374	494	1,880	6,346
3	6,346	2,374	381	1,993	4,352
4	4,352	2,374	261	2,113	2,239
5	2,239	2,374	134	2,240	0
Total		11,870	1,870	10,000	

C1 = A1×0.06, D1 = B1 − C1, E1 = A1 − D1, A2 = E1

Example2-6

(1) You borrow $85,000; the annual loan payments are $8,273.59 for 30 years. What interest rate are you being charged?

(2) You want to buy a car, and a local bank will lend you $20,000. The loan would be fully amortized over 5 years, and the nominal interest rate would be 12 percent, with loan paid annually. What would be the annual loan payment?

(3) You want to buy a car, and a local bank will lend you $20,000. The loan would be fully amortized over 60 months, and the nominal interest rate would be 12 percent, with loan paid monthly. What would be the monthly loan payment?

Solution

(1) Effective interest rate

Spreadsheet Solution : [EXCEL] 함수선택 RATE

$$\text{Nper} = 30, \ \text{Pmt} = -8,274, \ \text{Pv} = 85,000 \rightarrow \text{RATE} = 9\%$$

(2) Loan amortization

1) Tabular Solution : $20,000 = \text{PMT} \times 3.6048 \rightarrow \text{PMT} = \$5,548$

2) Spreadsheet Solution : [EXCEL] 함수선택 PMT

$$\text{Rate} = 12\%, \ \text{Nper} = 5, \ \text{Pv} = -20,000 \rightarrow \text{PMT} = 5,548$$

(3) Loan amortization

Spreadsheet Solution : [EXCEL] 함수선택 PMT

$$\text{Rate} = 1\%, \ \text{Nper} = 60, \ \text{Pv} = -20,000 \rightarrow \text{PMT} = 445$$

04 Perpetuities

1 Perpetuity

A stream of equal payments expected to continue forever.

영구연금(perpetuity)이란 일정한 금액의 현금흐름이 영원히 계속되는 것을 말한다. 만기가 없고 무한히 이자만 주는 영구채권이나 무한히 배당만 주는 우선주가 이러한 현금흐름에 해당하는 예이다.

2 Present value of perpetuity

영구연금의 현재가치는 다음과 같은 식으로 표현된다.

$$PV = \frac{PMT}{(1+R)^1} + \frac{PMT}{(1+R)^2} + \frac{PMT}{(1+R)^3} + \dots = \frac{PMT}{R}$$

즉, 매년 말 동일한 금액(PMT)을 무한히 받게 되는 무한연금의 현재가치는 그냥 PMT를 이자율(R)로 나누어주면 된다. 영구연금의 현재가치 공식은 주로 만기가 없고 무한히 이자만 주는 영구채권이나 무한히 배당만 주는 우선주의 가치평가에 사용된다.

3 Present value of growing perpetuity

영구연금 중에서 매기 말 수령액이 일정한 비율(g)로 증가하는 형태가 있다. 이러한 영구연금의 현재가치는 다음과 같은 식으로 표현된다.

$$PV = \frac{PMT}{(1+R)^1} + \frac{PMT \times (1+g)^1}{(1+R)^2} + \frac{PMT \times (1+g)^2}{(1+R)^3} + \dots = \frac{PMT}{R-g}$$

이때 현재가치가 일정한 값으로 존재하려면 R > g, 즉 증가율이 할인율보다 작아야 한다.

Example 2-7

(1) What is the present value of a $100 perpetuity if the interest rate is 7 percent? If interest rates doubled to 14 percent, what would its present value be?

(2) Assume that Amazon is expected to pay a $2.00 dividend per share one year from now. After that, the dividend is expected to increase at a constant rate of 5%. If you require a 12% return on stock, what is the value of the stock?

Solution

(1) Present value of a perpetuity

$$R = 7\% \rightarrow PV = \frac{\$100}{0.07} = \$1,429$$

$$R = 14\% \rightarrow PV = \frac{\$100}{0.14} = \$714$$

(2) Present value of constant growth stock

$$PV = \frac{\$2.00}{0.12 - 0.05} = \$28.57$$

05 ▶ Effective Annual Rate(EAR)

1 Nominal rate or Stated rate (R_S)

1기간에 2회 이상의 이자계산이 행해질 때 1기간 내에서 이자의 재투자효과를 고려하지 않은 1기간 단위의 이자율을 표면이자율(stated rate)이라고 한다.

2 Effective annual rate (R_e)

1기간에 2회 이상의 이자계산이 행해질 때 1기간 내에서 이자의 재투자효과를 고려한 1기간 단위의 이자율을 실효이자율(effective rate)이라고 한다. 1기간에 m회 이자계산이 행해질 때 다음 공식을 사용하여 표면이자율을 실효이자율로 변경한다.

$$R_e = (1 + \frac{R_S}{m})^m - 1$$

> **Example 2-8**

(1) If the nominal rate is 6% and semiannual compounding is used, find the effective interest annual rate.

(2) If the nominal rate is 6% and quarterly compounding is used, find the effective interest annual rate.

Solution

(1) $R_e = (1 + \dfrac{0.06}{2})^2 - 1 = 6.09\%$

(2) $R_e = (1 + \dfrac{0.06}{4})^4 - 1 = 6.14\%$

1 Bond valuation

(1) Coupon Bond (이자부채권)

채권을 보유함으로써 기대되는 미래의 현금흐름은 만기까지 일정시점마다 지급되는 이자(C)와 만기에 지급되는 원금(F)의 두 가지이다. 그리고 이에 알맞은 할인율은 채권수익률(YTM, Yield-To-Maturity)인데 이 두 가지 현금흐름에 채권수익률 적용한 현재가치를 각각 산출하여 합한 값이 채권의 균형가격이(B_0)된다.

$$B_0 = \frac{C}{1+R} + \frac{C}{(1+R)^2} + ... + \frac{C+F}{(1+R)^n} = \sum_{t=1}^{n} \frac{C}{(1+R)^t} + \frac{F}{(1+R)^n}$$

C : Coupon interest, F : Face value, n : Maturity, R : YTM

Tabular Solution 방법으로 채권의 가격을 구하면 다음과 같다.

$$PV = F \times PVIF_{R,n} + C \times PVIFA_{R,n}$$

Spreadsheet Solution 방법으로 채권의 가격을 구하면 다음과 같다.

[EXCEL] 함수선택 PV
Rate = R, Nper = n, Pmt = C, Fv = F

채권가격은 채권수익률과 액면이자율의 크기에 따라 다음과 같이 구분한다.

- Discount (할인가격) : 채권수익률 〉 액면이자율 → $B_0 \langle F$
- Premium (할증가격) : 채권수익률 〈 액면이자율 → $B_0 \rangle F$
- Par (액면가격) : 채권수익률 = 액면이자율 → $B_0 = F$

(2) Discount Bond (할인채권)

할인채권은 채권을 보유함으로써 기대되는 미래의 현금흐름이 만기에 지급되는 원금(F)이므로 원금에 채권수익률 적용한 현재가치를 산출한 값이 채권의 균형가격이 된다.

$$B_0 = \frac{F}{(1+R)^n}$$

(3) Relationship between bond price and market interest rate

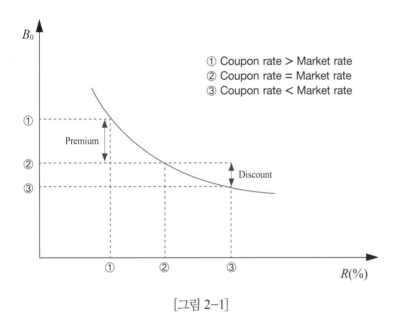

[그림 2-1]

다음 조건이 일정하면
채권수익률이 상승하면 채권가격은 하락,
채권수익률이 하락하면 채권가격은 상승.

Example 2-9

Walt Disney Co.'s bonds have 5 years remaining to maturity. Interest is paid annually, the bonds have a $1,000 par value and the coupon interest rate is a 8%. The bonds have a yield to maturity of 10%. What is the current market price of these bonds?

Solution

(1) Numeric Solution : $B_0 = \sum_{t=1}^{5} \frac{80}{(1.10)^t} + \frac{1,000}{1.10^5} = \$924$

(2) Tabular Solution : PV = 80×3.7908 + 1,000×0.6209 = $924

(3) Spreadsheet Solution : [EXCEL] 함수선택 PV

$$\text{Rate}=10\%, \ \text{Nper}=5, \ \text{Pmt}=80, \ \text{Fv}=1,000 \rightarrow \text{PV} = -924$$

※ 10% = 투자자의 채권수익률 = 발행자(기업)의 타인자본비용(k_d)

2 Stock valuation

주식을 보유함으로써 기대되는 미래의 현금흐름은 배당금(D)인데 이는 일반적으로 계속기업을 전제로 하기 때문에 무한히 계속되는 영구연금의 성격을 갖는다. 따라서 주식의 균형가격(P_0)는 이러한 영구연금에 주식수익률(R)을 적용하여 산출한 현재가치가 된다. 주식평가에 대한 자세한 공식은 4장에서 설명한다.

$$P_0 = \frac{D}{R}$$

Example 2-10

KIMCPA has preferred stock outstanding that pays a dividend of $10 per year. The required rate of return on the preferred stock is 12%. What is the value of the stock?

Solution

$$P_0 = \frac{10}{0.12} = \$83.33$$

※ 12% = 투자자의 주식수익률 = 발행자(기업)의 자기자본비용(k_e)

3 Capital budgeting

실물투자와 관련된 의사결정 문제를 자본예산이라고 하는데 자세한 내용은 6장에서 다룰 것이다. 먼저 자본예산에서 사용되는 두 가지 개념을 간단하게 소개하면 다음과 같다.

(1) NPV (Net present value)

순현가(NPV)란 투자안에서 기대되는 현금유입의 현재가치에서 투자비용을 차감한 값을 말하며 할인율은 투자안의 자본비용을 사용한다.

$$NPV = PV \text{ of cash inflows} - PV \text{ of cash outflows}$$

$$NPV = - CF_o + \sum_{t=1}^{n} \frac{CF_t}{(1+k)^t}$$

CF_t : t시점에서의 예상실물현금흐름, k : 기업의 자본비용

이렇게 산출한 NPV가 0보다 크면 투자안을 채택하고, 0보다 작으면 기각한다.

- NPV > 0 → 투자안 채택
- NPV < 0 → 투자안 기각

(2) IRR (Internal rate of return)

내부수익률 (IRR)이란 투자안에서 얻게 되는 수익률이다. 구체적으로는 투자로부터 기대되는 현금유입의 현재가치와 투자비용을 같게 하여 산출한다. 따라서 이를 할인율로 해서 NPV를 계산하게 되면 0이 되므로 다음 식이 성립한다.

$$CF_o = \sum_{t=1}^{n} \frac{CF_t}{(1+IRR)^t} \quad \rightarrow \quad NPV = -CF_o + \sum_{t=1}^{n} \frac{CF_t}{(1+IRR)^t} = 0$$

이렇게 산출한 내부수익률이 자금조달에 따른 자본비용보다 크면 투자안을 채택하고 자본비용보다 작으면 기각한다.

- IRR 〉 자본비용 → 투자안 채택
- IRR 〈 자본비용 → 투자안 기각

Example 2-11

Project K has a cost of $7,000, its expected cash inflow at year 2 is $9,000 and its cost of capital is 10%. What is the project's NPV and IRR?

Solution

(1) Calculate NPV

$$NPV = -\$7,000 + \frac{\$9,000}{(1+0.1)^2} = \$438$$

(2) Calculate IRR

1) Numeric Solution : $7,000 = \dfrac{\$9,000}{(1+IRR)^2}$ 에서 IRR = 13.39%

2) Spreadsheet Solution : [EXCEL] 함수선택 RATE

　　　　　　　　Nper = 2, Pv = −7,000, Fv = 9,000 → RATE = 13.39%

※ 내부수익률이 자금조달에 따른 자본비용보다 크면 NPV는 항상 0보다 크다.

　IRR 〉 k → NPV 〉 0

　IRR = k → NPV = 0

　IRR 〈 k → NPV 〈 0

4 Firm Value

현금흐름을 기준으로 보면 손익계산서의 영업이익(EBIT)의 현재가치가 자산(기업), 이자비용(I)의 현재가치가 부채(타인자본), 순이익(NI)의 현재가치가 자본(자기자본)이 된다. 법인세가 없고, 영구연금 현금흐름을 가정하면 기업가치는 다음과 같다.

$$V_{firm} = Debt + Equity = \frac{EBIT}{WACC} \leftarrow Debt = \frac{I}{k_d}, \; Equity = \frac{NI}{k_e}$$

k_e: 자기자본비용, k_d : 타인자본비용

$WACC$ (Weighted Average Cost of Capital) : 가중평균자본비용(총자본에 대한 평균조달비용)

Example 2-12

- 영업이익(EBIT) = 4, 이자비용(I) = 1, 순이익(NI) = 3
- k_e = 20%, k_d = 10%

타인자본의 시장가치 : Debt = $\dfrac{1}{0.1}$ = 10

자기자본의 시장가치 : Equity = $\dfrac{3}{0.20}$ = 15

기업가치 : V = 10 + 15 = 25 = $\dfrac{4}{WACC}$ → WACC = 0.16

가중평균자본비용 : $WACC = k_d \times \dfrac{D}{V} + k_e \times \dfrac{E}{V}$ = 10% × $\dfrac{10}{25}$ + 20% × $\dfrac{15}{25}$ = 16%

07 ›› Multiple Choice

01. Alibaba purchased a $20,000, 8% 5 year note that required five equal annual year-end payments of $5,009. The note was discounted to yield a 9% rate. At the date of purchase, the present value of the note was $19,485. What should be the total interest revenue earned by Alibaba over the life of this note?

a. $5,045

b. $5,560

c. $8,000

d. $9,000

02. On January 1, Year 1, General Electric sold goods to Boeing. Boeing signed a non-interest-bearing note requiring payment of $60,000 annually for seven years. The first payment was made on January 1, Year 1. The prevailing rate of interest for this type of note at date of issuance was 10%. Information on present value factors is as follows :

Periods	Present value of 1 at 10%	Present value of ordinary annuity of 1 at 10%
6	.56	4.36
7	.51	4.87

General Electric should record sales revenues in January Year 1 of

a. $321,600

b. $292,200

c. $261,600

d. $214,200

03. Apple Inc. adopted a plan to accumulate $1,000,000 by September 1, Year 5. Apple plans to make four equal annual deposits to a fund that will earn interest at 10% compounded annually. Apple made the first deposit on September 1, Year 1. Future value and future amount factors are as follows :

Future value of 1 at 10% for 4 periods	1.46
Future amount of ordinary annuity of 1 at 10% for 4 periods	4.64
Future amount of annuity in advance of 1 at 10% for 4 periods	5.11

Apple Inc. should make four annual deposits (rounded) of

a. $250,000

b. $215,500

c. $195,700

d. $146,000

04. Facebook, Inc. has $75,000 in a bank account as of December 31, Year 1. If the company plans on depositing $4,000 in the account at the end of each of the next three years and all amounts in the account earn 8 percent per year, what will the account balance be at December 31, Year 4? Information on future value factors is as follows

Periods	Future value of 1 at 8%	Future value of ordinary annuity of 1 at 8%
1	1.08	1.00
2	1.17	2.08
3	1.26	3.25
4	1.36	4.51

a. $88,000

b. $96,070

c. $107,500

d. $120,400

Items 5 through 7

IBM leases computer equipment to customers under leases on January 1, Year 1 and wishes to earn 8% interest on a 5-years lease of equipment with a fair value of $323,400. The present value of ordinary annuity of $1 at 8% for five years is 3.99. The present value of a $1 at 8% for five years is 0.68.

05. The equipment has no residual value at the end of the lease and the first lease payment will be paid on January 1, Year 1. What is the interest revenue that IBM will earn over the life of the lease?

a. $23,822

b. $51,845

c. $75,049

d. $139,450

06. The equipment has no residual value at the end of the lease and the first lease payment will be paid on December 31, Year 1. What is the interest revenue that IBM will earn over the life of the lease?

a. $23,822

b. $51,600

c. $81,053

d. $81,865

07. The equipment has $5,000 residual value at the end of the lease and the first lease payment will be paid on January 1, Year 1. What is the interest revenue that IBM will earn over the life of the lease?

a. $47,654

b. $52,900

c. $74,260

d. $75,000

08. BlackRock has preferred stock outstanding that pays a dividend of $5 per year. The preferred stock sells for $60 a share. What is the required rate of return on the preferred stock?

a. 8%

b. 8.3%

c. 10%

d. 12%

09. The following information pertains to Boeing's issuance of bonds on July 1, Year 1:

Face amount	$800,000
Term	10 years
Stated interest rate	6%
Interest payment dates	Annually on July 1
Yield	9%

	At 6%	At 9%
Present value of 1 for 10 periods	0.558	0.422
Future value of 1 for 10 periods	1.791	2.367
Present value of ordinary annuity of 1 for 10 periods	7.360	6.418

What should be the issue price for each $1,000 bond?

a. $1,000   b. $864

c. $807   d. $700

10. General Electric is planning an energy saving proposal :

Investment cost ： $100,000
Residual value of end of 5 years : $20,000
Present value of an annuity of 1 at 12% for 5 years : 3.60
Present value of $1 due in 5 years at 12% : 0.57

What would be the annual savings to realize a 12% yield?

a. $22,222   b. $24,611

c. $27,777   d. $33,333

Items 11 through 12

On January 1, Year 1, Amazon received a $50,000 note receivable. The note is due in 5 years. The market interest rate for similar notes was 12%.

Present value of an annuity of 1 at 12% for 5 years : 3.60
Present value of $1 due in 5 years at 12% : 0.57
Future value of an annuity of 1 at 8% for 5 years : 5.867
Future value of $1 due in 5 years at 8% : 1.469

11. If interest is calculated in the outstanding balance at the interest rate of 8% compounded annually and payable at maturity. what amount should the note be reported in Amazon's as of January 2, Year 1, balance sheet?

a. $28,500   b. $39,900

c. $41,867   d. $42,900

12. If Interest is calculated in the outstanding balance at the interest rate of 8% compounded annually and payable annually, what amount should the note be reported in Amazon's as of January 2, Year 1, balance sheet?

a. $28,500   b. $39,900

c. $41,867   d. $42,900

13. Consider a 5-year bond with a 10% coupon that has a present yield-to-maturity of 8%. If interest rates remain constant, one year from now the price of this bond will be

a. higher.   b. lower.

c. the same.   d. cannot be determined.

14. In applying the bond valuation, lowering the yield-to-maturity on bond will cause a bond's intrinsic value to

a. decrease.   b. increase.

c. remain unchanged.   d. decrease or increase, depending upon other factors.

15. In applying the bond valuation, lowering the coupon interest rate on bond will cause a bond's intrinsic value to

a. decrease.   b. increase.

c. remain unchanged.   d. decrease or increase, depending upon other factors.

16. Lang National Bank offered a one-year loan to a commercial customer. The instrument is a discounted note with a nominal rate of 12%. What is the effective interest rate to the borrower? (CMA)

a. 10.71%   b. 12.00%

c. 13.20%   d. 13.64%

17. WalMart borrowed $100,000 from a bank on a one-year 8% term loan, with interest compounded quarterly. What is the effective annual interest on the loan?

a. 2%   b. 8%

c. 8.16%   d. 8.24%

Solution

1	2	3	4	5	6	7	8	9	10
B	A	C	C	A	D	B	B	C	B

11	12	13	14	15	16	17
C	B	B	B	A	D	D

1. 총이자수익 = Inflows − outflows = $5,009 \times 5 - 19,485 = \$5,560$

2. Annuity in advance이므로 PV = $\$60,000 \times (4.36 + 1) = \$321,600$

3. Annuity in advance이므로 PMT = $\$1,000,000 \div 5.11 = \$195,695$

4. FV= $\$75,000 \times 1.26 + \$4,000 \times 3.25 = \$107,500$

5. Annuity in advance이므로 PMT = $\$323,400 \div (3.99 \times 1.08) = \$75,049$
   총이자수익 = Inflows − outflows = $75,049 \times 5 - 323,400 = \$51,845$

6. Ordinary annuity 이므로 PMT = $\$323,400 \div 3.99 = \$81,053$
   총이자수익 = Inflows − outflows = $81,053 \times 5 - 323,400 = \$81,865$

7. PMT = $(\$323,400 - 5,000 \times 0.68) \div (3.99 \times 1.08) = \$74,260$
   총이자수익 = Inflows − outflows = $74,260 \times 5 + 5,000 - 323,400 = \$52,900$

8. $\$60 = \$5 \div R \rightarrow R = \$5 \div \$60 = 0.0833$

9. PV = $(\$1,000 \times 0.422) + (\$1,000 \times 6\% \times 6.418) = \$807$

10. PMT = $(\$100,000 - 20,000 \times 0.57) \div 3.60 = \$24,611$

11. FV = $\$50,000 \times 1.469 = \$73,450 \rightarrow$ PV = $\$73,450 \times 0.57 = \$41,867$

12. PV = $(\$50,000 \times 0.57) + (\$50,000 \times 8\% \times 3.60) = \$42,900$

13. 액면이자율 〈 시장이자율(만기수익률) : 할증발행
    다른 조건이 변하지 않고, 시간이 경과하면 할증금액은 감소

14. 채권이나 주식의 가격은 요구수익률이 감소하면 증가한다.

15. 채권의 액면이자율이 감소하면 현금흐름이 감소하여 가격은 감소한다.

16. EAR = $12 \div (100 - 12) = 0.1364$

17. Re $=(1+\dfrac{0.08}{4})^{4}= 8.24\%$

08 ⟩⟩ Tasked-Based Simulation

Problem-1

A $25,000 loan to be repaid in equal installments at the end of each of the next 3 years. The interest rate is 10 percent, compounded annually.

Required

1. Set up an amortization schedule for a $25,000 loan
2. What percentage of the payment represents interest and what percentage represents principal for each of the 3 years?
3. Why do these percentages change over time?

Problem-2

Your father is 50 years old and will retire in 10 years. He expects to live for 25 years after he retires, until he is 85. He wants a fixed retirement income that has the same purchasing power at the time he retires as $40,000 has today. (The real value of his retirement income will decline annually after he retires.) His retirement income will begin the day he retires, 10 years from today; and he will then receive 24 additional annual payments. Annual inflation is expected to be 5 percent. He currently has $100,000 saved, and he expects to earn 8 percent annually on his savings.

Required

How much must he save during each of the next 10 years (end-of-year deposits) to meet his retirement goal?

Problem-3

A father is now planning a savings program to put his daughter through college. She is 13, she plans to enroll at the university in 5 years, and she should graduate in 4 years. Currently, the annual cost (for everything—food, clothing, tuition, books, transportation, and so forth) is $15,000, but these costs are expected to increase by 5 percent annually. He want a college savings account that has the same purchasing power at the time she enrolls at the university as $15,000 has today. The college requires that this amount be paid at the start of the year. She now has $7,500 in a college savings account that pays 6 percent annually. The father will make 5 equal annual deposits into her account during each of the next 5 years (end-of-year deposits).

Required

How large must each of the 5 payments be?

Problem-4

Bond X is noncallable, has 20 years to maturity, a 9 percent annual coupon, and a $1,000 par value. Your required return on Bond X is 10 percent, and if you buy it you plan to hold it for 5 years. You, and the market, have expectations that in 5 years the yield to maturity on a 15-year bond with similar risk will be 8.5 percent.

Required

How much should you be willing to pay for Bond X today?

Problem-5

Taylor Swift recently received a credit card with a 12 percent nominal interest rate. With the card, she purchased a new smart LED TV for $350. The minimum payment on the card is only $10 per month.

Required

1. If she makes the minimum monthly payment and makes no other charges, how long will it be before she pays off the card? Round to the nearest month.

2. If she makes monthly payments of $30, how long will it take her to pay off the debt? Round to the nearest month.

3. How much more in total payments will he make under the $10-a-month plan than under the $30-a-month plan?

Financial Management For the US CPA Exam

Chapter 03

Financial Statement Analysis

Volume
8

1 Income Statement

KIM Corporation
Income Statement for Year Ended December 31, Year 2
($ in millions)

Sales	$2,311
Cost of goods sold	1,144
Gross profit	1,167
Operating expenses excluding depreciation	200
Depreciation expenses	276
Earnings before interest and taxes (EBIT)	691
Interest expense	141
Earnings before taxes (EBT)	550
Federal and state income taxes (34%)	187
Net income	**$ 363**

Additional information

Total dividends : $121 millions

Shares outstanding : 33 millions

Stock price per share at the end of the year : $88

2 Balance Sheet (Financial Position)

KIM Corporation
Balance Sheet as of December 31, Year 1and Year 2
($ in millions)

Accounts	Year 1	Year 2
Cash	84	98
Accounts receivable	165	188
Inventory	393	422
Total current assets	$642	$708
Net plant & equipment	$2,731	$2,880
Total assets	**$3,373**	**$3,588**

Accounts	Year 1	Year 2
Accounts payable	312	344
Notes payable	231	196
Total current liabilities	$543	$540
Long-term debt	531	457
Total liabilities	$1,074	$997
Common stock	500	550
Retained earnings	1,799	2,041
Total equity	$2,299	$2,591
Total liabilities and equity	**$3,373**	**$3,588**

3 Statement of Cash Flows

KIM Corporation
Statement of Cash Flows for Year Ended December 31, Year 2
($ in millions)

Operating activity	
Net income	$363
Depreciation	276
Increase in accounts receivable	−23
Increase in inventory	−29
Increase in accounts payable	32
Net cash from operating activity	**$619**
Investing activity	
Plant & equipment acquisition	−$425
Net cash from investing activity	**−$425**
Financing activity	
Decrease in notes payable	−$35
Decrease in long-term debt	−74
Dividend paid	−121
Increase in common stock	50
Net cash from financing activity	**−$180**
Net increase in cash	$14
Cash, beginning of year	$84
Cash, end of year	$98

02 > Financial Statement Analysis

1 Time-Series

A time series is a sequence of numerical data points in successive order.

시계열분석이란 두 기간이상에 걸쳐 재무제표를 분석하는 기법으로, 미래에 대한 추세를 예측하는데도 유용한 정보를 제공하는 방법이다.

2 Cross-Sectional Analysis

Cross-sectional analysis compares one company against the industry in which it operates.

횡단면분석이란 특정시점에서 동일업종내의 다른 기업과 재무제표의 금액을 비교하는 방법으로, 주로 동종업종의 유사기업이나 산업평균과 비교한다.

3 Horizontal Analysis

Horizontal analysis is used in financial statement analysis to compare historical data, over a number of accounting periods. Horizontal analysis can either use absolute comparisons or percentage comparisons, where the numbers in each succeeding period are expressed as a percentage of the amount in the baseline year, with the baseline amount being listed as 100%. This is also known as base-year analysis.

기준연도의 각 항목을 100%로 놓고 그 이후 년도의 항목을 기준년도에 대한 비율로 표시한다. 예를 들면 기준년도의 매출액이 150억이고 비교년도의 매출액이 250억이라면 기준년도의 매출액을 100%으로 놓으면 비교년도의 매출액은 167%이 된다.

4 Vertical Analysis (= Common–Size Statements)

Vertical analysis is a method of financial statement analysis in which each line item is listed as a percentage of a base figure within the statement. Thus, line items on an income statement can be stated as a percentage of gross sales, while line items on a balance sheet can be stated as a percentage of total assets, and vertical analysis of a cash flow statement shows each cash inflow or outflow as a percentage of the total cash inflows.

common-size income statement ratios	$\dfrac{\text{income statement account}}{\text{sales}}$
common-size balance sheet ratios	$\dfrac{\text{balance sheet account}}{\text{total assets}}$
common-size cash flow ratios	$\dfrac{\text{cash flow statement account}}{\text{total cash inflows}}$

KIM Corporation
Common-Size Income Statement

Sales	100%
Cost of goods sold	49.5
Gross profit	50.5
Operating expenses excluding depreciation	8.7
Depreciation expenses	11.9
Earnings before interest and taxes (EBIT)	29.9
Interest expense	6.1
Earnings before taxes (EBT)	23.8
Federal and state income taxes (34%)	8.1
Net income	**15.7**

KIM Corporation

Common-Size Balance Sheet as of December 31, Year 2 and Year 1

Accounts	Year 1	Year 2	Horizontal analysis
Cash	2.5	2.7	1.17
Accounts receivable	4.9	5.2	1.14
Inventory	11.7	11.8	1.07
Total current assets	19.1	19.7	1.10
Net plant & equipment	80.9	80.3	1.05
Total assets	100 %	100 %	1.06

Accounts	Year 1	Year 2	Horizontal analysis
Accounts payable	9.2	9.6	1.10
Notes payable	6.8	5.5	0.85
Total current liabilities	16.1	15.1	0.99
Long-term debt	15.7	12.7	0.86
Total liabilities	31.8	27.8	0.94
Common stock	14.8	15.3	1.10
Retained earnings	53.3	56.9	1.13
Total equity	68.2	72.2	1.13
Total liabilities and equity	100 %	100 %	1.06

Example 3-1

In financial statements analysis, expressing all financial statements items as a percentage of base-year amounts is called?

a. Horizontal analysis　　　　b. Vertical analysis
c. Cross-sectional analysis　　d. Ratio analysis

Solution

수평적 분석은 기준년도를 100으로 설정하고 분석하는 기법이고 수직적 분석은 당기 매출액과 자산을 100으로 설정하고 분석하는 기법이다.

정답 : a

Example 3-2

In financial statements analysis, benchmarking with other firms is called?

a. Horizontal analysis　　　　b. Vertical analysis
c. Cross-sectional analysis　　d. Ratio analysis

Solution

경쟁업체를 벤치마킹하는 기법을 횡단면 분석이라고 한다.

정답 : c

Example 3-3

An example of vertical analysis is?

a. An assessment of the relative stability of a firm's level of vertical integration.

b. A comparison in financial ratio from between two or more firms in the same industry.

c. Advertising expense is 2% greater compared with the previous year.

d. Advertising expense for the current year is 2% of sales.

Solution

vertical analysis는 매출액과 자산을 100으로 설정하고 분석하는 기법이다.

b : cross−sectional analysis

c : horizontal analysis

정답 : d

03 ⟩ Ratio Analysis

Ratio analysis is a quantitative method of gaining insight into a company's liquidity, operational efficiency, and profitability by comparing information contained in its financial statements.

(1) Liquidity ratio

(2) Long-term solvency (Leverage) ratio

(3) Activity ratio

(4) Profitability ratio

(5) Growth ratio

(6) Market value ratio

1 Liquidity Measures

유동성 비율(Liquidity ratios)은 기업의 단기 채무를 상환할 수 있는 능력을 측정하는 재무비율로 단기 안정성(short-term solvency)라고도 한다. 유동성 비율이 높을수록 단기적인 채무지급능력은 뛰어나지만 수익성은 낮아지기 때문에 적정수준은 기업의 상황에 따라 달라진다.

(1) Working Capital

순운전자본은 유동자산에서 유동부채를 차감한 잔액으로 일상적인 영업활동에 필요한 자금을 말하며, 단기부채를 지급하기 위해 단기자산의 여력이 얼마나 되는가를 판단하는 지표로 활용된다.

working capital	current assets - current liabilities

For KIM, the Year 2 working capital = \$708 - \$540 = \$168

the Year 1 working capital = \$642 - \$543 = \$99

(2) Current Ratio

유동비율은 유동자산을 유동부채로 나눈 비율이다. 회사의 지불능력을 판단하기 위해서 사용하는 분석지표로 유동부채의 몇 배의 유동자산을 가지고 있는가를 나타내며 이 비율이 높을수록 지불능력이 커진다.

current ratio (working capital ratio)	$\dfrac{\text{current assets}}{\text{current liabilities}}$

For KIM, the Year 2 current ratio = \$708 ÷ \$540 = 1.31 times

- If a current ratio is less than one, a company has negative working capital with potential liquidity problems.
- A high current ratio isn't always a good thing. It might indicate that the business has too much inventory or is not investing its excess cash.

(3) Quick Ratio

당좌비율은 당좌자산을 유동부채로 나눈 비율이다. 당좌자산은 유동자산에서 재고자산과 선급비용을 제외한 자산으로 단기간에 환금할 수 있는 자산만을 포함한다. 당좌비율을 계산하는 데 있어서 재고자산을 제외하는 이유는 재고자산은 판매과정을 거쳐야 현금화할 수 있으므로 현금, 예금 또는 외상매출금 등과 같은 당좌자산과 비교할 때 유동성이 낮으며, 재고자산은 평가방법에 따라 그 가치가 다르게 나타나는 경우가 있기 때문이다.

※ Quick assets = current assets − inventory − prepaid expenses

= cash & equivalents + marketable securities + accounts receivable

Quick ratio (Acid-test ratio)	$\dfrac{\text{quick assets}}{\text{current liabilities}}$

For KIM, the Year 2 quick ratio = ($708 − 422) ÷ $540 = 0.53 times

- The quick ratio indicates a company's capacity to pay its current liabilities without needing to sell its inventory or get additional financing.
- The quick ratio is considered a more conservative measure than the current ratio.

(4) Cash Ratio

현금비율은 현금자산을 유동부채로 나눈 비율로 기업의 초단기 채무지급능력을 가늠할 수 있는 지표이다. 현금자산은 현금, 현금성자산 및 단기금융상품을 말하며, 당좌자산에서 매출채권을 제외한 자산이다.

cash ratio	$\dfrac{\text{cash \& cash equivalents} + \text{marketable securities}}{\text{current liabilities}}$

For KIM, the Year 2 cash ratio = $98 ÷ $540 = 0.18 times

- The cash ratio is more conservative than other liquidity ratios because it only considers a company's most liquid resources.

(5) Other Liquidity Ratio

operating cash flow ratio	$\dfrac{\text{cash flow from operations}}{\text{current liabilities}}$
working capital to total assets	$\dfrac{\text{working capital}}{\text{total assets}}$
defensive interval	$\dfrac{\text{quick assets}}{\text{average daily expenditures}}$

Example 3-4

JOHNSON & JOHNSON has current assets equal to $3 million. The company's current ratio is 1.5 and its quick ratio is 1.0. What is the firm's level of inventories.

Solution

Current liabilities = $3 million ÷ 1.5 = $2 million.

Quick assets = 1.0 × $2 million = $2 million.

Inventory = Current assets − Quick assets

= $3 million − $2 million = $1 million

Example 3-5

American Express Co. has $1,400,000 in current assets and $500,000 in current liabilities. Its initial inventory level is $500,000 and it will raise funds as additional notes payable and use them to increase inventory. How much can the firm's short-term debt increase without pushing its current ratio below 2.0? What will be the firm's quick ratio after the firm has raised the maximum amount of short-term funds?

Solution

Current assets = $1,400,000 + X

Current liabilities = $500,000 + X

$1,400,000 + X = 2 × ($500,000 + X) → X = $400,000

After refinancing

Quick assets = $1,400,000 − $500,000 = $900,000

Current liabilities = $500,000 + $400,000 = $900,000

Quick ratio = $900,000 ÷ $900,000 = 1.00 (100%)

2 Long-term Solvency Measures

　장기안정성 비율은 기업의 장기채무지급능력의 측정치로 재무레버리지 비율(financial leverage ratios) 또는 레버리지 비율(leverage ratios, gearing ratio)이라고도 한다.

(1) Debt ratio

　부채비율은 타인자본과 자산 또는 자기자본 간의 관계를 나타내는 대표적인 안정성 지표로서 이 비율이 낮을수록 재무구조가 건전하다고 판단할 수 있다.

total debt ratio	$\dfrac{\text{total liabilities}}{\text{total assets}}$
debt-to-equity ratio	$\dfrac{\text{total liabilities}}{\text{total equity}}$
equity multiplier	$\dfrac{\text{total assets}}{\text{total equity}}$

For KIM, the Year 2

total debt ratio = $997 ÷ $3,588 = 0.28 times

debt-to-equity ratio = $997 ÷ $2,591= 0.39 times

equity multiplier = $3,588 ÷ $,591= 1.39 times

- Investors can use the debt ratio to evaluate how much leverage a company is using.

- Higher leverage ratios tend to indicate a company with higher risk to shareholders.

- Ambiguity between the terms "debt" and "liabilities"

　Total debt = long−term and shirt−term debt

　Total liabilities = total debt + operating liabilities such as accounts payable

　For KIM, the Year 2

　total debt ratio = ($997 − 344) ÷ $3,588 = 0.18 times

(2) Times-Interest-Earned (Interest Coverage) Ratio

이자보상비율은 이자지급에 필요한 수익의 창출능력을 측정하기 위한 지표로 이자부담능력을 판단하는데 유용하게 쓰인다.

TIE ratio (times-interest-earned)	$\dfrac{\text{EBIT}}{\text{interest expense}}$

For KIM, the Year 2 TIE ratio = $691 ÷ $141 = 4.9 times

(3) EBITDA Coverage Ratio (=Cash Coverage)

현금보상비율은 기업의 영업현금흐름을 측정치인 EBITDA를 이용한 현금주의 이자보상비율이다.

EBITDA coverage ratio	$\dfrac{\text{EBITDA}}{\text{interest expense}}$

For KIM, the Year 2 cash coverage = ($691 + 276) ÷ $141 = 6.9 times

(4) Other Leverage Ratio

debt-to-capital ratio	$\dfrac{\text{total debt}}{\text{total capital}}$
비유동장기적합률	$\dfrac{\text{non-current assets}}{\text{equity + non-current liabilities}}$
fixed charge coverage	$\dfrac{\text{EBIT + lease payments}}{\text{interest payments + lease payments}}$

Example 3-6

WELLS FARGO has a total debt ratio of 0.62.

What is its debt-equity ratio? What is its equity multiplier??

Solution

$D/A = D/E \times E/A = D/E \times (1 - D/A)$

$0.62 = D/E \times (1-0.62) \rightarrow D/E = 1.63$

$A/E = 1 + D/E = 1 + 1.63 = 2.63$

Example 3-7

Caterpillar Inc. has $500,000 of debt outstanding and it pays an interest rate of 10% annually. The company's sales are $2 million, its average tax rate is 30% and its net profit margin on sales is 7%. If the company does not maintain a TIE ratio of at least 4 times, its bank will refuse to renew loan, and bankruptcy will result. What is the company's ratio?

Solution

Net income = $2,000,000 \times 7\% = \$140,000$

$EBT = \$140,000 \div 0.7 = \$200,000$

Interest = $\$500,000 \times 10\% = \$50,000$

$EBIT = \$200,000 + \$50,000 = \$250,000$

$TIE = \$250,000 \div \$50,000 = 5$ times

$\rightarrow$ The bank will not refuse to renew loan.

Example 3-8

When compared to a debt-to-assets ratio, a debt-to-equity ratio is
a. the same as the debt-to-assets ratio.
b. higher than the debt-to-assets ratio.
c. lower than the debt-to-assets ratio.
d. unrelated to the debt-to-assets ratio.

Solution

Assets $>$ Equity $\rightarrow$ D/A $<$ D/E
정답 : b

Example 3-9

Calvin Klein's net income for the most recent year was $8,175. The tax rate was 34 percent. The firm paid $2,380 in total interest expense and deducted $1,560 in depreciation expense. What was Calvin Klein's interest coverage ratio and cash coverage ratio for the year?

Solution

EBIT = $8,175 $\div$ 0.66 + 2,380 = $14,766
interest coverage ratio = $14,766 $\div$ $2,380 = 6.2 times
EBITDA = 14,766 + 1,560 = $16,326
cash coverage ratio = $16,326 $\div$ $2,380 = 6.9 times

3 Activity Measures

활동성 비율은 기업에 투하된 자본이 기간 중 얼마나 활발하게 운용되었는가를 나타내는 비율로서 회전율(turnover ratio) 또는 자산 이용률(asset utilization ratios)이라고도 한다. 활동성 분석의 재무상태표 항목은 일반적으로 평균금액을 기준으로 구한다. 하지만 AICPA 시험에서는 기말금액을 기준으로 회전율을 계산하도록 요구하기도 한다.

(1) Asset Turnover Ratios

총자산회전율(total asset turnover)은 총자산이 1년 동안 몇 번 회전하였는가를 나타내는 비율로서 기업에 투하한 총자산의 운용효율을 총괄적으로 표시하는 지표이다.

total asset turnover	$\dfrac{\text{sales}}{\text{average total assets}}$

For KIM, the Year 2

average total assets = (3,373 + 3,588) ÷ 2 = $3,480

total asset turnover = $2,311 ÷ $3,480 = 0.66 times

유형자산 회전율(fixed asset turnover) 유형자산의 이용도를 나타내는 지표로서 기업이 보유하고 있는 설비자산의 적정성 여부를 판단하는데 유용하다.

fixed asset turnover	$\dfrac{\text{sales}}{\text{average net fixed assets}}$

For KIM, the Year 2

average net fixed assets = (2,731 + 2,880) ÷ 2 = $2,806

fixed asset turnover = $2,311 ÷ $2,806 = 0.82 times

운전자본 회전율(working capital turnover) 운전자본의 이용도를 나타내는 지표로서 기업이 보유하고 있는 운전자본의 적정성 여부를 판단하는데 유용하다.

working capital turnover	$\dfrac{\text{sales}}{\text{average working capital}}$

For KIM, the Year 2

average working capital = (99 + 168) ÷ 2 = $134

working capital turnover = $2,311 ÷ $134 = 17.3 times

(2) Receivables Turnover and Days Sales Outstanding (DSO)

　매출채권 회전율은 매출채권의 현금화 속도를 측정하는 비율로서 높을수록 매출채권의 현금화 속도가 빠르다는 것을 의미한다. 매출채권회전율의 역수를 취하여 365일을 곱하면 평균회수기간을 계산할 수 있는데 이 기간이 짧을수록 매출채권이 효율적으로 관리되어 판매자금이 매출채권에 오래 묶여 있지 않음을 뜻하며, 반대의 경우에는 가공매출 또는 고객의 지급불능의 신호가 된다.

　그러나 기업이 시장점유율 확대를 위해 판매 전략을 강화하는 경우에도 매출채권회전율이 낮게 나타날 수 있으므로 기업의 목표회수기간이나 판매조건과 비교하여 적정성을 평가하여야 할 것이다.

receivable turnover	$\dfrac{\text{sales}}{\text{average A/R}}$
days sales outstanding (DSO)	$\dfrac{365}{\text{receivable turnover}}$
	$\dfrac{\text{average A/R}}{\text{sales per day}}$
	$\dfrac{\text{ending A/R(net)}}{\text{sales per day}}$

For KIM, the Year 2

average receivable = (165 + 188) ÷ 2 = $177

receivable turnover = $2,311 ÷ $177 = 13.1 times

days sales outstanding = 365 ÷ 13.1 times = 28 days (평균 매출채권기준)

days sales outstanding = 188 ÷ (2,311 ÷ 365) = 30 days (기말 매출채권기준)

(3) Inventory Turnover and Days Inventory Outstanding (DIO)

재고자산회전율은 매출액을 재고자산으로 나눈 비율로서 재고자산의 회전속도, 즉 재고자산이 현금 등 당좌자산으로 변화하는 속도를 나타낸다. 일반적으로 이 비율이 높을수록 상품의 재고손실 방지 및 보험료, 보관료의 절약 등 재고자산의 관리가 효율적으로 이루어지고 있음을 의미한다. 이 비율이 낮다는 것은 재고자산이 과다하다는 것을 의미하며, 이 비율이 높다는 것은 생산 및 판매활동이 효율적으로 수행되고 있다는 의미이다. Just-in-time (JIT) system을 도입한 기업은 재고자산 회전율은 높아지고, 재고자산 회전기간은 짧아진다.

그러나 재고를 정상적인 영업활동에 필요한 적정수준 이하로 유지하여 수요변동에 적절히 대처하지 못하는 경우에도 이 비율은 높게 나타날 수가 있으므로 해석에

유의할 필요가 있다.

또한 원재료의 가격이 상승추세에 있는 기업이나 재고자산의 보유수준이 크게 높아지는 기업들의 경우에는 주로 후입선출법(LIFO)에 의해 재고자산을 평가함으로써 재고자산회전율이 높게 나타나는 경향이 있다.

따라서 재고자산회전율에 대한 상대적인 차이에 대해서는 실제로 재고자산이 효율적으로 관리되었는지, 생산기간이 단축되어 재공품이 감소하였는지, 기업의 재고보유 방침이 바뀌었는지, 또한 재고자산 평가방법을 다르게 채택하고 있는지를 비교 분석하여 판단하여야 할 것이다.

inventory turnover	$\dfrac{\text{cost of goods sold}}{\text{average inventory}}$
days inventory outstanding (DIO)	$\dfrac{365}{\text{inventory turnover}}$
	$\dfrac{\text{average inventory}}{\text{COGS per day}}$
	$\dfrac{\text{ending inventory}}{\text{COGS per day}}$

For KIM, the Year 2

average inventory = (393 + 422) ÷ 2 = $408

inventory turnover = \$1,144 ÷ \$408 = 2.8 times

days inventory outstanding = 365 ÷ 2.8 times = 130 days (평균 재고자산 기준)

days inventory outstanding = 422 ÷ (1,144 ÷ 365) = 134 days (기말 재고자산 기준)

(4) Payable Turnover and Days Payable Outstanding (DPO)

매입채무회전율은 매입채무의 지급속도를 측정하는 지표로서 기업의 부채 중에서도 특히 매입채무가 원활히 결제되고 있는가의 여부를 나타낸다. 매입채무회전율을 측정하는 기본항목은 매출원가 또는 매입금액이다.

매입채무회전율이 높을수록 결제속도가 빠름을 의미하나 회사의 신용도가 저하되어 신용 매입기간을 짧게 제공받는 경우에도 이 비율이 높게 나타날 수 있기 때문에 운전자본의 압박가능성 등을 보다 정확하게 분석하기 위해서는 매출채권회전율도 함께 비교·검토하는 것이 요구된다.

payable turnover	$\dfrac{\text{cost of goods sold}}{\text{average A/P}}$
days payable outstanding (DPO)	$\dfrac{365}{\text{payable turnover}}$
	$\dfrac{\text{average A/P}}{\text{COGS per day}}$
	$\dfrac{\text{ending A/P}}{\text{COGS per day}}$

For KIM, the Year 2

average A/P = (312 + 344) ÷ 2 = \$328

payable turnover = \$1,144 ÷ \$328 = 3.5 times

days payable outstanding = 365 ÷ 3.5 times = 104 days (평균 매입채무 기준)

days payable outstanding = 344 ÷ (1,144 ÷ 365) = 110 days (기말 매입채무 기준)

(5) Cash Conversion Cycle (CCC)

The Cash Conversion Cycle (CCC) is a metric that shows the amount of time it takes a company to convert its investments in inventory to cash. The cash conversion cycle formula measures the amount of time, in days, it takes for a company to turn its resource inputs into cash.

The cash conversion cycle formula is aimed at assessing how efficiently a company is managing its working capital. The shorter the cash conversion cycle, the better the company is at selling inventories and recovering cash from these sales while paying suppliers.

DIO

the average number of days that a company holds its inventory before selling it.

DSO

the average number of days for a company to collect payment after a sale.

DPO

the average number of days for a company to pay its invoices from suppliers.

cash conversion cycle	DIO + DSO - DPO

For KIM, the Year 2

Cash Conversion Cycle = 130 + 28 - 104 = 54 days

→ it takes approximately 54 days to turn its initial cash investment in inventory back into cash.

Example 3-10

The following financial ratios and calculations were based on information from Boeing Co.'s financial statements for the current year :

Accounts receivable turnover : Ten times during the year

Total assets turnover : Two times during the year

Average receivables during the year : $200,000

What was firm's average total assets for the year?

Solution

Sales = $200,000 × 10 times = $2,000,000

Total average assets = $2,000,000 ÷ 2.0 times = $1,000,000

Example 3-11

Accounts receivable turnover will normally decrease as a result of

a. The write-off of an uncollectible account.

b. A significant sales volume decrease near the end of the accounting period.

c. An increase in cash sales in proportion to credit sales.

d. A change in credit policy to lengthen the period for cash discounts.

Solution

a. 이미 대손충당금을 설정하였기 때문에 매출채권의 순액에 영향을 주지 않는다.

b. 기말의 매출감소는 기말매출채권을 급격히 감소시키므로 매출채권 회전율이 증가.

c. 현금매출의 증가는 매출채권의 감소이므로 회전율의 증가.

d. 현금할인 기간이 증가하면 회수기간이 길어지므로 회전율은 감소.

정답 : d

Example 3-12

CHANEL's receivable turnover is ten times, the inventory turnover is five times and the payable turnover is nine times. What is firm's cash conversion cycle?

Solution

DIO = 365 ÷ 5 times = 73 days
DSO = 365 ÷ 10 times = 37 days
DPO = 365 ÷ 9 times = 41 days
CCC = 73 + 37 − 41 = 69 days

4 Profitability Measures

수익성 비율은 일정기간 동안의 기업의 경영성과를 측정하는 비율로서 투자된 자본 또는 자산, 매출수준에 상응하여 창출한 이익의 정도를 나타내므로 자산이용의 효율성, 이익창출능력 등에 대한 평가는 물론 영업성과를 요인별로 분석 · 검토

하기 위한 지표로 이용된다. 수익성 분석의 재무상태표 항목은 일반적으로 평균금액을 기준으로 구한다. 하지만 AICPA 시험에서는 기말금액을 기준으로 수익성 비율을 계산하도록 요구하기도 한다.

(1) Profit Margin Ratios

매출액 이익률은 일정기간 동안의 기업의 경영성과를 측정하는 비율로서 매출수준에 상응하여 창출한 이익의 정도를 나타낸다.

gross profit margin	$\dfrac{\text{gross profit}}{\text{sales}}$
operating profit margin	$\dfrac{\text{operating profit}}{\text{sales}}$
net profit margin	$\dfrac{\text{net income}}{\text{sales}}$

For KIM, the Year 2

gross profit margin = 1,167 ÷ 2,311 = 50.5%

operating profit margin = 691 ÷ 2,311 = 29.9%

net profit margin = 363 ÷ 2,311 = 15.7%

(2) Return on Assets (ROA)

총자산순이익률은 당기순이익의 총자산에 대한 비율로, 기업 관점에서의 투자수익률을 의미한다. 기업의 계획과 실적 간 차이 분석을 통한 경영활동의 평가나 경영전략 수립 등에 많이 활용된다.

return on assets (ROA)	$\dfrac{\text{net income}}{\text{average total assets}}$

For KIM, the Year 2

average assets = (3,373 + 3,588) ÷ 2 = $3,481

return on assets = $363 ÷ $3,481 = 10.43%

(3) Return on Equity (ROE)

자기자본순이익률은 자기자본에 대한 당기순이익의 비율로서, 주주 관점에서의 투자수익률을 의미한다. 자본조달 특성에 따라 동일한 자산구성 하에서도 서로 다른 결과를 나타낼 수 있으므로 자본구성과의 관계도 동시에 고려해야 한다.

return on equity (ROE)	$\dfrac{\text{net income}}{\text{average equity}}$

For KIM, the Year 2

average equity = (2,299 + 2,591) ÷ 2 = $2,445

return on equity = $363 ÷ $2,445 = 14.85%

Du Pont identity (듀퐁항등식)

화학업체 듀퐁에서 근무하던 Donaldson Brown이 1920년대 고안한 재무 분석 기법

ROE = NI / Equity = (NI / Sales) × (Sales / Assets) × (Assets / Equity)

return on equity (ROE)	profit margin × asset turnover × equity multipliers
	ROA × equity multipliers

For KIM, the Year 2

profit margin = 15.7%, asset turnover = 0.664 times,

average equity multipliers = $3,481 ÷ $2,445 = 1.42 times

ROE = 15.7% × 0.664 × 1.42 = 14.8%

Popular expression breaking ROE into three parts:

1. Operating efficiency (as measured by profit margin)
2. Asset use efficiency (as measured by total asset turnover)
3. Financial leverage (as measured by the equity multiplier)

Example 3-13

Dimler-Benz Corp. has a profit margin of 7 percent, total asset turnover of 1.09, and ROE of 23.70 percent. What is this firm's debt-equity ratio?

Solution

$23.70\% = 7\% \times 1.09 \times$ equity multipliers → equity multipliers = 3.1

$A/E = 1 + D/E \rightarrow 3.1 = 1 + D/E \rightarrow D/E = 2.1$

Example 3-14

PRADA has a debt-equity ratio of 1.10. Return on assets is 8.4 percent, and total equity is $440,000. What is the equity multiplier? Return on equity? Net income?

Solution

equity multipliers = $1 + D/E = 1 + 1.10 = 2.10$

ROE = $8.4\% \times 2.10 = 17.64\%$

NI = $\$440,000 \times 0.1764 = \$77,616$

Example 3-15

Coca-Cola Co.'s ROE last year was only 3%, but its management has developed a new operating plan designed to improve things. The new plan calls for a total debt ratio of 60%, which will result in interest charge of $300,000 per year. Management projects an EBIT of $1,000,000 on sales of $10,000,000 and it expects to have a total assets turnover of 2.0. Under these condition, the tax rate will be 40%. If the changes are made, what ROE will the company earn?

Solution

net income = ($1,000,000 − $300,000) × (1 − 0.4) = $420,000

profit margin = $420,000 ÷ $10,000,000 = 4.2%

equity multiplier = Assets ÷ Equity = 100% ÷ 40% = 2.5times

ROE = 4.2% × 2.0 × 2.5 = 21%

5 Growth Measures

(1) Sales Growth

매출액 증가율은 전기 매출액에 대한 당기 매출액의 증가율로서 기업의 외형 신장세를 판단하는 대표적인 지표이다.

sales growth	$\dfrac{\text{current sales - prior sales}}{\text{prior sales}}$

(2) Profit Growth

순이익증가율은 전기 순이익에 대한 당기 순이익의 증가율로서 기업의 수익성 신장세를 판단하는 대표적인 지표이다.

profit growth	$\dfrac{\text{current net income - prior net income}}{\text{prior net income}}$

(3) Assets Growth

자산증가율은 기업에 투하된 총자산이 얼마나 증가하였는가를 나타내는 비율로서 기업의 전체적인 성장성을 측정하는 지표이다.

assets growth	$\dfrac{\text{current assets - prior assets}}{\text{prior assets}}$

(4) Payout Ratio

배당성향은 기업이 당기순이익 중 어느 정도를 배당금으로 지급하였는가를 나타내는 지표로 배당금을 당기순이익으로 나누어 측정하거나 주당배당금을 주당이익으로 나누어 측정한다.

payout ratio	$\dfrac{\text{total dividends}}{\text{net income}}$
	$\dfrac{\text{dividend per share (DPS)}}{\text{earning per share (EPS)}}$

For KIM, the Year 2 payout ratio = 121 ÷ 363 = 33.3%

(5) Retention Ratio (RR)

유보율은 당기순이익 중에서 배당으로 처분되지 않고 기업내부에 유보된 금액의 비율을 나타내며, 1001에서 배당성향을 차감하여 산출된다.

retention ratio	1 - payout ratio

For KIM, the Year 2 retention ratio = 100% − 33.3% = 66.7%

(6) Sustainable Growth Rate (SGR)

배당 성장률은 당기 배당대비 향후 배당이 얼마나 증가할 것인지를 나타내는 비율로서, 기업의 유보율에 자기자본이익률(ROE)을 곱하여 측정한다.

sustainable growth rate	ROE × retention ratio

For KIM, the Year 2 SGR = 66.7% × 14.85% = 9.9%

Examplet 3-16

Volvo has a dividend payout ratio of 40%, a net profit margin of 10%, an asset turnover of 0.9 times and a equity multiplier of 1.2times. What is the firm's sustainable growth rate?

Solution

ROE = 10% × 0.9 × 1.2 = 10.8%

Retention rate = 1 − 0.4 = 0.6

SGR = 10.8% × 0.6 = 6.48%

Example 3-17

Two companies are identical except for different dividend payout ratio. The company with the lower dividend payout ratio is most likely to have?

a. lower stock price   b. higher debt-to-equity ratio

c. less rapid growth of EPS   d. more rapid growth of EPS

Solution

배당성향이 낮은 기업은 자기자본이 더 크기 때문에 부채비율은 작고, 유보율이 높기 때문에 이익성장률이 높으며, 주가는 더 높을수도 있고 낮을 수도 있다.

정답 : d

6 Market Value Measures

(1) Price-to-Earnings Ratio (P/E Ratio)

주가수익률은 주가를 주당이익(EPS)으로 나눈 값을 말하며, 이는 기업의 주당순이익이 증권시장에서 몇 배의 주가로 평가되고 있는가를 나타낸다. 예를 들어, 주당이익이 1,000원이고 주가가 12,000원이라면 PER는 12이다.

P/E ratio	$\dfrac{\text{price per share}}{\text{earning per share}}$
	$\dfrac{\text{market value}}{\text{net income}}$

For KIM, the Year 2

EPS = $363 ÷ 33 = $11

P/E = $88 ÷ $11 = 8 times

- High P/E : 주식의 시장가격이 과대평가 또는 성장주(growth stock)

- Low P/E : 주식의 시장가격이 과소평가 또는 가치주(value stock)

- Forward P/E : uses forecasted earnings for the P/E calculation

- Trailing P/E : uses last 12 months of actual earnings for the P/E calculation

- TTM : Trailing 12 Months

- MRQ : Most Recent Quarter

목표기업의 주가를 추정하는 경우 목표기업의 주당이익에 목표기업이 속한 산업평균 P/E ratio를 곱하여 산출할 수 있다.

$$\text{Price}^{\text{target}} = \text{EPS}^{\text{target}} \times \text{P/E}^{\text{industry}}$$

The earnings yield (which is the inverse of the P/E ratio) shows the percentage of each dollar invested in the stock that was earned by the company.

earnings yield (EY)	$$\dfrac{\text{earning per share}}{\text{price per share}}$$

For KIM, the Year 2 earnings yield = $11 ÷ $88 = 12.5%

The price/earnings to growth ratio (PEG ratio) is a stock's price-to-earnings (P/E) ratio divided by the growth rate of its earnings for a specified time period. The PEG ratio is considered to be an indicator of a stock's true value, and a lower PEG may indicate that a stock is undervalued.

PEG ratio	$$\dfrac{\text{price-to-earnings ratio}}{\text{EPS growth}}$$

For KIM, the Year 2 PEG ratio = 8 ÷ 9.9 = 0.81

(2) Price-to-Book Ratio (P/B ratio, Market-to-Book Ratio)

주가순자산배율은 주가를 주당순자산으로 나눈 값을 말하며, 이는 기업의 주당순자산이 증권시장에서 몇 배의 주가로 평가되고 있는가를 나타낸다.

P/B ratio	$$\dfrac{\text{price per share}}{\text{book value per share}}$$
	$$\dfrac{\text{market value}}{\text{equity}}$$

For KIM, the Year 2
book value per share = $2,591 ÷ 33 = $78.5
P/B = $88 ÷ $78.5 = 1.12 times

- High P/B : 주식의 시장가격이 과대평가 또는 성장주(growth stock)
- Low P/B : 주식의 시장가격이 과소평가 또는 가치주(value stock)

목표기업의 주가를 추정하는 경우 목표기업의 주당순자산에 목표기업이 속한 산업평균 P/B ratio 를 곱하여 산출할 수 있다.

$$\text{Price}^{\text{target}} = \text{BPS}^{\text{target}} \times \text{P/B}^{\text{industry}}$$

The P/B ratio can also be used for firms with positive book values and negative earnings since negative earnings render price-to-earnings ratios useless, and there are fewer companies with negative book values than companies with negative earnings. However, when accounting standards applied by firms vary, P/B ratios may not be comparable, especially for companies from different countries. Additionally, P/B ratios can be less useful for service and information technology companies with little tangible assets on their balance sheets. Finally, the book value can become negative because of a long series of negative earnings, making the P/B ratio useless for relative valuation.

(3) Price-to-Sales Ratio (P/S Ratio)

주가매출배율은 주가를 주당매출액으로 나눈 값을 말하며, 이는 기업의 주당매출액이 증권시장 에서 몇 배의 주가로 평가되고 있는가를 나타낸다.

P/S ratio	$\dfrac{\text{price per share}}{\text{sales per share}}$
	$\dfrac{\text{market value}}{\text{sales}}$

For KIM, the Year 2

sales per share = $2,311 ÷ 33 = $70.0

P/S = $88 ÷ $70 = 1.26 times

The P/S ratio provides a way to value a company with little or no profits. A higher (lower) P/S ratio relative to peers or the industry may suggest a company is overvalued (undervalued).

(4) Price-to-Cash Flow Ratio (P/CF Ratio)

주가현금흐름배율은 주가를 주당영업현금흐름으로 나눈 값을 말하며, 이는 기업의 주당영업현금흐름이 증권시장에서 몇 배의 주가로 평가되고 있는가를 나타낸다.

P/CF ratio	$\dfrac{\text{price per share}}{\text{operating cash flow per share}}$
	$\dfrac{\text{market value}}{\text{operating cash flow}}$

The price-to-cash flow multiple works well for companies that have large non-cash expenses such as depreciation. A low multiple implies that a stock may be undervalued.

Example 3-18

LVMH group had additions to retained earnings for the year just ended of $275,000. The firm paid out $150,000 in cash dividends, and it has ending total equity of $6 million. If LVMH currently has 125,000 shares of common stock outstanding, what are earnings per share? Book value per share? If the stock currently sells for $95 per share, what is the market-to-book ratio? The price-earnings ratio?

Solution

net income = 275,000 + 150,000 = $425,000

EPS = $425,000 ÷ 125,000 = $3.4

BPS = $6,000,000 ÷ 125,000 = $48

market-to-book ratio = $95 ÷ $48 = 1.98 times

price-earnings ratio = $95 ÷ $3.4 = 27.9 times

Example 3-19

A company has an EPS of $2.00, a cash flow per share of $3.00, and a price/cash flow ratio of 8.0. What is its P/E ratio?

Solution

price per share = $3 × 8 = $24
price−earnings ratio = $24 ÷ $2 = 12 times

Example 3-20

Volkswagen recently reported net income of $2 million. It has 500,000 shares of common stock, which currently trades at $40 a share. Volkswagen continues to expand and anticipates that 1 year from now its net income will be $3.25 million. Over the next year it also anticipates issuing an additional 150,000 shares of stock, so that 1 year from now it will have 650,000 shares of common stock. Assuming its price/earnings ratio remains at its current level, what will be its stock price 1 year from now?

Solution

EPS = $2,000,000 ÷ 500,000 = $4
price−earnings ratio = $40 ÷ $4 = 10 times
EPS 1 year from now = $3,250,000 ÷ 650,000 = $5
price per share = $5 × 10 = $50
market value = $50 × 650,000 = $32,500,000

7 Limitations of Financial Statement Analysis

(1) Different accounting practices

기업마다 회계처리 방법이 다르기 때문에 비율분석을 통한 비교만으로는 충분하지 않다. 비교대상 기업의 재고자산 평가방법이나 감가상각 방법이 상이하다면 정확한 비교정보를 얻을 수 없을 것이다. 예를 들면 물가 상승시에 FIFO방법은 LIFO방법보다 기말재고와 이익을 더 높게 보고한다.

(2) Large firms operating different divisions in different industries.

다양한 산업을 영위하는 대기업의 경우 적절한 벤치마킹을 결정하기가 어렵다. 예를 들면 삼성전자의 비교대상이 되는 산업평균은 반도체인지 가전제품인지의 판단이 어려울 것이다.

(3) It is difficult to generalize about whether a particular ratio is good or bad.

종합적인 재무비율이 양호한지 불량한지의 여부를 일반화하기가 어렵다. 예를 들면 현금을 많이 보유하고 있으면 유동성은 좋지만, 수익성은 감소한다.

(4) Window dressing technique.

회계연도 말에 경영자가 재무제표의 수치를 고의로 왜곡시키는 분식회계를 말한다.

예를 들면 연말에 기업이 은행으로부터 장기차입을 하여 현금을 보유하고 있다면, 유동성은 양호해 보인다. 그리고 다음연도 초에 차입금을 상환한다면, 또한 이러한 행위를 매년 반복한다면, 이 기업의 유동성 비율은 매년 분식을 하는 셈이다.

(5) Only financial measures.

재무비율 분석은 기업의 재무적인 성과만을 보는 것이다. 하지만 경영자의 자질, 시장점유율, 브랜드 가치 등의 비재무적인 질적 요인들은 재무제표에 수치화 할 수 없다.

Example 3-21

Which of the following is not a limitation of ratio analysis?

a. Different accounting practices   b. Different fiscal years.

c. Window dressing   d. Liquidity cannot be analyzed.

Solution

유동비율이나 당좌비율 등으로 기업의 유동성을 평가할 수 있다.

정답 : d

04 Multiple Choice

01. For a given level of sales, and holding all other financial statement items constant, a company's return on equity (ROE) will (CMA)

a. increase as their debt ratio decreases.

b. decrease as their cost of goods sold as a percent of sales decrease.

c. decrease as their total assets increase.

d. increase as their equity increases.

02. The following financial information applies to Sycamore Company.

Cash	$10,000
Marketable securities	18,000
Accounts receivable	120,000
Inventories	375,000
Prepaid expenses	12,000
Accounts payable	75,000
Long-term debt — current portion	20,000
Long-term debt	400,000
Sales	1,650,000

What is the acid-test (or quick) ratio for Sycamore? (CMA)

a. 1.56   b. 1.97

c. 2.13   d. 5.63

03. A bondholder would be most concerned with which one of the following ratios? (CMA)

a. Inventory turnover

b. Times interest earned

c. Quick ratio

d. Earnings per share

04. Anderson Cable wishes to calculate their return on assets. You know that the return on equity is 12% and that the debt ratio is 40%. What is the ROA? (CMA)

a. 4.8%

b. 7.2%

c. 12.0%

d. 20.0%.

05. Peggy Monahan, controller, has gathered the following information regarding Lampasso Company.

	Beginning of the year	End of the year
Inventory	$6,400	$7,600
Accounts receivable	2,140	3,060
Accounts payable	3,320	3,680

Total sales for the year were $85,900, of which $62,400 were credit sales. The cost of goods sold was $24,500. Lampasso's accounts receivable turnover ratio for the year was (CMA)

a. 9.4 times

b. 20.4 times

c. 24.0 times

d. 33.0 times

06. Davis Retail Inc. has total assets of $7,500,000 and a current ratio of 2.3 times before purchasing $750,000 of merchandise on credit for resale. After this purchase, the current ratio will (CMA)

a. remain at 2.3 times.

b. be higher than 2.3 times.

c. be lower than 2.3 times.

d. be exactly 2.53 times.

07. Markowitz Company increased its allowance for uncollectable accounts. This adjustment will (CMA)

a. increase the acid test ratio.

b. increase working capital.

c. reduce debt-to-asset ratio.

d. reduce the current ratio.

08. Birch Products Inc. has the following current assets.

Cash	$250,000
Marketable securities	100,000
Accounts receivable	800,000
Inventories	1,450,000
Total current assets	$2,600,000

If Birch's current liabilities are $1,300,000, the firm's (CMA)

a. current ratio will decrease if a payment of $100,000 cash is used to pay $100,000 of accounts payable.

b. current ratio will not change if a payment of $100,000 cash is used to pay $100,000 of accounts payable.

c. quick ratio will decrease if a payment of $100,000 cash is used to purchase inventory.

d. quick ratio will not change if a payment of $100,000 cash is used to purchase inventory.

09. Garstka Auto Parts must increase its acid test ratio above the current 0.9 level in order to comply with the terms of a loan agreement. Which one of the following actions is most likely to produce the desired results? (CMA)

a. Expediting collection of accounts receivable.

b. Selling auto parts on account.

c. Making a payment to trade accounts payable.

d. Purchasing marketable securities for cash.

10. The owner of a chain of grocery stores has bought a large supply of mangoes and paid for the fruit with cash. This purchase will adversely impact which one of the following? (CMA)

a. Working capital   b. Current ratio

c. Quick or acid test ratio   d. Price earnings ratio

11. Both the current ratio and the quick ratio for Spartan Corporation have been slowly decreasing. For the past two years, the current ratio has been 2.3 to 1 and 2.0 to 1. During the same time period, the quick ratio has decreased from 1.2 to 1 to 1.0 to 1. The disparity between the current and quick ratios can be explained by which one of the following? (CMA)

a. The current portion of long-term debt has been steadily increasing.

b. The cash balance is unusually low.

c. The accounts receivable balance has decreased.

d. The inventory balance is unusually high.

12. Globetrade is a retailer that buys virtually all of its merchandise from manufacturers in a country experiencing significant inflation. Globetrade is considering changing its method of inventory costing from first-in, first-out (FIFO) to last-in, first-out (LIFO). What effect would the change from FIFO to LIFO have on Globetrade's current ratio and inventory turnover ratio? (CMA)

a. Both the current ratio and the inventory turnover ratio would increase.

b. The current ratio would increase but the inventory turnover ratio would decrease.

c. The current ratio would decrease but the inventory turnover ratio would increase.

d. Both the current ratio and the inventory turnover ratio would decrease.

13. Which one of the following is the best indicator of long-term debt paying ability? (CMA)

a. Working capital turnover   b. Asset turnover

c. Current ratio   d. Debt-to-total assets ratio

14. The interest expense for a company is equal to its earnings before interest and taxes (EBIT). The company's tax rate is 40%. The company's times-interest earned ratio is equal to (CMA)

a. 2.0   b. 1.0

c. 0.6   d. 1.2

Items through 15 and 16

Bull & Bear Investment Banking is working with the management of Clark Inc. in order to take the company public in an initial public offering. Selected financial information for Clark is as follows.

Long-term debt (8% interest rate)	$10,000,000
Common equity : Par value ($1 per share)	3,000,000
Additional paid-in-capital	24,000,000
Retained earnings	6,000,000
Total assets	55,000,000
Net income	3,750,000
Dividend (annual)	1,500,000

15. If public companies in Clark's industry are trading at twelve times earnings, what is the estimated value per share of Clark? (CMA)

a. $9.00

b. $12.00

c. $15.00

d. $24.00.

16. If public companies in Clark's industry are trading at a market to book ratio of 1.5, what is the estimated value per share of Clark? (CMA)

a. $13.50

b. $16.50

c. $21.50

d. $27.50.

Solution

1	2	3	4	5	6	7	8	9	10
C	A	B	B	C	C	D	C	B	C

11	12	13	14	15	16
D	C	D	B	C	B

1. ROE = Profit margin × asset turnover × financial leverage

   a. 부채비율의 감소 → financial leverage의 감소 → ROE의 감소

   b. 매출원가율의 감소 → Profit margin의 증가 → ROE의 증가

   c. 자산의 증가 → asset turnover의 감소 → ROE의 감소

   d. 자본의 증가 → financial leverage의 감소 → ROE의 감소

2. Quick assets = 10,000 + 18,000 + 120,000 = 148,000

   Current liabilities = 75,000 + 20,000 = 95,000

   Quick ratio = 148,000 ÷ 95,000 = 1.56

3. 채권자가 관심을 가지는 재무비율은 레버리지 (장기 안정성) 비율이다.

4. ROE = ROA × equity multipliers

   D/A = 0.4 → equity multipliers = A ÷ E = 10 ÷ 6 = 1.67

   ROA = 12% ÷ 1.67 = 7.2%

5. 외상매출과 현금매출이 구분되는 경우 매출채권회전율은 외상매출 기준으로 측정한다.

   Average AR = (2,140 + 3,060) ÷ 2 = 2,600

   AR turnover = 62,400 ÷ 2,600 = 24

6. 재고자산 증가, 매입채무 증가

   Current ratio 〉 1 → Current ratio 감소

7. 대손충당금 증가, net A/R 감소

   → 순운전자본, Current ratio, Quick ratio 모두 감소

   → 부채 변동없음, 부채비율 증가

8. Current ratio 〉 1, Quick ratio 〈 1

   매입채무 감소, 현금 감소 → Current ratio 증가, Quick ratio 감소

   재고자산 증가, 현금 감소 → Current ratio 변동없음, Quick ratio 감소

9. Quick ratio ⟨ 1

  a : 당좌자산 변동없음, Quick ratio 변동없음

  b : 재고자산 감소, 매출채권 증가, 당좌자산 증가, Quick ratio 증가

  c : 당좌자산 감소, 유동부채 감소, Quick ratio 감소

  d : 당좌자산 변동없음, Quick ratio 변동없음

10. 재고자산 증가, 현금 감소

  → 유동자산 변동없음, 당좌자산 감소,

    Current ratio 변동없음. Quick ratio 감소

11. 유동비율과 당좌비율의 차이가 큰 원인은 재고자산의 많기 때문이다.

12. 물가상승시 : FIFO → LIFO

  재고자산 감소, 매출원가 증가, 매출총이익 감소 .

13. 장기 지급능력은 레버리지 비율로 측정한다.

14. TIE = EBIT ÷ Interest = 1

15. EPS = \$3,750,000 ÷ 3,000,000 shares = \$1.25

  Price = P/E × EPS = 12 × 1.25 = \$15

16. BPS = (3,000,000 + 24,000,000 + 6,000,000) ÷ 3,000,000 = \$11

  Price = P/B × BPS = 1.5 × \$11 = \$16.5

05 ▶ Task-Based Simulation

Problem-1

Financial data (Calculation is based on a 365-day year) :

Debt ratio : 50%

Current ratio : 1.8

Total assets turnover : 1.5

Days sales outstanding : 36.5 days

Gross profit margin on sales : 25%

Inventory turnover ratio : 5

Balance Sheet

Accounts	Amount	Accounts	Amount
Cash		Accounts payable	
Accounts receivable		Long-term debt	60,000
Inventories		Common stock	
Fixed assets		Retained earnings	97,500
Total assets	$300,000	Total liabilities and equity	

Income statement

Accounts	Amount
Sales	
Cost of goods sold	

Required

Complete the balance sheet and sales information using the above financial data.

Problem-2

Data for KIM Co. follow.

Balance Sheet as of December 31, 20X1 (In Thousands)

Accounts	Amount	Accounts	Amount
Cash	$ 77,500	Accounts payable	$129,000
Accounts receivable	336,000	Notes payable	84,000
Inventories	241,500	Other current liabilities	117,000
Total current assets	$655,000	Total current liabilities	$330,000
Net fixed assets	292,500	Long-term debt	256,500
		Common equity	361,000
Total assets	$947,500	Total liabilities and equity	$947,500

Income Statement for Year Ended December 31, 20X1 (In Thousands)

Accounts	Amount
Sales	$1,607,500
Cost of goods sold	1,392,500
Gross profit	$ 215,000
Selling expenses	115,000
General and administrative expenses	30,000
Earnings before interest and taxes (EBIT)	$ 70,000
Interest expense	24,500
Earnings before taxes (EBT)	$ 45,500
Federal and state income taxes (40%)	18,200
Net income	$ 27,300

Required

1. Calculate the indicated ratios for KIM. Calculation is based on a 365−day year.

   (1) Current

   (2) Quick

   (3) Days sales outstanding

   (4) Inventory turnover

   (5) Total assets turnover

   (6) Net profit margin

   (7) ROA

   (8) ROE

   (9) Total debt/total assets

2. Construct the Du Pont equation for Barry.

At the end of last year, KIM reported the following income statement
(in millions of dollars):

Accounts	Amount
Sales	$3,000
Operating costs excluding depreciation	2,450
EBITDA	$ 550
Depreciation	250
Earnings before interest and taxes (EBIT)	$ 300
Interest expense	125
Earnings before taxes (EBT)	$ 175
Income taxes (40%)	70
Net income	$ 105

Looking ahead to the following year, the company's CFO has assembled the following
information:

- Year–end sales are expected to be 10 percent higher than the $3 billion in sales generated
  last year.
- Year–end operating costs, excluding depreciation, are expected to equal 80 percent of
  year–end sales.
- Depreciation is expected to increase at the same rate as sales.
- Interest costs are expected to remain unchanged.
- The tax rate is expected to remain at 40 percent.

Required

On the basis of this information, what will be the forecast for KIM's year–end net income?

Financial Management For the **US CPA** Exam

Chapter 04

Interest Rate and Risk

Volume
8

Chapter

4

Interest Rate and Risk

---

01 ❯ Interest Rate

1 The Factors Affecting the Cost of Money

사람들은 일반적으로 동일한 금액에 대해서 미래의 현금흐름 보다는 현재의 현금흐름을 더 선호하며, 그 차이가 이자율을 결정하게 되는데 그 원인은 다음과 같다.

(1) Production opportunities

The investment opportunities in productive (cash-generating) assets.

현재의 현금을 가지고 주어진 생산기회를 이용하여 새로운 가치를 창출 할 수 있기 때문에 현재 현금 흐름을 더 선호한다.

(2) Time preference for consumption

The preferences of consumers for current consumption as opposed to saving for future consumption.

사람들은 미래의 소비보다 현재의 소비를 더 선호하는 시차선호의 경향을 가지고 있다.

(3) Risk

If an investor perceives high degree of risk from a given investment alternative, he or she will demand higher rate of return, and hence the cost of money will increase.

동일한 금액에 대해서는 위험한 현금흐름 보다는 위험하지 않은 현금흐름을 선호하게 되므로, 위험이 증가하면 이자율도 증가한다.

(4) Inflation

Increasing in rate of inflation results in decline in purchasing power of investors. The investors will demand higher rate of return to commensurate against decline in purchasing power because of inflation.

인플레이션이 증가하면 이자율도 증가한다.

2 The Components of Market Interest Rate

채권의 시장이자율은 무위험이자율과 위험 프리미엄으로 구성이 된다.

$$R = \text{Risk-free rate} + \text{Risk premium}$$
$$= r^* + IP + DRP + LP + MRP$$

r^* : the real risk−free rate of interest
IP = inflation premium
DRP = default risk premium
LP = liquidity (or marketability) premium
MRP = maturity risk premium

(1) The real risk−free rate (r^*)

This is defined as the interest rate that would exist on a riskless security if no inflation were expected. → Indexed Treasury securities

인플레이션 없는 경우 무위험 이자율을 의미한다.

(2) Nominal risk−free rate (R_F)

This is the real risk−free rate plus a premium for expected inflation.

→ Treasury Bill (T−Bill) securities

인플레이션 프리미엄이 포함된 무위험 이자율을 의미한다.

Fisher effect is the relationship between nominal returns, real returns, and inflation.

$$R_F = r^* + IP$$
$$(1 + R_F) = (1 + r^*) \times (1 + IP)$$

실질 이자율(r*)과 명목 이자율(R_F)의 관계를 피셔효과라고 하며 명목금리는 실질금리와 예상 인플레이션율의 합계와 같다는 것을 말한다. 예를 들어 시중의 명목금리가 5%라고 할 때 예상되는 인플레이션율이 연 3%라고하면 실질금리는 2%에 해당한다고 말할 수 있다. 시중의 명목금리가 상승한다고 할 때 그 원인은 실질금리의 상승 때문일 수도 있고 앞으로 인플레이션율이 높아질 것이라는 예상 때문에 그렇게 될 수도 있다.

❖ Treasury securities

미국 재무성(treasury department)이 발행하는 채무 증권

- Treasury Bills (T-Bills)

  1년 이하의 재무성 증권(무이자 할인발행방식)

- Treasury Notes (T-Notes)

  1년 이상 10년 미만의 재무성 중기 채권 (연 2회 이자지급)

- Treasury Bonds (T-Bonds)

  10년 이상의 재무성 장기 채권 (연 2회 이자지급)

- Treasury Inflation-Protected Securities (TIPS)

  물가연동채권은 투자 원금에 물가상승률을 반영한 뒤 그에 대한 이자를 지급하는 채권으로, 인플레이션이 일어나더라도 채권의 실질가치를 보전해준다.

(3) Default Risk Premium (DRP)

Default risk (= Credit risk) is the risk that a borrower will default on a loan interest or principal.

채무불이행 위험은 채권의 발행자가 이자와 원금을 약속한 대로 지급하지 못할 가능성을 말한다.

The greater the default risk, the higher the interest rate.

채무불이행 위험이 증가하면 이자율은 증가하고 채권의 가격은 하락한다.

Default Risk Premium (DRP) is the difference between the interest rate on a Treasury bond and a corporate bond of equal maturity and marketability.

Treasury security는 채무불이행 위험이 없기 때문에 만기와 시장성 조건이 동일한 회사채 수익률과 Treasury security 수익률의 차이는 채무불이행 위험프리미엄이 된다.

채무불이행 위험에 대한 정보는 S&P 또는 Moody's 같은 신용평가기관에서 평가하는 채권등급평가 (bond rating)를 통하여 투자자들은 알 수 있다. 채권 등급의 분류와 그 의미를 살펴보면 다음과 같다.

구 분		Moody's	S&P	Fitch
투자적격	최우수	Aaa	AAA	AAA
	우수	Aa	AA	AA
	중상	A	A	A
	중하	Baa	BBB	BBB
투자부적격	투기적	Ba	BB	BB
	매우 투기적	B, Caa	B,CCC,CC	B,CCC,CC,C
	채무불이행	Ca,C	D	DDD,DD,D

(4) Liquidity Premium (LP)

Liquidity risk is the risk that an asset cannot be sold on short notice for its fair market value.

유동성 위험이란 자산 보유자가 자산을 용이하게 공정가치로 현금화 할 수 없는 위험을 말한다.

Real assets are generally less liquid than financial assets, but different financial assets vary in their liquidity.

실물자산은 금융자산보다 유동성이 작으며, 금융자산은 거래금액이 클수록 유동성 위험이 작다. Treasury security는 발행시장과 유통시장의 거래금액이 크기 때문에 유동성 위험이 없다.

Liquidity Premium (LP) is a premium added to the equilibrium interest rate on a security if that security cannot be converted to cash on short notice and at close to its "fair market value."

(5) Maturity Risk Premium (MRP)

Interest rate risk is the risk of capital losses to which investors are exposed because of changing interest rates.

이자율 위험이란 이자율의 변동으로 투자자의 자산 가치가 변동하여 손실이 발생할 위험이다.

As a general rule, the bonds have more interest rate risk the longer the maturity of the bond. Therefore, a maturity risk premium (MRP), which is higher the greater the years to maturity, must be included in the required interest rate.

일반적으로 만기가 길수록 이자율 위험은 커지게 되므로 만기가 긴 채권일수록 만기위험프리미엄이 반영되어야 한다.

(6) Investing overseas

Country risk is the risk that arises from investing or doing business in a particular country. This risk depends on the country's economic, political and social environment.

Exchange rate risk is the risk that a foreign currency transaction will be negatively exposed to fluctuations in exchange rates.

Example 4-1

The real risk-free rate is 3% and inflation is expected to be 3% for next 2 years. A 2-year Treasury security yields 6.2%. What is the maturity risk premium (MRP) for the 2-year security?

Solution

Treasury security is the security that has no default risk, no liquidity risk, no country risk and no exchange rate risk.

2-year Treasury security yields = r* + IP + MRP

6.2% = 3% + 3% + MRP = 6.2% → MRP = 0.2%

Example 4-2

A Treasury bond that matures in 10 years has a yield of 6%. A 10-year corporate bond has a yield of 8%. Assume that the liquidity premium on the corporate bond is 0.5%. What is the default risk premium (DRP) on the corporate bond?

Solution

만기가 10년인 국채와 회사채는 이자율 위험은 동일하므로 수익률의 차이는 유동성 위험과 채무불이행 위험의 차이에 기인한 것이다.

yield of the corporate bond − yield of the treasury bond = DRP + LP

2% = DRP + 0.5% → DRP = 1.5%

3 The Term Structure of Interest Rate

(1) The relationship between bond yield and maturities.

Term structure of interest rates is the relationship between bond yields and maturities.

이자율의 기간구조는 채권의 만기가 채권의 수익률에 어떤 영향을 주는지를 설명하는 이론이다.

Yield curve is a graph showing the relationship between bond yields and maturities.

수익률 곡선은 채권 수익률과 만기와의 그래프이므로 이자율의 기간구조는 수익률 곡선의 형태를 분석하는 것이다.

[Figure 4-1] U.S. Treasury Bond Interest Rates on Different Dates

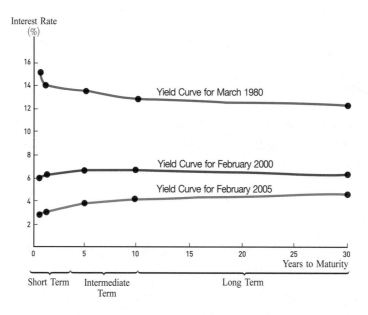

Term to Maturity	INTEREST RATE		
	March 1980	February 2000	February2005
6 months	15.0%	6.0%	2.9%
1 year	14.0	6.2	3.1
5 years	13.5	6.7	3.8
10 years	12.8	6.7	4.2
30 years	12.3	6.3	4.6

Figure 4–1에서 보여주는 것처럼 미국의 국채 수익률과 만기와의 관계를 실증적으로 관찰해본 결과 다양한 수익률 곡선을 볼 수 이었다. 1980년 3월에는 장기채권의 수익률이 단기채권의 수익률보다 낮은 우하향 수익률 곡선이었으며 2005 2월년에는 장기채권의 수익률이 단기채권의 수익률보다 높은 우상향 수익률 곡선이었다.

Normal yield curve is an upward-sloping yield curve. (February 2005)

Inverted (abnormal) yield curve is a downward-sloping yield curve. (March 1980)

Humped yield curve is a yield curve where interest rates on medium-term maturities are higher than rates on both short- and long-term maturities. (February 2000)

(2) Pure expectations theory

A theory that states that the shape of the yield curve depends on investors' expectations about future interest rates. If the maturity risk premium (MRP) would be zero, and long-term interest rates would simply be a weighted average of current and expected future short-term interest rates.

투자자들이 예상하는 미래의 기대이자율에 따라서 단기채권과 장기채권의 수익률의 차이가 발생한다는 이론이다. 이자율의 상승이 예측된다면 우상향 수익률 곡선이 나타나며, 향후 이자율의 하락이 예측된다면 우하향 수익률 곡선이 나타난다. 장기채권의 수익률은 단기채권 수익률과 미래의 기대이자율의 가중평균으로 결정된다.

(3) Market segmentation theory

채권 시장은 구조적으로 경직되어 투자자들이 채권 만기에대해 서로 다르게 선호하는 몇 개의 하부시장으로 구성되는데, 채권수익률은 이들 각 하부 시장에서의 수요, 공급의 원리에 의해서 결정된다는 주장이다. 은행은 보유하고 있는 부채가 단기이기 때문에 자산운용에 있어서도 단기채권을 선호하게 되고 반면에 보험회사나 연금기금은 장기부채를 보유하고 있어서 장기채권을 선호하게 된다.

Example 4-3

One-year Treasury securities yield 5%. The market anticipates that 1 year from now, 1-year Treasury securities will yield 6%. If the pure expectation theory is correct, what should be the yield today for 2-year Treasury securities?

Solution

Option 1:
Buy a one—year security, hold it for one year, and then at the end of the year reinvest the proceeds in another one—year security.
FV at end of Year 2 = $1 × (1.05) × (1.06) = $1.113

Option 2:
FV at end of Year 2 = $1 × (1 + R)^2 = $1.113 → R = 5.5%
기대이론에 따르면 만기 2년의 국채수익률은 시장에서 5.5%로 결정된다.

02 > A Single Asset's Return and Risk

1 Investment Rate of Return

주식을 1기간 보유함으로써 얻게 되는 수익률은 다음과 같이 측정된다.

$$\text{Rate of return} = \frac{\text{amount received} - \text{amount invested}}{\text{amount invested}}$$

$$\text{Rate of return} = \frac{P_1 + D_1 - P_0}{P_0} = \frac{P_1 + D_1}{P_0} - 1$$

P_0 : 현재주가, D_1 : 1기간후의 주당 배당금, P_1 : 1기간후의 주가

2 Average Return

- Arithmetic average : Average annual return ignoring compounding
  산술평균은 복리를 고려하지 않은 평균 수익률이다.

- Geometric average : Average annual return considering compounding
  기하평균은 복리를 고려한 평균 수익률이다.

- Arithmetic average ≥ geometric average
  산술평균은 기하평균 이상이며, 수익률의 표준편차가 증가할수록 두 평균의 차이는 증가한다.

Example 4-4

Investment rate of return in Year 1 : 10%
Investment rate of return in Year 2 : 20%
What is the average rate of return?

Solution

Arithmetic average $= (10\% + 20\%) \div 2 = 15\%$
Geometric average $= (1.10 \times 1.20)^{1/2} - 1 = 14.89\%$

3 Risk Attitude

투자자들의 위험에 대한 태도에 따라 다음과 같이 세 가지로 분류할 수 있다.

	Risk and return relationship	Risk premium
Risk averse	Direct	Positive
Risk neutral	No effect	Zero
Risk seeking	Inverse	Negative

Risk-averse investors dislike risk and require higher rates of return as an inducement to buy riskier securities. Risk premium (RP) is the difference between the expected rate of return on a given risky asset and that on a less risky asset.

In a market dominated by risk-averse investors, the higher a security' risk the lower its price and the higher its required return.

Economic Thinking

Selected Realized Returns, 1926-2007

	Average Return	Standard Deviation
Small–company stocks	17.1%	32.6%
Large–company stocks	12.3%	20.0%
L–T corporate bonds	6.2%	8.4%
L–T government bonds	5.8%	9.2%
U.S. Treasury bills	3.8%	3.1%

Source: Based on Stocks, Bonds, Bills, and Inflation: (Valuation Edition) 2008 Yearbook (Chicago: Morningstar, Inc., 2008), p 28.

4 Stand-Alone Risk

Example 4-5

Stock A has the following probability distribution :

Situation	Probability	Expected return
Optimistic	0.6	20%
Pessimistic	0.4	−10%

(1) Expected Rate of Return

The rate of return expected to be realized from an investment;

the weighted average of the probability distribution of possible results.

기대수익률은 각 상황에 따른 확률분포의 평균값으로 산출한다.

$$E(R_i) = P_1 \times R_1 + P_2 \times R_2 + \ldots + P_N \times R_N = \sum_{i=1}^{N} P_i \times R_i$$

$E(R_i)$: 기대수익률, P_i : 상황 i가 발생할 확률, R_i : 상황 i에서의 수익률

$E(R_A) = (0.6 \times 20\%) + (0.4 \times -10\%) = 8\%$

(2) Variance

A measurement of the spread between numbers in a data set. It measures how far each number in the set is from the mean.

분산은 확률분포가 주어져 있을 때 각 실현가능 수익률과 기대수익률과의 차이를 제곱하여 이를 확률로 가중 평균한 값이다.

$$Var(R_i) = \sigma_i^2 = \sum P_i \times (R_i - E(R_i))^2$$

$Deviation = R_i - E(R_i)$

$Var(R_A) = \sigma_A^2 = \{0.6 \times (20\% - 8\%)^2\} + \{0.4 \times (-10\% - 8\%)^2\} = 216\%^2 = 0.0216$

(3) Standard Deviation

The square root of variance is the standard deviation (σ).

표준편차는 분산의 양의 제곱근을 구한 것이다.

$$\sigma_i = \sqrt{Var(R_i)}$$

$\sigma_A = (0.0216)^{1/2} = 0.147 = 14.7\%$

(4) Coefficient of variation (CV)

Standardized measure of the risk per unit of return;

calculated as the standard deviation divided by the expected return.

변동계수는 표준편차를 기대수익률로 나눈 값으로 수익률 단위당 위험을 의미한다.

$$CV = \frac{\sigma_i}{E(R_i)}$$

$CV = 0.147 \div 0.08 = 1.84$

Example 4-6

An investment has a 50 percent chance of producing a 20 percent return, a 25 percent chance of producing an 8 percent return, and a 25 percent chance of producing a 12 percent return. What is its expected return, standard deviation and coefficient of variation?

Solution

$E(R) = (0.5 \times 20\%) + (0.25 \times 8\%) + (0.25 \times 12\%) = 15\%$

$Var(R) = \{0.5 \times (20\% - 15\%)^2\} + \{0.25 \times (8\% - 15\%)^2\} + \{0.25 \times (12\% - 15\%)^2\}$

$\qquad = 27\%^2 = 0.0027$

$\sigma = (27)^{1/2} = 5.20\%$

$CV = 5.20 \div 15 = 0.35$

(5) Dominance principle

Among investments with the same rate of return, the one with the least risk is most desirable. In addition, given a group of investments with the same level of risk, the one with the highest return is most desirable.

지배원리는 동일한 수익률에 대해서는 위험이 낮은 자산을, 동일한 위험에 대해서는 수익률이 높은 자산을 투자하는 원칙을 말한다.

Example 4-7

Intel Co. has the following investment portfolio.

	Expected return	Standard deviation
Investment A	15%	25%
Investment B	10%	17%
Investment C	8%	12%
Investment D	15%	12%

If management decided to buy one of the investments, which one should be selected?

Solution

C와 D는 위험은 동일하지만 기대수익률이 D가 더 크기 때문에 D를 선택

A와 D는 기대수익률은 동일하지만 위험이 D가 더 작기 때문에 D를 선택

D는 B와 비교하여 기대수익률은 더 크지만 위험이 더 작기 때문에 D를 선택

03 ➤ Portfolio's Return and Risk

1 Portfolio of Two Assets

Example 4-8

Stock A and B have the following probability distribution :

Situation	Probability	Return (A)	Return (B)
Optimistic	0.6	20%	−5%
Pessimistic	0.4	−10%	10%

If we formed a $100,000 portfolio, investing $50,000 in each stock, what is the expected rates of return and the standard deviations for the portfolio?

(1) Expected Portfolio Return

The weighted average of the expected returns on the assets held in the portfolio.

포트폴리오의 기대수익률은 각 주식의 기대수익률에 대하여 투자비율을 가중치로 평균을 구한다.

$$E(R_p) = \sum_{i=1}^{N} w_i \times E(R_i)$$

$E(R_p)$: 포트폴리오의 기대수익률, w : 각 주식의 투자비중

$E(R_A) = (0.6 \times 20\%) + (0.4 \times -10\%) = 8\%$

$E(R_B) = (0.6 \times -5\%) + (0.4 \times 10\%) = 1\%$

$E(R_p) = W_A \times E(R_A) + W_B \times E(R_B) = (0.5 \times 8\%) + (0.5 \times 1\%) = 4.5\%$

(2) Portfolio Risk

Although the expected return on a portfolio is simply the weighted average of the expected returns of the individual assets in the portfolio, the riskiness of the portfolio is not the weighted average of the individual assets'standard deviations. The portfolio' risk is generally smaller than the average of the assets.

$$\sigma_A^2 = \{0.6 \times (20\% - 8\%)^2\} + \{0.4 \times (-10\% - 8\%)^2\} = 216 \ \rightarrow \sigma_A = (216)^{1/2} = 14.7\%$$

$$\sigma_B^2 = \{0.6 \times (-5\% - 1\%)^2\} + \{0.4 \times (10\% - 1\%)^2\} = 54 \rightarrow \sigma_B = (54)^{1/2} = 7.4\%$$

$$\sigma_P^2 = \{0.6 \times (7.5\% - 4.5\%)^2\} + \{0.4 \times (0\% - 4.5\%)^2\} = 13.5 \rightarrow \sigma_P = (13.5)^{1/2} = 3.7\%$$

weighted average of standard deviations = $0.5 \times 14.7\% + 0.5 \times 7.35\% = 11.03\%$

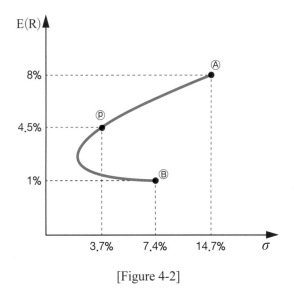

[Figure 4-2]

주식 A와 주식 B에 각각 50%씩 투자한 포트폴리오의 기대수익률은 주식B의 기대수익률보다 크지만 위험은 더 작기 때문에 더 효율적 투자안이다. 따라서 지배원리에 의하여 주식 B는 비효율적 투자안이며, 주식A는 효율적 투자안이다.

2 Correlation Coefficient

The tendency of two variables to move together is called correlation, and the correlation coefficient, ρ(pronounced "rho"), measures this tendency. The correlation coefficient(ρ) can range from +1.0, denoting that the two variables move up and down in perfect synchronization, to -1.0, denoting that the variables always move in exactly opposite directions. A correlation coefficient of zero indicates that the two variables are not related to each other—that is, changes in one variable are independent of changes in the other.

상관관계(correlation)는 한 변수가 다른 변수와 동시에 움직이는 성향을 말하며, 상관계수 (correlation coefficient)는 상관관계를 측정한 통계적 지수로 두 변수가 얼마나 밀접한 선형관계를 가지고 있는지를 나타내며, −1과 1사이의 값을 가진다. 두 변수가 완전 + 상관관계를 가지면 상관 계수는 1이 되며, 두 변수가 완전 − 상관관계를 가지면 상관계수는 −1이 된다. 두 변수가 상관관 계가 없으면 상관계수는 0이 된다.

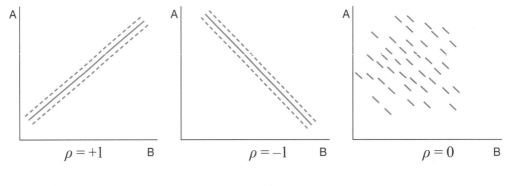

[Figure 4-3]

3 Portfolio Effect

The extent to which adding stocks to a portfolio reduces its risk depends on the degree of correlation among the stocks:

- The smaller the correlation coefficients, the lower the risk in a large portfolio.
- Diversification does nothing to reduce risk if the portfolio consists of perfectly positively correlated stocks.

투자자가 포트폴리오를 구성하는 이유는 일정한 기대 수익률 하에서 투자위험을 최소화시킬 수 있는 포트폴리오의 위험분산효과 때문이다. 이러한 위험분산효과는 두 주식의 상관계수가 감소할수록 증가한다. 두 주식의 상관계수가 1인 경우 위험분산효과는 없다.

If we could find a set of stocks whose correlations were zero or negative, all risk could be eliminated. However, in the real world, the correlations among the individual stocks are generally positive but less than 1.0, so some but not all risk can be eliminated.

현실에서는 주식간의 상관계수는 1보다 작은 양수이므로 위험분산효과는 있지만 위험을 완전히 제거할 수는 없다.

N개의 주식으로 구성된 포트폴리오의 위험분산 효과는 다음과 같다.

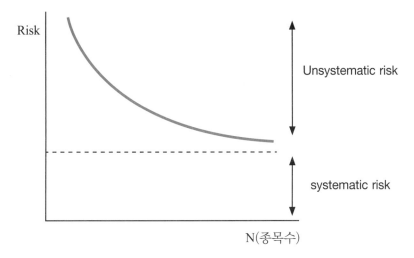

[Figure 4-4]

포트폴리오를 구성하는 주식수가 증가하면 각 주식의 비체계적 감소하지만, 모든 주식에 공통적으로 영향을 미치는 체계적 위험(시장위험)은 제거되지 않는다.

> Total risk = Nonsystematic risk + Systematic risk

(1) Nonsystematic risk (= firm-specific risk or diversifiable risk)

Risk that can be eliminated by proper diversification.

투자자의 입장에서 볼 때 개별주식의 위험은 체계적 위험과 비체계적 위험으로 구성되어 있다. 비체계적 위험은 경영진의 변동, 파업, 법적소송, 새로운 해외진출계획 등과 같이 어느 특정기업만이 가지는 사건이나 상황의 변동 등에서 발생되는 위험이다. 투자자는 여러 개의 주식으로 포트폴리오를 구성함으로 써 비체계적 위험을 제거할 수 있다. 즉, 한 주식으로부터의 불리한 상황을 다른 주식으로부터의 유리한 상황으로 상쇄시킬 수 있기 때문이다.

(2) Systematic risk (= market risk or non-diversifiable risk)

Risk that cannot be eliminated by proper diversification.

체계적 위험은 주식의 위험을 크게 분산 가능한 위험과 분산 불가능한 위험으로 분류할 때 분산투자를 통하여 제거할 수 없는 위험을 말한다. 체계적 위험은 시장전체의 변동위험으로서 이에 영향을 미치는 요인은 경기변동, 인플레이션, 경상수지, 사회 · 정치적 환경 등 거시적 변수들이다.

(3) Relevant Risk

The risk of a security that cannot be diversified away. This is the risk that affects portfolio risk and thus is relevant to a rational investor.

분산투자가 가능한 상황에서는 비체계적 위험보다는 체계적 위험을 투자의사 결정변수로 고려하게 된다.

(4) Market portfolio

A portfolio consisting of all stocks.

모든 주식에 투자하여 비체계적 위험을 완전히 제거한 포트폴리오를 시장포트폴리오라고 하며
이 포트폴리오는 체계적 위험만을 반영한다.

4 Modern Portfolio Theory (MPT)

Modern portfolio theory (MPT) is a theory on how risk-averse investors can construct portfolios to optimize or maximize expected return based on a given level of market risk, emphasizing that risk is an inherent part of higher reward. This theory was pioneered by Harry Markowitz in his paper "Portfolio Selection," published in 1952.

포트폴리오 이론은 분산투자를 통하여 투자위험을 감소하는 투자자산의 구성방법을 제시하는 이론으로 1952년 Markowitz에 의하여 제시된 이래 CAPM모형으로 발전한 투자론의 핵심적인 이론이다.

According to the theory, it's possible to construct an "efficient frontier" of optimal portfolios offering the maximum possible expected return for a given level of risk.

투자기회집합에서 실제 투자대상으로 고려되는 것은 지배원리(Dominance principle)를 충족하는 포트폴리오 집합인데 이를 효율적 투자선(efficient frontier)이라고 한다.

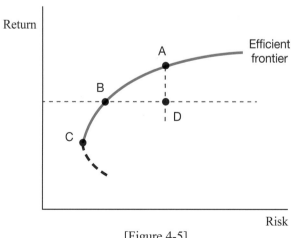

[Figure 4-5]

Figure 4-5에서 투자안 A, B, C는 투자안 D를 지배하지만, 서로는 지배되지 않으므로 효율적 투자선위에 위치하고 있다. 이러한 효율적 투자선상의 투자안중에서 투자자의 효용을 가장 극대화 시키는 포트폴리오를 optimal portfolio라고 한다. 이는 투자자의 indifferent curve(무차별곡선)와 efficient frontier가 만나는 접점에서 선택이 된다.

04 CAPM (Capital Asset Pricing Model)

1 Introduction

자본자산 가격결정모형(Capital Asset Pricing Model)은 흔히 CAPM으로 불리는데, 현대 금융경제학과 투자론의 핵심 이론이다. CAPM은 1952년 Harry Markowitz에 의해 포트폴리오 선택이론(portfolio selection theory)이 개발된 이후 12년이 지난 1964년부터 샤프(Sharpe), 린트너(Lintner), 그리고 모신(Mossin) 등에 의해 개발되었다. 이 모형은 주식이나 채권 등 자본자산들의 기대수익률과 위험과의 관계를 이론적으로 정립시킨 균형 모델로서 커다란 의미를 지니고 있다.

CAPM에 의하면 자본시장이 균형을 이룰 때, 어떤 자산의 기대수익률은 그 자산의 체계적 위험을 나타내는 베타계수(b)와 선형적 증가함수의 관계를 갖는다. CAPM에서는 주식의 요구수익률에 반영하여야 할 위험은 총위험이 아닌 체계적 위험이 적절하다는 것이다. (relevant risk)

2 Beta

The tendency of a stock to move up and down with the market, and thus its market risk is reflected in its beta coefficient (b). Beta is a measure of market risk, which is extent to which the returns on a stock move with the stock market as measured by some index such as the Dow Jones Industrials, the S&P 500, or the New York Stock Exchange Index.

An average stock has beta=1.0.

The stock will move up by 10% if the market moves up by 10%, while if the market falls by 10%, the stock will likewise fall by 10%.

A high-beta stock is more volatile than an average stock.

b = 2.0: Stock is twice as risky as an average stock.

The stock will move up by 20% if the market moves up by 10%, while if the market falls by 10%, the stock will likewise fall by 20%.

A low-beta stock is less volatile than an average stock.

b=0.5: Stock is only half as volatile, or risky, as an average stock.

The stock will move up by 5% if the market moves up by 10%, while if the market falls by 10%, the stock will likewise fall by 5%.

주가시장이 추세적으로 상승할 때에는 베타가 높은 주식들에 투자함으로써 주식시장 전체보다 높은 수익을 올릴 수 있으며, 반대로 하락국면에서는 베타가 낮은 주식들에 투자함으로써 주식시장 전체보다 낮은 손실을 올릴 수 있다.

3 Portfolio Beta

k개 주식으로 구성된 포트폴리오의 베타(b_p)는 다음과 같이 각 주식의 베타를 구성비율로 가중평균한 합계가 된다.

$$b_p = \sum_{i=1}^{k} w_i \times b_i$$

An individual has \$30,000 invested in a stock with a beta of 0.8 and another \$45,000 invested in a stock with a beta of 1.4. If these are the only two investments in his portfolio, what is his portfolio' beta?

$$b_p = 0.8 \times \frac{30,000}{75,000} + 1.4 \times \frac{45,000}{75,000} = 1.16$$

4　SML (Security Market Line)

(1) What is the SML?

The line on a graph that shows the relationship between risk as measured by beta and the required rate of return for individual securities.

증권시장선(SML)은 각 개별증권의 수익률과 베타계수와의 선형관계를 나타내는 식이며 다음과 같이 결정된다.

> Required return on a stock
> = Risk-free return + Premium for the stock's risk
>
> $$R_i = R_F + (R_M - R_F) \times b_i$$

R_i : i 주식의 요구수익률
R_M : 시장포트폴리오의 요구수익률
b_i : i 주식의 베타계수
Market risk premium : $R_M - R_F$
Risk Premium for stock i = $(R_M - R_F) \times b_i$

Example 4-9

Assume that the risk-free rate is 6% and the expected return on the market is 13%. What is the required rate of return on a stock that has a beta of 0.7?

Solution

$$R_i = R_F + (R_M - R_F) \times b_i = 6\% + (13\% - 6\%) \times 0.7 = 10.9\%$$

앞의 예제를 그림으로 나타내면 다음과 같다.

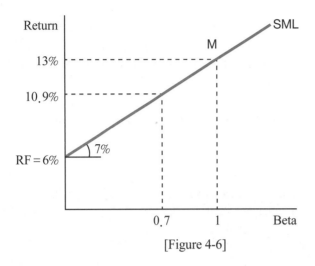

[Figure 4-6]

Example 4-10

Assume that the risk-free rate is 5% and the market risk premium is 6%. What is the expected return on the market? What is the required rate of return on a stock that has a beta of 1.5?

Solution

Market risk premium $= R_M - R_F = 6\%$에서 $R_M = 11\%$

$R_i = R_F + (R_M - R_F) \times b_i = 5\% + (11\% - 5\%) \times 1.5 = 14\%$

(2) Using the SML

- If the security plots above the SML
  - ✔ expected rate of return is greater than required rate of return
  - ✔ the investor will buy the stock because the stock is considered undervalued

- If the security plots below the SML
  ✓ expected rate of return is less than required rate of return
  ✓ the investor will sell the stock because the stock is considered overvalued

- Cost of equity
  증권시장을 이용해서 산출한 요구수익률은 기업이 주식을 발행해서 자금을 조달할 때 자금 사용의 대가로 부담하는 비용이 된다. 즉, 주식의 자기자본비용을 산출하는 데에 증권시장선 이 이용된다.

(3) Shift in the SML and required return on a stock

주식의 요구수익률과 SML의 결정변수와의 관계는 다음과 같다.

Inflation	Direct relationship
Beta	Direct relationship
Investor's aversion to risk	Direct relationship

- The Impact of Inflation
  물가 상승 → 무위험이자율 증가 → SML 기울기는 변하지 않고 위로 평행이동
  → 요구수익률 증가

- Changes in Risk Aversion
  투자자 위험 회피도 증가 → SML 기울기 증가 → 요구수익률 증가

- Changes in a Stock' Beta Coefficient
  개별주식의 베타 증가 → SML 이동 없음, 요구수익률 증가

Example 4-11

Bradford Manufacturing Company has a beta of 1.45, while Farley Industries has a beta of 0.85. The required return on an index fund that holds the entire stock market is 12.0 percent. The risk-free rate of interest is 5 percent. By how much does Bradford' required return exceed Farley' required return?

Solution

$R_{Bradford} = 5\% + (12\% - 5\%) \times 1.45 = 15.15\%$

$R_{Farley} = 5\% + (12\% - 5\%) \times 0.85 = 10.95\%$

$R_{Bradford} - R_{Farley} = 15.15\% - 10.95\% = 4.20\%$

Example 4-12

Calculate the required rate of return for Manning Enterprises, assuming that investors expect a 3.5 percent rate of inflation in the future. The real risk-free rate is 2.5 percent and the market risk premium is 6.5 percent. Manning has a beta of 1.7.

Solution

$R_F = 2.5\% + 3.5\% = 6\%$

$R_{Manning} = 6\% + 6.5\% \times 1.7 = 17.05\%$

Example 4-13

You have been managing a $5 million portfolio that has a beta of 1.25 and a required rate of return of 12 percent. The current risk-free rate is 5.25 percent. Assume that you receive another $500,000. If you invest the money in a stock with a beta of 0.75, what will be the required return on your $5.5 million portfolio?

Solution

$R_p = 12\% = 5.25\% + MRP \times 1.25 \rightarrow MRP = 5.4\%$

$b_p = 1.25 \times \dfrac{5}{5.5} + 0.75 \times \dfrac{0.5}{5.5} = 1.20$

$R_p = 5.25\% + 5.4\% \times 1.20 = 11.73\%$

Example 4-14

A stock has a required return of 15 percent; the risk-free rate is 7 percent; and the market risk premium is 4 percent. If the market risk premium increased to 6 percent, what would happen to the stock' required rate of return? Assume the risk-free rate and the beta remain unchanged.

Solution

$R_i = 15\% = 7\% + 4\% \times b_i \rightarrow b_i = 2$

$R_i = 7\% + 6\% \times 2 = 19\% \rightarrow 4\%$ increase

05 ⟩⟩ Valuation of Stock

1 Valuation Approaches

(1) Income Approach (Absolute Value)

The income approach to measuring fair value converts future amounts to a single current amount (such as would be determined by using the discounted cash flow).

- Free cash flow approach (FCF)
- Dividend discount model (DDM)

(2) Market Approach (Relative Value)

The market approach to measuring fair value uses prices and other relevant information generated by market transactions involving identical or similar assets or liabilities.

- Valuation using multiples

  P/E ratio, P/B ratio, P/S ration, P/CF ratio

(3) Top-Down Approach

An investment analysis approach that involves looking first at the macro picture of the economy, and then looking at the smaller factors in finer detail. Top - down approaches prioritize macroeconomic or market-level factors most.

(4) Bottom-Up Approach

An investment approach that focuses on a specific company and its fundamentals, rather than on the industry in which that company operates or on the greater economy as a whole. Bottom-up investing forces investors to consider microeconomic factors first and foremost.

2 **DDM** (Dividend Discount Model)

(1) Dividend discount model

주식의 가격은 주식을 보유함으로써 기대되는 미래의 현금흐름을 적절한 할인율로 산출한 현재가치이다. 그런데 주식보유로 예상되는 현금흐름은 보유기간 동안 수령하게 되는 배당금과 주식처분시점에서 얻게 되는 처분가격이다. 따라서 이러한 주가결정모형을 배당평가모형 또는 배당할인모형(DDM)이라고 한다.

$$P_o = \sum_{t=1}^{n} \frac{D_t}{(1+R)^t} + \frac{P_n}{(1+R)^n}$$

D_t : t시점에서의 배당, P_n : n시점에서의 주가, R: 주식의 요구수익률

(2) Zero-growth model

매년 배당금이 일정하여 증가하지 않는 경우에 적용되는 주가결정공식을 제로성장모형이라고 하며, 일반적으로 우선주의 평가에 사용한다.

$$P_0 = \frac{D}{R}$$

D : 매년 일정한 배당금, R: 주식의 요구수익률

(3) One period – Dividend discount model

$$P_o = \frac{D_1 + P_1}{(1+R)^1} \quad \rightarrow \quad R = \frac{D_1}{P_0} + \frac{P_1 - P_0}{P_0}$$

주식을 1년 보유한 후 처분한다고 가정한 평가모형으로 주식의 투자수익률은 배당수익률과 자본수익률의 합으로 분석이 된다.

3 Constant Growth Model

배당금액이 일정한 비율로 계속적인 증가를 하는 경우의 평가모형을 고정성장모형이라고 하며 이 경우 성장률은 주식의 요구수익률보다 작아야 하는 전제조건이 필요하다.

$$P_o = \frac{D_1}{R-g} \qquad (단, \ R > g)$$

D_1 : 1년 후의 예상주당 배당금 → $D_1 = D_0 \times (1 + g)^1$

g : 주당이익의 고정성장율 → g = ROE × RR

ROE (return on equity) = NI ÷ Equity

Retention rate = 1 − payout

R : 주식의 요구수익률 → $R_i = R_F + (R_F - R_f) \times b_i$

Example 4-15

An investor plans to buy a common stock and hold it for one year. The investor expects to receive both $2.75 in dividends and $26 from the sale of stock at the end of the year. If the investor wants to earn a 15% return, the maximum price the investor would pay for the stock today is?

Solution

$$P_o = \frac{D_1 + P_1}{(1 + R)^1} = \frac{\$2.75 + \$26}{(1.15)^1} = \$25$$

$$R = \frac{D_1}{P_0} + \frac{P_1 - P_0}{P_0} = \frac{\$2.75}{\$25} + \frac{\$26 - \$25}{\$25} = 11\% + 4\% = 15\%$$

→ 요구수익률 15%는 11%의 배당수익률과 4%의 자본수익률로 구성됨

Example 4-16

Assume that Johnson & Johnson is expected to pay a $2.10 dividend per share one year from now, an increase from the current dividend of $2.00 per share. After that, the dividend is expected to increase at a constant rate. If you require a 12% return on stock, what is the value of the stock?

Solution

$D_1 = \$2.10$, $R = 12\%$, $g = 2.10 \div 2.00 - 1 = 5\%$

$$P_0 = \frac{\$2.10}{12\% - 5\%} = \$30$$

Example 4-17

Assume that McDonald's Corp. is expected to pay a $1.20 dividend per share one year from now and continue to pay out 40% of its earnings as dividends for the foreseeable future. If the firm is expected to generate a 10% return on equity in the future and if you require a 12% return on stock, what is the value of the stock?

Solution

$D_1 = \$1.20$, $R = 12\%$, $g = 10\% \times (1 - 0.4) = 6\%$

$$P_0 = \frac{\$1.20}{12\% - 6\%} = \$20$$

06 ⟫ Multiple Choice

01. The systematic risk of an individual security is measured by the (CMA)

    a. standard deviation of the security's rate of return.

    b. covariance between the security's returns and the general market.

    c. security's contribution to the portfolio risk.

    d. standard deviation of the security's returns and other similar securities.

02. Which one of the following would have the least impact on a firm's beta value? (CMA)

    a. Debt-to-equity ratio.   b. Industry characteristics.

    c. Operating leverage.   d. Payout ratio.

03. If Dexter Industries has a beta value of 1.0, then its (CMA)

    a. return should equal the risk-free rate.

    b. price is relatively stable.

    c. expected return should approximate the overall market.

    d. volatility is low.

04. Stock J has a beta of 1.2 and a required return of 15.6%, and stock K has a beta of 0.8 and a required return of 12.4%. What is the expected return on the market and the risk-free rate of return, consistent with the capital asset pricing model?

	Expected return on the market	Risk-free rate of return
a.	14%	6%
b.	12.4%	0%
c.	14%	4%
d.	14%	1.6%

05. If Treasury bills yield 4.0%, and the market risk premium is 9.0%, a portfolio with a beta of 1.5 is expected to yield

a. 9.0%   b. 13.5%

c. 17.5%   d. 19.50%.

06. Short-term interest rates are

a. usually lower than long-term rates.

b. usually higher than long-term rates.

c. lower than long-term rates during periods of high inflation only.

d. not significantly related to long-term rates.

07. According to the expectations theory, if the yield curve on the New York money market is upward sloping while that on the Tokyo money market is downward sloping, then inflation in

a. the United States is expected to decrease.

b. the United States is expected to remain constant.

c. Japan is expected to decrease.

d. Japan is expected to remain constant.

08. Which of the following describes the flow of the top-down valuation process?

a. Economic analysis, industry analysis, company analysis.

b. Company analysis, industry analysis, economic analysis.

c. Economic analysis, company analysis, industry analysis.

d. Pick the best stocks regardless of the industry and economic conditions.

09. An analyst used the infinite period valuation model to determine that XYZ Corporation should be valued at $20. The current market price is $30. The analyst should do which of the following?

a. Issue a buy recommendation on XYZ.

b. Issue a sell recommendation on XYZ.

c. Issue a hold recommendation on XYZ.

d. Do nothing since the results conflict each other.

10. What would an investor be willing to pay for a share of preferred stock that paid an annual $7 dividend if the yield on preferred was 25 basis points below the AA bond yield of 8%? (1% = 100 basis points)

a. $77.50   b. $87.50

c. $90.32   d. $110.71

11. An analyst projects that a stock will pay a $2 dividend next year and that it will sell for $40 at year-end. If the required rate of return is 15%, what is the value of the stock?

a. $25.00   b. $33.54

c. $36.52   d. $43.95

12. An analyst expects a stock selling for $25 per share to increase to $30 by year-end. The dividend last year was $1, but the analyst expects next year's dividend to be $1.50. What is the expected holding period yield on this stock?

a. 20.00%   b. 21.67%

c. 24.00%   d. 26.00%.

13. A stock paid a $2 dividend last year. An investor projects that next year's dividend will be 10% higher and that the stock will be selling for $40 at the end of the year. The risk-free rate of interest is 8%, the market return is 13%, and the stock's beta is 1.2. Determine the value of the stock.

a. $35   b. $37

c. $39   d. $42.

14. A stock will pay a $2 dividend next year, $2.25 the year after, and $2.50 the following year. An investor believes that she can then sell the stock for $50 at the end of a 3-year holding period. The risk-free rate of interest is 7%, the market return is 13%, and the stock's beta is 1. What is the value of the stock?

a. $35.76   b. $37.44

c. $39.92   d. $47.99.

15. The infinite period DDM implies that a stock's value will be greate :

a. the larger its expected dividend

b. the higher the expected growth rate

c. the lower the required rate of return

d. all of the above

16. Holding all other factors constant, which of the following is expected to grow at the same rate as dividends in the infinite period DDM?

a. Sales   b. ROE

c. Stock price   d. All of the above

17. The infinite period DDM assumes which of the following?

    a. g < k   b. g = k

    c. g > k   d. g ≠ k

18. What is the intrinsic value of a company's stock if next year's expected dividend is projected to be 5% greater than today's $1 dividend? The sustainable growth rate is 5%, and investor's required rate of return for this stock is 10%.

    a. $20.00   b. $21.00

    c. $21.05   d. $22.05

19. Next year's dividend is expected to be $2; g=7%; and k=12%. What is the stock's intrinsic value?

    a. $16.67   b. $28.57

    c. $40.00   d. $42.80

20. A stock paid a $1 dividend last year. The risk-free rate is 5%; the expected return on the market is 12%; and the stock's beta is 1.5. If dividends are expected to grow at a 5% rate forever, what is the value of the stock?

    a. $10.00   b. $15.25

    c. $21.50   d. $25.75

21. The Hatch Sausage Company is projecting an annual growth rate for the foreseeable future of 9%. The most recent dividend paid was $3.00 per share. New common stock can be issued at $36 per share. Using the constant growth model, what is the approximate cost of capital for retained earnings? (CMA)

a. 9.08%   b. 17.33%

c. 18.08%   d. 19.88%

22. At year-end, Appleseed Company reported net income of $588,000. The company has 10,000 shares of $100 par value, 6% preferred stock and 120,000 shares of $10 par value common stock outstanding and 5,000 shares of common stock in treasury. There are no dividend payments in arrears, and the market price per common share at the end of the year was $40. Appleseed's price-earnings ratio is (CMA)

a. 9.47   b. 9.09

c. 8.50   d. 8.16

23. The dividend yield ratio is calculated by which one of the following methods? (CMA)

a. Market price per share divided by dividends per share.

b. Earnings per share divided by dividends per share.

c. Dividends per share divided by market price per share.

d. Dividends per share divided by earnings per share.

24. The constant-growth dividend discount model will not produce a finite value for a stock if the dividend growth rate is

a. above its historical average

b. below its historical average

c. above the required rate of return on stock

d. below the required rate of return on stock

25. In applying the constant-growth dividend discount model, lowering the required rate of return on stock will cause a stock's intrinsic value to

a. decrease.

b. increase.

c. remain unchanged.

d. decrease or increase, depending upon other factors.

26. Management of Kelly, Inc. uses CAPM to calculate the estimated cost of common equity. Which of the following would reduce the firm's estimated cost of common equity?

a. A reduction in the risk-free rate.

b. An increase in the firm's beta.

c. An increase in expected inflation.

d. An increase in risk aversion.

Solution

1	2	3	4	5	6	7	8	9	10
B	D	C	A	C	A	C	A	B	C

11	12	13	14	15	16	17	18	19	20
C	D	B	C	D	C	A	B	C	A

21	22	23	24	25	26
C	B	C	C	B	A

1. 체계적 위험은 개별증권의 주식시장에 대한 상대적 민감도를 의미한다.

2. 베타는 영업위험과 재무위험으로 구성되며 배당성향과는 무관하다.

3. 베타 = 1인 주식은 주식시장과 동일한 민감도를 갖는다.

4. $R_J = 15.6\% = R_F + MRP \times 1.2$
   $R_K = 12.4\% = R_F + MRP \times 0.8$
   $MRP = (15.6\% - 12.4\%) \div (1.2 - 0.8) = 8\%$
   $R_J = 15.6\% = R_F + 8\% \times 1.2 \rightarrow R_F = 6\% \rightarrow R_M = 6\% + 8\% = 14\%$

5. $R_i = 4\% + 9\% \times 1.5 = 17.5\%$

6. Normal yield curve : upward curve → 단기금리 〈 장기금리

7. Normal yield curve : upward curve → increase in inflation
   Abnormal yield curve : downward curve → decrease in inflation

8. Top−down approach: 경제분석 → 산업분석 → 기업분석

9. Intrinsic value 〈 Current price → Sell the stock

10. $R = 8\% - 0.25\% = 7.75\%$

   $$P_0 = \frac{D}{R} = \$7 \div 0.0775 = \$90.32$$

11. $P_o = \dfrac{D_1 + P_1}{(1+R)^1} = \$42 \div 1.15 = \$36.52$

12. $R = \dfrac{D_1 + P_1}{P_0} - 1 = \$31.50 \div \$25 - 1 = 26\%$

13. $R_i = 8\% + (13\% - 8\%) \times 1.2 = 14\%$

$P_o = \dfrac{2 \times 1.10 + 40}{(1.14)^1} = \$37$

14. $R_i = 7\% + (13\% - 7\%) \times 1 = 13\%$

$P_o = \dfrac{2}{(1.13)^1} + \dfrac{2.25}{(1.13)^2} + \dfrac{2.50 + 50}{(1.13)^3} = \$39.92$

15. $P_0 = \dfrac{D_1}{R - g}$

다른 조건이 일정한 경우,

주가는 기대배당과 성장률에 비례하고, 요구수익률에 반비례한다.

16. $P_0 = \dfrac{D_1}{R - g}$ 이며 $P_1 = \dfrac{D_1 \times (1 + g)}{R - g}$ 이므로 주가는 배당과 동일한 성장을 한다.

17. $P_0 = \dfrac{D_1}{R - g}$ 에서 R $>$ g 의 가정이 필요하다.

18. $P_0 = \dfrac{D_1}{R - g} = \dfrac{\$1 \times 1.05}{0.10 - 0.05} = \$21$

19. $P_0 = \dfrac{D_1}{R - g} = \dfrac{\$2}{0.12 - 0.07} = \$40$

20. $R_i = 5\% + (12\% - 5\%) \times 1.5 = 15.5\%$

$P_0 = \dfrac{D_1}{R - g} = \dfrac{1.05}{0.155 - 0.05} = \$10$

21. $R = k_e = \dfrac{D_1}{P_0} + g = \dfrac{\$3 \times 1.09}{36} + 0.09 = 0.1808$

22. EPS = $(\$588,000 - 10,000 \times \$100 \times 6\%) \div 120,000$ shares = $\$4.40$

P/E = $\$40 \div \$4.40 = \$9.09$

23. DPS ÷ Price per share = dividend yield

DPS ÷ EPS = payout

24. $P_0 = \dfrac{D_1}{R-g}$ 에서 R ＜ g 인 경우에는 DDM은 성립하지 않는다.

25. $P_0 = \dfrac{D_1}{R-g}$ 에서 요구수익률(R)이 감소하면 주식의 내재가치(P)는 증가한다.

26. SML에서 주식의 요구수익률(자기자본비용)은 무위험이자율, 베타, 인플레이션, 투자자의 위험회피도의 변수에 대하여 모두 비례한다.

07 ⟩ Tasked-Based Simulation

Problem-1

You read in The Wall Street Journal that 30-day T-bills are currently yielding 5.5 percent. Your brother-in-law, a broker at Safe and Sound Securities, has given you the following estimates of current interest rate premiums:

Inflation premium =3.25%

Liquidity premium =0.6%

Maturity risk premium = 1.8%

Default risk premium = 2.15%

Required

On the basis of these data, what is the real risk−free rate of return?

Problem-2

A Treasury bond that matures in 10 years has a yield of 6 percent. A 10-year corporate bond has a yield of 8 percent. Assume that the liquidity premium on the corporate bond is 0.5 percent.

Required

What is the default risk premium on the corporate bond?

Problem-3

The real risk-free rate is 3 percent, and inflation is expected to be 3 percent for the next 2 years. A 2-year Treasury security yields 6.2 percent.

Required

What is the maturity risk premium for the 2−year security?

Problem-4

A stock's returns have the following distribution:

Demand for the Company's Products	Probability of This Demand Occurring	Rate of Return If This Demand Occurs
Weak	0.1	(50%)
Below average	0.2	(5)
Average	0.4	16
Above average	0.2	25
Strong	0.1	60

Required

Calculate the stock's expected return, standard deviation, and coefficient of variation.

Problem-5

Suppose you are the money manager of a $4 million investment fund. The fund consists of 4 stocks with the following investments and betas:

Stock	Investment	Beta
A	$ 400,000	1.50
B	600,000	(0.50)
C	1,000,000	1.25
D	2,000,000	0.75

Required

If the market"s required rate of return is 14 percent and the risk-free rate is 6 percent, what is the fund"s required rate of return?

Problem-6

Kim Mining Company's ore reserves are being depleted, so its sales are falling. Also, its pit is getting deeper each year, so its costs are rising. As a result, the company"s earnings and dividends are declining at the constant rate of 5 percent per year.

Required

If the dividend last year was $5 and the required rate of return is 15%, what is the value of Kim Mining's stock?

Problem-7

A stock is expected to pay a dividend of $0.50 at the end of the year, and it should continue to grow at a constant rate of 7 percent a year.

Required

If its required return is 12 percent, what is the stock's expected price 4 years from today?

Problem-8

KIM Corporation is expanding rapidly and currently needs to retain all of its earnings, hence it does not pay dividends. However, investors expect KIM to begin paying dividends, beginning with a dividend of $1.00 coming 1 years from today. The dividend should grow rapidly at a rate of 50 percent per year during Years 2 and 3, but after Year 3 growth should be a constant 8 percent per year.

Required

If the required return on KIM is 15 percent, what is the value of the stock today?

Problem-9

Consider the following information for three stocks,
Stocks X, Y, and Z. The returns on the three stocks are positively correlated, but they are not perfectly correlated.

Stock	Expected Return	Beta
X	9.00%	0.8
Y	10.75	1.2
Z	12.50	1.6

Fund P has half of its funds invested in Stock X and half invested in Stock Y. Fund Q has one-third of its funds invested in each of the three stocks. The risk-free rate is 5.5 percent, and the market is in equilibrium.

Required

What is the differences in the required return for Fund P and Fund Q?

Problem-10

A mutual fund manager has a $20,000,000 portfolio with a beta of 1.5. The risk-free rate is 4.5 percent and the market risk premium is 5.5 percent. The manager expects to receive an additional $5,000,000, which she plans to invest in a number of stocks. After investing the additional funds, she wants the fund' required return to be 13 percent.

Required

What should be the average beta of the new stocks added to the portfolio?

Problem-11

Stock X has a 10 percent expected return, a beta coefficient of 0.9, and a 35 percent standard deviation of expected returns. Stock Y has a 12.5 percent expected return, a beta coefficient of 1.2, and a 25 percent standard deviation. The risk-free rate is 6 percent, and the market risk premium is 5 percent.

Required

1. Calculate each stock' coefficient of variation.

2. Which stock is riskier for a diversified investor?

3. Calculate each stock' required rate of return.

4. On the basis of the two stocks'expected and required returns, which stock would be more attractive to a diversified investor?

5. Calculate the required return of a portfolio that has $7,500 invested in Stock X and $2,500 invested in Stock Y.

6. If the market risk premium increased to 6 percent, which of the two stocks would have the larger increase in its required return?

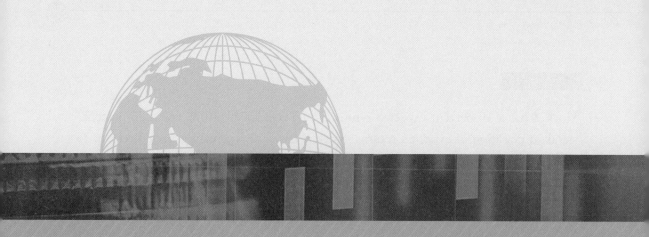

Financial Management For the **US CPA** Exam

Chapter 05

Capital Structure

Volume
8

Capital Structure

01 >> Long-Term Debt

1 Bond

(1) Basic components

- Par value (액면금액)

- Coupon interest rate (표시이자율)

- Coupon payment date (이자지급시기)

- Maturity date (만기)

(2) Bond indenture

A formal agreement between the issuer of a bond and the bondholders detailing the terms of the debt issue. It contains restrictive covenants intended to prevent the issuer from taking actions contrary to the interests of bondholders. (채권발행약정서)

(3) Protective covenants

A part of the indenture limiting certain actions that might be taken during the term of the loan, usually to protect the lender's interest.

1) Positive (Affirmative) covenants

They specify what the issuer must do. (Requirements)

- The company must maintain its working capital at or above some specified minimum level.

- The company must periodically furnish audited financial statements to the lender.

- The firm must maintain any collateral or security in good condition.

2) Negative covenants

They specify actions the issuer cannot take. (Restrictions)

- The firm must limit the amount of dividends it pays according to some formula.

- The firm cannot pledge any assets to other lenders.

- The firm cannot merge with another firm.

- The firm cannot sell or lease any major assets without approval by the lender.

- The firm cannot issue additional long−term debt

(4) Public and private debt

1) Private debt

- Loan from financial institution

- High interest rate

2) Public debt

- SEC registered bonds directly sold to investors.

- Low interest rate but SEC regulation.

2 Types of Bonds

(1) Who issue bonds?

1) Treasury bond (T-Bond)

A bond issued by the federal government. These bonds have no default risk.

2) Municipal bond (Munis)

A bond issued by state and local governments. The interest earned on these bonds is exempt from federal income taxes.

3) Corporate bond

A bond issued by corporations. These bonds have default risk.

(2) Security provision

1) Mortgage bond (담보부채권)

A bond by a mortgage on the real property of the borrower.

2) Collateral trust bond (유가증권 담보채권)

A bond secured by financial asset.

3) Debenture (무담보채권)

Unsecured debt, usually with a maturity of 10 years or more.

(3) Seniority

1) Senior debt (우선순위채권)

A bond that a company must repay first if it goes out of business.

2) Subordinated debenture (후순위채권)

A bond having a claim on assets only after senior debt holders and general debt holders have been paid off in case of bankruptcy.

(4) Repayment

1) Term bond (일시상환채권)

A bond that matures on a specific date.

2) Serial bond (연속상환채권)

A bond that matures in installments over a period of time. payments.

3) Sinking fund provision (감채 기금부 채권)

A provision in a bond contract that requires the issuer to accumulate cash in sinking fund to retire debt.

(5) Embedded option

1) Callable bond (수의상환채권)

A bond that can be redeemed by the issuer prior to its maturity. If the interest rates decline, the issuer can replace high−interest bond with low−interest bond.

→ 채권가격이 상승 할 때 발행자가 행사하기 때문에 투자자에게는 불리한 조항이다.

2) Puttable bond (상환청구권부채권)

A bond that can be redeemed by the bondholders prior to its maturity. If the interest rates increase, the investors can replace low−interest bond with high−interest bond.

→ 채권가격이 하락 할 때 투자자가 행사하기 때문에 투자자에게는 유리한 조항이다.

※ 일반채권과 옵션채권의 채권가격과 채권수익률의 크기는 다음과 같다.

Price : Puttable > Straight > Callable

Yield : Puttable < Straight < Callable

3) Convertible bond (C/B) (전환사채)

A bond that is exchangeable, at the option of the holder, for the issuing firm' common stock. Convertibles have lower coupon rates than nonconvertible debt, but they offer investors the chance for capital gains as compensation for the lower coupon rate.

4) Exchangeable bond (E/B) (교환사채)

A bond that gives the holder the option to exchange the bond for the stock of a company other than the issuer at some future date.

교환사채는 채권 발행자가 보유하고 있는 제3의 주식으로 교환할 수 있는 사채로써, 발행회사의 주식으로 교환하는 전환사채와는 구별된다.

5) Warrant (신주인수권)

An option to buy a stated number of shares of common stock at a specific price. Bonds issued with warrants, carry lower coupon rates than regular bonds.

(6) Coupon payment

1) Coupon interest rate

The stated annual interest rate on a bond.

2) Floating rate bond (변동 금리채권)

A bond whose interest rate fluctuates with shifts in the general level of interest rates.

Coupon rate = Reference Rate + Margin

e.g.) Coupon rate = LIBOR(SOFR) + 200 bps.

※ LIBOR (London Inter-bank Offered Rate)

런던 금융시장에서 한 은행이 다른 은행에 자금을 대출할 때 적용되는 이자율

※ SOFR (Secured Overnight Financing Rate)

LIBOR의 대체금리로 미국 국채를 담보로 하는 1일물 환매조건부채권(RP) 금리

※ BP (basis point)

금리나 수익률을 나타내는 데 사용하는 기본단위로 0.01%를 뜻한다.

The advantage of floating rate bonds, compared to traditional bonds, is that interest rate risk is largely removed.

변동금리채권은 시장 이자율 변동에 따라 액면이자가 변동하므로 채권가격의 변동성이 적다. 즉, 변동금리 채권은 이자율위험이 대부분 제거된 채권이다.

3) Indexed (purchasing power) bond (물가연동채권)

A bond that has interest payments based on an inflation index so as protect the holder from inflation.

물가연동채권은 투자 원금에 물가상승률을 반영한 뒤 그에 대한 이자를 지급하는 채권으로, 인플레이션이 일어나더라도 채권의 실질가치를 보전해준다는 점에서 대표적인 인플레이션 헤지 상품이다.

4) Income bond (이익채권)

A bond that pays interest only if it is earned.

기업의 이익이 이자를 지급할 수 없을 만큼 적을 때 이자지급을 이행하지 않아도 되는 채권

5) Zero-coupon bond (무이자할인채)

A bond that has no interest payments and is sold at a deep discount. The difference between maturity value and current price is interest portion.

(7) International bonds

1) Eurobonds (유로본드)

International bonds denominated in the currency other than that of the country in which they are sold.

2) Foreign bonds (외국채)

International bonds denominated in the currency of the country in which they are sold.

✔ Yankee bond : 미국자본시장에 발행되는 달러화표시 채권

✔ Samurai bond : 일본자본시장에 발행되는 엔화표시 채권

✔ Bulldog bond : 영국자본시장에 발행되는 파운드표시 채권

(8) Bond rating

1) Investment grade bonds (투자등급채권)

Bonds rated triple-B or higher

2) Junk (speculative) bonds (정크본드)

Bonds rated double-B or lower. High-risk, high-yield bonds.

(9) Record of ownership

1) Registered bonds (기명채권)

Bonds that are issued in the name of owner. When the owner sells the bonds, the bond certificates must be surrendered.

2) Bearer bonds (무기명채권)

Bond that can be freely transferred and have a detachable coupon for each interest payment.

4 Advantages and Disadvantages of Debt Financing

(1) Advantages

1) Debt is less costly than equity
2) Interest expense is tax-deductible
3) The stockholders do not give up control of the firm.
4) During inflation, the firm can repay debt at cheaper price

(2) Disadvantages

1) Debt financing has a fixed charge.
2) Debt covenants give restrictions to the firm.
3) Excessive debt adds risk to a firm.

Example 5-1

All else being equal, which one of the following bonds most likely would sell for the highest price (or lowest yield)?

a. Callable debenture   b. Puttable mortgage bond
c. Callable mortgage bond   d. Puttable debenture

Solution

Price : callable 〈 puttable , unsecured bond 〈 secured bond
정답 : b

Example 5-2

If an investor is concerned about inflation risk, the investor should invest in

a. Treasury bond   b. Floating rate bond
c. Indexed bond   d. Investment grade bond

Solution

Treasury bond : no default risk
Floating rate bond : no interest rate risk
Indexed bond : no inflation risk
정답 : c

5 Bond Yield

(1) Coupon rate

Coupon rate = Stated rate = Interest payments ÷ Par value

(2) Current yield

Current yield = Interest payments ÷ Bond price

(3) Yield-to-maturity (YTM)

- The rate of return earned on a bond if it is held to maturity.

- Interest rate that will make present value of cash inflows equal to market price.

$$\text{Price of bond} = \sum_{t=1}^{n} \frac{C}{(1+YTM)^t} + \frac{F}{(1+YTM)^m}$$

(4) Yield to Call (YTC)

The rate of return earned on a bond if it is called before its maturity date.

$$\text{Price of callable bond} = \sum_{t=1}^{m} \frac{C}{(1+YTC)^t} + \frac{callprice}{(1+YTC)^m}$$

m = the number of years until the company can call the bond

Example 5-3

A bond has a $1,000 par value, 5 years to maturity, a 7 percent annual coupon, and sells for $959. What is its current yield? What is its yield to maturity (YTM)?
Assume that the yield to maturity remains constant for the next 2 years. What will the price be 2 years from today?

Solution

(1) Current yield

CY = interest payments ÷ current price = $70 ÷ $959 = 7.3%

(2) Yield to maturity

[EXCEL] 함수선택 RATE

Nper = 5, Pmt = 70, Pv = −959, Fv = 1000 → Rate = 8%

(3) Bond price

[EXCEL] 함수선택 PV

Rate = 8%, Nper = 3, Pmt = 70, Fv = 1000 → PV = −974

Example 5-4

Zara Corporation' outstanding bonds have a $1,000 par value, a 9 percent semiannual coupon, 8 years to maturity, and an 8.5 percent YTM. What is the bond' price?

Solution

Bond price
[EXCEL] 함수선택 PV
Rate = 4.25%, Nper = 16, Pmt = 45, Fv = 1000 → PV = −1,029

Example 5-5

An 8 percent semiannual coupon bond matures in 5 years. The bond has a face value of $1,000 and a current yield of 8.21 percent. What are the bond' price and YTM?

Solution

Bond price = $80 × 8.21% = $974

[EXCEL] 함수선택 RATE

Nper = 10, Pmt = 40, Pv = −974, Fv = 1000 → Rate = 4.33%

YTM = 4.33% × 2 = 8.66%

Example 5-6

The Henderson Company' bonds currently sell for $1,275. They pay a $120 annual coupon, a par value of $1,000 and have a 20-year maturity, but they can be called in 5 years at $1,120. What is their YTM and their YTC, and which is "more relevant" in the sense that investors should expect to earn it?

Solution

[EXCEL] 함수선택 RATE

Nper = 20, Pmt = 120, Pv = −1275, Fv = 1000 → Rate = 8.99% (YTM)

[EXCEL] 함수선택 RATE

Nper = 5, Pmt = 120, Pv = −1275, Fv = 1120 → Rate = 7.31% (YTC)

YTC is more relevant.

6 Lease

(1) Lessee's accounting of US GAAP

Theres are two different forms: operating leases and finance leases.

A lessee should classify a lease as a finance lease when the lease meets any of the following criteria at lease commencement:

1) The lease transfers ownership of the underlying asset to the lessee by the end of the lease term.

2) The lease grants the lessee an option to purchase the underlying asset that the lessee is reasonably certain to exercise.

3) The lease term is for the major part of the remaining economic life of the underlying asset.

4) The present value of the sum of the lease payments and any residual value guaranteed by the lessee equals or exceeds substantially all of the fair value of the underlying asset.

5) The underlying asset is of such a specialized nature that it is expected to have no alternative use to the lessor at the end of the lease term.

(2) Comprehensive example

On January 1, Year 1, United Airlines enters into a lease contract with annual payments of $20,000 per tear. The first payment will be made December 31 and the interest rate implicit in the lease is 8%. The present value of ordinary annuity of $1 at 8% for five years is 3.99. The present value of a $1 at 8% for five years is 0.68.

1) Amortization tale

present value of lease payments $= 3.99 \times 20,000 = \$79,800$

Year	A Beginning Balance	B PMT	C Interest	D Payment of Principal	E Remaining Balance
1	79,800	20,000	6,384	13,616	66,184
2	66,184	20,000	5,295	14,705	51,479
3	51,479	20,000	4,118	15,882	35,597
4	35,597	20,000	2,848	17,152	18,445
5	18,445	20,000	1,555	18,445	0
Total		100,000	20,200	79,800	

$C1 = A1 \times 0.08, D1 = B1 - C1, E1 = A1 - D1, A2 = E1$

2) Operating lease

Date	Accounts	Dr	Cr
1/1/Year 1	Right-of-use asset	$79,800	
	Lease liability		79,800
12/31/Year 1	Lease expense	20,000	
	Cash		20,000
	Lease liability	13,616	
	Accumulated amortization		13,616

	Accounts	Dr	Cr
12/31/Year 2	Lease expense	20,000	
	Cash		20,000
	Lease liability	14,705	
	Accumulated amortization		14,705

	B/S		I/S
	right-of-use asset	lease liability	lease expense
Year 1	66,184	66,184	20,000
Year 2	51,479	51,479	20,000
Year 3	35,597	35,597	20,000
Year 4	18,445	18,445	20,000
Year 5	0	0	20,000

3) Finance lease

Date	Accounts	Dr	Cr
1/1/Year 1	Right-of-use asset	$79,800	
	Lease liability		79,800
12/31/Year 1	Interest expense	6,384	
	Lease liability	13,616	
	Cash		20,000
	Amortization expense	15,960	
	Accumulated amortization		15,960
12/31/Year 2	Interest expense	5,295	
	Lease liability	14,705	
	Cash		20,000
	Amortization expense	15,960	
	Accumulated amortization		15,960

	B/S		I/S
	right-of-use asset	lease liability	interest + amortization
Year 1	63,840	66,184	22,344
Year 2	47,880	51,479	21,255
Year 3	31,920	35,597	20,078
Year 4	15,960	18,445	18,808
Year 5	0	0	17,515

(3) Sales and leaseback (판매후리스)

An arrangement in which the owner of the property sells the property to another and simultaneously eases it back. This contract provides financing and tax advantages.

(4) Advantages of lease

1) Less initial expense

A firm can lease an asset when it does not have enough funds. Because equipment leases rarely require a down payment, you can obtain the goods you need without significantly affecting your cash flow.

2) Tax deductible

Lease payments can usually be deducted as business expenses on tax return, reducing the net cost of your lease.

3) Hedge Obsolescence

Leasing helps equipment users (lessees) avoid the burdens of ownership, one of them being equipment obsolescence.

4) Flexible terms.

Leases are usually easier to obtain and have more flexible terms than loans for buying equipment.(such as the number and amount of rent payments, the term, various purchase options, etc.)

(5) Disadvantages of lease

The cost of lease is higher than cost of purchasing an asset.

02 > Equity Financing

1 Common Stock

(1) Shareholder's rights

1) Voting rights

2) Dividends rights

3) Preemptive right

The right to purchase on a pro rata basis new issues of common stock

4) They are entitled to share in final distribution of assets.

Last priority in receiving the assets after creditors and preferred stockholders

(2) Advantages

1) No contractual obligation
2) Increased equity will reduce cost of borrowing
3) Common stock is attractive to investor due to capital gain potential

(3) Disadvantages of common stock

1) Higher issuance cost than debt
2) The stockholders give up control of the firm.
3) Dividend is not tax deductible

(4) Closely-held corporation

A corporation that is owned by a few individuals who are typically associated with the firm's management.

(5) Publicly-owned corporation

A corporation that is owned by a relatively large number of individuals who are not actively involved in firm's management.

1) OTC (Over-the-counter) market : Unlisted

2) Exchanges market : Listed

2 Preferred Stock

(1) Preferred stock

1) Preferred stock is a hybrid security.

   It is similar to bonds in some respects and to common stocks in other ways.

2) Preferred stockholders receive dividend before dividend payment to common stockholders

3) Preferred stockholders have priority over common stockholder in liquidation.

(2) Types of preferred stock

1) Cumulative preferred stock(누적적우선주)

   If dividend is not paid this year, it is accumulated for next year payment.

2) Participating preferred stock(참가적우선주)

   Preferred stockholder may share dividend with common stockholders.

3) Callable preferred stock(수의상환 우선주)

   Preferred stock that can be retired at specified date at the option of issuer.

4) Convertible preferred stock(전환 우선주)

   Preferred stock that can be convertible into common stock at the option of investor.

3 Financial Market

(1) Function of financial market (금융시장의 기능)

- 자금의 수요와 공급을 중개

- 자금의 가격(이자율)을 탄력적으로 결정

- 금융자산의 유동성을 높여서 거래활성화

- 다양한 금융상품과 리스크 회피수단 제공

- 금융거래에 필요한 정보의 수집시간 및 비용 절감

(2) Financial intermediary (중개기관의 유무)

1) Direct Market (직접금융시장)
자금수요자(기업)가 주식이나 채권을 발행 또는 판매함으로써 투자자들로부터 직접 자금을 조달하는 금융시장

2) Indirect Market (간접금융시장)
불특정다수의 예금자가 은행 등의 금융기관에 맡긴 자금이 이를 필요로 하는 다수의 개인이나 기업에게 대출되는 금융시장

(3) Maturity of financial instrument (금융상품의 만기)

1) Money Market (자금시장 : 단기금융시장)
취급하는 금융상품의 기간이 1년 이내인 시장으로 기업은 일반적으로 영업활동에 소요되는 운전자금을 단기금융시장에서 조달한다.

2) Capital Market (자본시장 : 장기금융시장)
취급하는 금융상품의 기간이 1년을 초과하는 시장으로 주로 주식 또는 채권 등을 취급하는 증권시장을 의미하기도 한다. 기업은 일반적으로 설비투자 등을 위한 투자자금을 장기금융시장에서 조달한다.

(4) Distribution stage of financial instrument (금융상품의 유통단계)

1) Primary market (issue market, 발행시장)

The market in which newly issued securities are sold

발행시장은 채권이나 주식 등의 증권이 신규로 발행되어 투자자에게 판매되는 시장으로 주로 증권 인수업자 (underwriter)를 통하여 모집 및 발행을 한다.

2) Secondary market (trading market, 유통시장)

The market in which previously issued securities are sold

유통시장은 증권이 투자자에게 발행되어 이후 투자자간에 매매되는 시장으로 주로 증권 거래소(exchange)를 통하여 매매가 이루어진다.

(5) Transaction Place (거래장소)

1) On-board market (장내시장)

금융거래가 구체적인 거래장소(거래소)에서 정해진 시간 중에 이루어지는 시장

2) Off-board market (장외시장)

금융거래가 특정한 시장 밖에서 상호 개별적 접촉에 의해 거래가 이루어지는 시장이며 Over-the-counter (OTC) market이라고도 한다.

(6) Stock market

1) Listing (상장)

증권을 증권거래소에서 매매할 수 있는 종목으로 지정하는 것

2) Bull market (강세시장)

A bull market is a period of several months or years during which asset prices consistently rise.

3) Bear market (약세시장)

A bear market is a period of several months or years during which securities prices consistently fall.

(7) Going pubic

1) Initial public offering (IPO)

The process for making shares of a private company available to the public for the first time to raise capital is called an initial public offering (IPO) or 'going public'. Businesses usually go public to raise capital in hopes of expanding. Venture capitalists may use IPOs as an exit strategy.

2) Advantages

- A public company can raise additional funds in the future through secondary offerings.
- Stock in a public company is more attractive to potential employees because shares can be sold more easily.
- Merger and acquisition activity may be easier for a public company that can use its shares to acquire another firm.
- Increase liquidity of owners' investments

3) Disadvantages

- A public company must file reports with the SEC that may reveal secrets and business methods that could help competitors.
- Puts pressure on short-term growth
- Imposes more restrictions on management
- Makes former business owners lose control of decision making

1. Securities Act of 1933

미국의 증권발행시장을 규제하기 위해 제정된 법률을 말한다. 동 법이 제정되기 이전에는 blue sky law가 발행시장을 규제하고 있었으나 1920년대 들어 다양한 변칙발행이 성행하자 각 주(州) 간 상이한 규제조치를 통일하여 신규증권발행을 공정히 하고 공시제도를 확충할 목적으로 제정되었다. 동 법률은 발행회사가 증권의 내용을 사전에 철저히 공개하고 증권발행의 목적, 회사내용 등 법정사항을 기재한 신고서를 증권거래위원회에 제출토록 하며, 투자자가 당해 증권의 내용을 알 수 있도록 신고서의 주요 내용을 기재한 안내서를 첨부하도록 규정하고 있다.

Registration forms
① Form S-1
② Form S-2 and S-3
③ Form SB-1 and SB-2

2. Securities Act of 1934

미국의 증권유통시장을 규제하기 위해 제정된 법률을 말한다.

Required reporting
① Form 10-K : Annual reports
② Form 10-Q : Quarterly reports
③ Form 8-K : 기업인수합병, 파산, 이사진 사임, 회계연도 변경 등

3. Sarbanes-Oxley Act

2002년 7월 제정된 미국의 기업회계개혁법으로, 회계부정에 대해 강력한 제재를 가할 수 있도록 하는 내용을 담고 있다. 회계감시를 강화하기 위한 회계감독위원회(PCAOB) 설립은 물론 기업경영진이 기업회계장부의 정확성을 보증하고 잘못이 있으면 처벌을 받도록 규정하고 있다. 이 위원회는 5명의 위원으로 구성되며, 기업들의 회계를 감사하고 윤리 규정을 채택토록 종용하는 역할을 맡는다. 또 회계법인에 대한 사찰도 가능하며 특정 기업의 회계 법규 위반시 조사권을 갖는다. 또 극히 일부 기업들의 재무제표를 조사하는데 그쳤던 증권거래위원회(SEC)는 대부분 대기업들의 재무제표를 감사할 수 있으며 CEO들은 고의적으로 사실과 다른 재무제표를 인증할 경우 형사처벌을 받게 되었다.

(8) Efficient market hypothesis (EMH)

주가에 모든 이용가능한 정보가 충분히 반영되는 시장을 효율적 자본시장이라고 하며, 이를 검증하는 가설을 효율적 시장가설 (EMH)이라고 한다. 효율적 시장 가설은 다음 세 가지로 구분한다.

1) Weak-form EMH

Current market prices reflect all past price movements.

약형 EMH란 현재의 증권가격에는 과거의 주가정보가 반영되어 있다는 것이다. 따라서 과거 주가정보를 이용해서는 평균적으로 초과수익을 얻을 수 없게 된다.

2) Semi-strong form EMH

Current market prices reflect all publicly available information.

준강형 EMH란 현재의 증권가격에는 공개된 모든 정보가 반영되어 있다는 것이다. 따라서 이미 공개된 정보를 이용해서는 평균적으로 초과수익을 얻을 수 없게 된다. 그리고 과거주가정보도 공개된 정보에 포함되므로 준강형 EMH이 성립하면 약형 EMH도 당연히 성립하게 된다.

3) Strong form EMH

Current market prices reflect all publicly available and privately held information.

강형 EMH란 현재의 증권가격에는 공개정보뿐만 아니라 공개되지 않은 내부정보까지 반영되어 있다는 것이다. 따라서 누구도 초과수익을 지속적으로 얻을 수 없게 된다.

(9) Developed market and developing market

1) Developed market

In investing, a developed market is a country that is most developed in terms of its economy and capital markets. The country must be high income, but this also includes openness to foreign ownership, ease of capital movement, and efficiency of market institutions. Emerging markets and frontier markets are types of developing markets.

2) Emerging market

An emerging market is a country that has some characteristics of a developed market, but does not satisfy standards to be termed a developed market.

→ BRIC countries (Brazil, Russia, India and China)

3) Frontier market

A type of developing country with smaller, riskier, or more illiquid capital markets than emerging market.

03 ▶ Leverage

1 Business Risk & Financial Risk

(1) Business risk (영업위험 또는 경영위험)

The riskiness inherent in the firm's operations if it uses no debt.

- Demand variability
- Sales price variability
- Input cost variability
- The extent to which costs are fixed (Operating Leverage)

(2) Financial risk (재무위험)

The additional risk placed on the common stockholders as a result of using debt.

An increase in stockholders'risk, over and above the firm' basic business risk, resulting from the use of financial leverage.

2 Operating Leverage

(1) 영업레버리지의 의미

The extent to which fixed costs are used in a company's operations.

영업레버리지는 총 영업비용중에서 고정영업비용이 차지하는 비중으로 측정된다.

(2) DOL (Degree of operating leverage)

The change in operating income resulting from a percentage change in sales.

> DOL = percentage change in EBIT ÷ percentage change in sales
>
> = contribution margin (CM) ÷ EBIT

if) DOL = 3

✔ 매출액이 1% 증가한다면 영업이익은 3% 증가

✔ 매출액이 1% 감소한다면 영업이익은 3% 감소

3 Financial Leverage

(1) 재무레버리지의 의미

The extent to which debt and preferred stock are used in a company's capital structure.

재무레버리지는 자본구조에서 부채와 우선주의 사용정도로 측정된다.

(2) DFL (Degree of financial leverage)

The change in earnings per share (EPS) resulting from changes in operating income (EBIT).

> DFL = percentage change in EPS ÷ percentage change in EBIT
>
> = EBIT ÷ EBT

if) DFL = 2

✔ 영업이익이 1% 증가한다면 EPS는 2% 증가

✔ 영업이익이 1% 감소한다면 EPS는 2% 감소

(3) DTL (Degree of total leverage)

The change in earnings per share (EPS) resulting from a percentage change in sales.

DTL = percentage change in EPS ÷ percentage change in EBIT

= contribution margin (CM) ÷ EBT

= DOL × DFL

if) DTL = 6

✔ 매출액이 1% 증가한다면 EPS는 6% 증가

✔ 매출액이 1% 감소한다면 EPS는 6% 감소

Example 5-7

The following information is available for Home Depot Inc.
Budgeted income statement

	100,000 units	105,000 units
Sales	$3,000,000	$3,150,000
EBIT	$200,000	$240,000
EPS	0.20	0.27

What is Home Depot Inc.'s DOL, DFL and DTL?

Solution

Percentage change in Sales = $(3,150,000 - 3,000,000) \div 3,000,000 = 5\%$

Percentage change in EBIT = $(240,000 - 200,000) \div 200,000 = 20\%$

Percentage change in EPS = $(0.27 - 0.20) \div 0.20 = 35\%$

DOL = 20% ÷ 5% = 4

DFL = 35% ÷ 20% = 1.75

DTL = 35% ÷ 5% = 7

DTL = DOL × DFL = 4 × 1.75 = 7

Example 5-8

Coca-Cola Co. currently sells 400,000 bottles each year. Each bottle variable costs $0.84 to produce and sells for $1.00. Fixed costs are $24,000 per year. The firm has annual interest expense of $8,000 and a 40% tax rate. What is the firm's DOL & DFL?

Solution

CM = 400,000 units $\times$ ($1.00 − $0.84) = $64,000

EBIT = CM − TFC = $64,000 − $24,000 = $40,000

EBT = EBIT − I = $40,000 − $8,000 = $32,000

DOL = = $64,000 ÷ $40,000 = 1.60

DFL = = $40,000 ÷ $32,000 = 1.25

DTL = DOL $\times$ DFL = 1.6 $\times$ 1.25 = 2.00

04 〉 **WACC**

1 Cost of Debt

타인자본비용은 부채를 사용하는 대가로 기업이 부담하는 비용을 말한다. 기업이 부채에 대하여 지급하는 이자는 비용으로 인정되기 때문에 법인세의 절감효과를 얻게 되므로 이를 고려한 타인자본비용은 다음과 같다.

$$
\begin{aligned}
\text{After tax cost of debt} &= \text{Interest rate} - \text{Tax savings} \\
&= k_d \times (1 - \text{tax rate})
\end{aligned}
$$

$k_d = \text{YTM or CY}$

2 Cost of Preferred Stock

우선주 자본비용은 자본을 사용하는 대가로 배당이 일정액으로 지급되는데 배당은 이자처럼 비용처리가 되지 않고 납세 후 이익에서 지급되기 때문에 법인세 감세효과는 없다.

$$
k_{ps} = \frac{D}{P_0 - F}
$$

F : flotation costs (발행비용) : underwriting fee, registration fee, etc

Example 5-9

Procter & Gamble Co. has preferred stock paying $8 dividend per share and sells for $100 per share. If the firm wants to issue new preferred shares, it would cost 5% flotation costs. What is the firm's cost of preferred stock with flotation costs considered?

Solution

Flotation cost = $100 × 0.05) = $5
Cost of preferred stock = $8 ÷ ($100 − $5) = 8.4%

3 Cost of Retained Earnings

보통주의 자금조달은 이익의 일부를 사내에 유보하여 적립하는 내부금융과 신규 주식을 발행하는 외부금융으로 구분된다. 배당 대신 재투자를 위해 유보시킨 유보이익의 자기자본비용은 다음과 같이 분류할 수 있다.

(1) Capital asset pricing model approach (CAPM)

SML을 통해서 산출한 주식의 요구수익률을 자기자본비용으로 이용한다.

$$k_e = R_F + (R_M - R_F) \times b_i$$

(2) Dividend Discount Model approach (DDM)

배당평가모형에서 주가를 산출하기 위해서 사용한 할인율을 자기자본비용으로 이용한다.

$$P_0 = \frac{D_1}{k_e - g} \rightarrow k_e = \frac{D_1}{P_0} + g$$

g = ROE × Retention rate

Example 5-10

As before, Apple's stock sells for $21, next year's dividend is expected to be $1, Apple's expected ROE is 12% and will pay out 40% of its earnings. What is the firm's cost of retained earnings?

Solution

g = (1 − 0.4) × 12% = 7.2% → $k_e = \frac{\$1}{\$21} + 0.072 = 11.96\%$

4 Cost of New Common Stock

신규 주식을 발행하여 자금을 조달하는 경우의 자기자본비용은 다음과 같이 결정한다.

$$k_e = \frac{D_1}{P_0 - F} + g$$

F : flotation costs (발행비용) : underwriting fee, registration fee, etc

Example 5-11

As before, Apple's stock sells for $21, next year's dividend is expected to be $1, Apple's expected ROE is 12% and will pay out 40% of its earnings. Flotation cost is 10%. What is the firm's cost of new common stock?

Solution

$$g = (1 - 0.4) \times 12\% = 7.2\% \rightarrow k_e = \frac{\$1}{21 - 21 \times 0.1} + 0.072 = 12.5\%$$

5 WACC

(1) WACC (weighted average cost of capital)

가중평균자본비용이란 원천별 자본비용을 각 자본의 총자본구성비율로 가중평균한 자본비용을 말하는데 총자본이 타인자본, 우선주자본 및 보통주자본으로 구성된 경우 다음 식을 통해서 측정된다.

$$\text{WACC} = w_d \times k_d \times (1-t) + w_{ps} \times k_{ps} + w_e \times k_e$$

w_d : the percentage of debt in the capital structure
w_{ps} : the percentage of preferred stock in the capital structure
w_e : the percentage of common stock in the capital structure

위와 같이 WACC를 산출할 때에 각 자본비용에 대한 가중치는 장부가치보다는 시장가치로 하는 것이 이론적으로 더 타당하다.

(2) Factors that affect the WACC

Factors the firm cannot control	Factors the firm can control
• Interest rates • Tax rates	• Capital structure policy • Dividend payout • Capital budgeting decision

Example 5-12

For example, a firm's capital structure consists of the following:

Capital component	Cost	Amount	Percentage (weight)
Long term debt	6%	$720,000	40%
Preferred stock	8%	180,000	10%
Common equity	9%	900,000	50%
		$1,800,000	

Assuming a marginal tax rate of 30 percent, what is the firm's WACC?

Solution

$$\text{WACC} = 0.40 \times (6\% \times 0.7) + 0.10 \times (8\%) + 0.50 \times (9\%) = 6.98\%$$

Example 5-13

LEVIS has the following capital structure, which it considers to be optimal:

Debt : 25%

Preferred stock : 15%

Common equity : 60%

LEVIS' established dividend payout ratio is 30 percent, its federal-plus-state tax rate is 40 percent, and investors expect earnings and dividends to grow at a constant rate of 9 percent in the future. LEIVIS paid a dividend of $3.60 per share last year, and its stock currently sells for $54 per share.

LEVIS can obtain new capital in the following ways:

- Preferred: New preferred stock with a dividend of $11 can be sold to the public at a price of $95 per share.
- Debt: Debt can be sold at an interest rate of 12 percent.

  What is its WACC?

Solution

$$k_e = \frac{D_1}{P_0} + g = (\$3.60 \times 1.09) \div \$54 + 9\% = 16.27\%$$

$$k_{ps} = \frac{D}{P_0 - F} = \$11 \div \$95 = 11.58\%$$

$$\text{WACC} = 0.25 \times (12\% \times 0.6) + 0.15 \times (11.58\%) + 0.60 \times (16.27\%) = 13.3\%$$

6 Optimal (Target) Capital Structure

The optimal capital structure is the proportion of debt and equity that will maximize the stock price and minimize the WACC. However, the optimal capital structure does not necessarily maximize EPS. Greater leverage maximizes EPS but also increases risk. Thus the highest stock price is not reached by maximizing EPS.

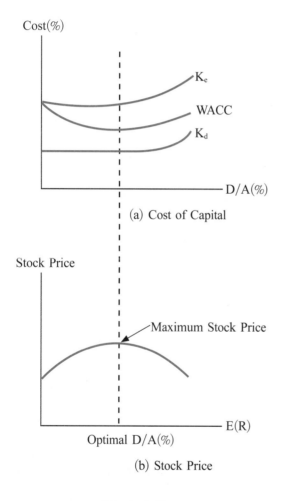

(a) Cost of Capital

(b) Stock Price

[Figure 5-1]

> **Example 5-14**

A firm's target or optimal capital structure is consistent with which one of the following?

a. Maximum earnings per share.
b. Minimum cost of debt
c. Minimum cost of equity
d. Minimum weighted-average cost of capital

Solution

최적 자본구조는 WACC를 최소화하여 기업 가치를 최대화시키는 자본구조이다. 타인 자본을 사용하지 않으면 타인자본비용이나 자기자본 비용만을 최소화할 수 있지만 기업가치 결정의 할인율이 WACC이므로 WACC을 최소화하는 자본구조가 목표자본구조가 되어야 한다.

정답 : d

7 Capital Structure Theory

(1) MM theory with no taxes

Under the assumption of no taxes, transaction costs or bankruptcy costs, the value of the firm is unaffected by leverage changes. According to MM propositions, capital structure is irrelevant for firm value and WACC.

F. Modigliani & M. H. Miller는 1958년에 발표한 논문에서 세금이 없는 완전자본시장이 존재하는 경우, 기업가치는 자본구조와 무관하다고 주장하였다. 즉 자본구조의 변동이 기업가치나 WACC에 영향을 주지 못한다.

(2) MM with taxes

Under the assumption of no transaction costs or bankruptcy costs, the tax deductibility of interest payments creates a tax shield that add value to the firm, and optimal capital structure is achieved with 100% debt. This theory says that WACC is minimized at 100% debt.

MM은 1963년에 법인세를 고려한 수정이론을 발표하였다. 법인세가 존재하면 부채에 대한 이자비용은 법인세를 절감시켜 준다. 따라서 부채를 많이 사용할수록 기업가치는 증가한다. 즉, 법인세가 존재하면 레버리지가 증가할수록 가중평균자본비용은 감소하고, 기업가치는 증가하게 되므로 100% 부채를 사용하는 경우에 기업가치가 극대화된다는 것이 MM수정이론이다.

(3) The trade-off theory

When taxes and bankruptcy costs are considered, there is a trade-off between the tax savings of increased debt (increasing firm value) and the increased bankruptcy risk of increased debt (decreasing firm value) so that there is an optimal debt level that maximizes firm value.

부채의 사용을 증가함에 따라 부채의 세금절감 효과에 의하여 기업이 가치가 증가하는 반면에 파산비용의 증가로 인하여 기업의 가치가 감소하게 된다.

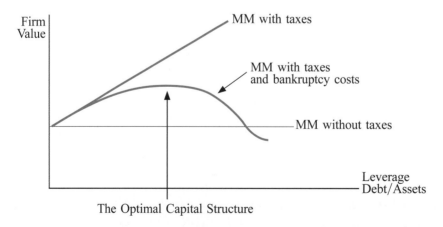

[Figure 5-2]

(4) Pecking order theory (자본조달순위이론)

- Symmetric Information

  The situation in which investors and managers have identical information about firms' prospects.

- Asymmetric Information

  The situation in which managers have different (better) information about firms'prospects than do investors.

- Signal

  An action taken by a firm' management that provides clues to investors about how management views the firm' prospects.

  Based on asymmetric Information, management sends signals to investors through its financing decision. The pecking order is

  - Internally generated equity (retained earnings)

  - Debt

  - External equity (newly issued shares)

05 ▶ Dividend Policy

1 Dividend Policy

(1) 배당정책의 의의

배당정책은 기업이 벌어들인 이익을 주주에 대한 배당금과 미래의 재투자를 위한 유보이익으로 나누는 결정을 의미한다. 여기에서 배당금은 주주가 자본을 출자한 대가로 받게 되는 보상이기는 하지만 배당금이 많이 지급되는 것이 반드시 좋은 것은 아니다. 왜냐하면 유보이익은 새로운 투자를 수행하기 위한 자금의 원천이 되기 때문에 배당을 많이 지급하여 유보이익이 적게 되면 기업의 성장기회가 제약받을 수 있기 때문이다. 그래서 배당과 유보의 조화로운 결정이 배당정책에서 가장 중요한 목표가 되는 것이다.

(2) 배당의 척도

기업이 어느 정도 수준의 배당을 지급하는가를 나타내는 척도로 다음과 같은 개념들이 이용된다.

dividend per share (DPS) = total dividends ÷ outstanding shares

dividend payout ratio = DPS ÷ EPS

retention ratio (RR) = 1 − dividend payout ratio

dividend yield (DY) = DPS ÷ price per share

dividend ratio = DPS ÷ par value per share

(3) Factors affecting dividend policy

1) Impairment of capital rule

상법에 의하여 납입자본은 배당이 불가능하며, 이익만이 배당이 가능하다.

2) Availability of cash

유동성이 양호 할수록 배당지급능력이 크다.

3) Access to capital market

자본시장에서의 자금조달이 어려울수록 배당을 감소하는 경향이 있다.

4) Tax positions of shareholder

주주는 배당 소득세를 부담하므로 주주들의 세율구조가 중요한 요인이다.

5) Investment opportunities

수익성이 큰 투자기회가 많을수록 배당은 감소하게 된다.

6) Restriction in debt agreement

채권자들은 자금을 제공할 때에 부채가치를 보호하기 위해서 배당제한조항을 포함하는 계약을 맺는 경우가 많다.

2 Dividend Policy Theory

배당정책에 대한 논의는 배당정책이 주주의 부(wealth)에 영향을 미치는가 아니면 아무런 영향을 주지 않는가에 대한 논의에서부터 시작된다. 주주가 주식을 보유함으로써 얻게 되는 소득은 배당소득과 자본이득소득으로 구성된다. 배당정책에 대한 논의는 결국 주주의 입장에서 배당소득이 유리한가 아니면 자본이득이 유리한가에 대한 논의로 귀결된다.

(1) Dividend irrelevance theory (MM theory)

MM의 배당무관련이론은 완전자본시장이라면 배당정책의 차이가 기업가치나 주주의 부에 영향을 주지 않는다는 것이다.

> **Example 5-15**

Nike Company has net income of $2,000,000 and it has 1,000,000 shares of common stock outstanding. The company' stock currently trades at $32 a share. Nike is considering a plan in which it will use available cash to pay a cash dividend of $1,600,000. What will be its stock price and EPS following the cash dividend?

Solution

Ex-dividend price per share
= $(1,000,000 \times \$32 - \$1,600,000) \div 1,000,000$ shares = $30.4
Ex-dividend EPS = $2,000,000 ÷ 1,000,000 shares = $2
Dividend per share = $1,600,000 ÷ 1,000,000 shares = $1.60
Total wealth from the ownership of one share = $30.4 + $1.60 = $32

(2) Tax preference theory

현실에서 나타나는 여러 가지 불완전요인들 중에 세금을 고려한 배당이론이다. 즉, 주주의 개인소득세는 배당소득에 대한 세율이 자본이득에 대한 세율보다 높으므로, 배당성향이 낮은 기업의 기업가치가 높게 나타난다는 이론이다.

(3) Bird-in-the-hand theory

Firm's value will be maximized by setting a high dividend payout because dividends are considered less risky when compared to future capital gains.

현실에서 나타나는 여러 가지 불완전요인들 중에 불확실성을 고려한 배당이론이다. 즉, 현재의 확실한 배당소득이 미래의 불확실한 자본이득보다 더 가치가 있으므로, 주주들은 현재의 배당을 선호하고, 고배당을 하는 기업의 가치가 더욱 크게 나타난다.

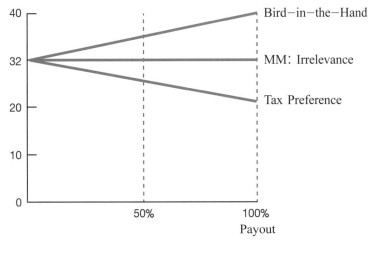

[Figure 5-3]

(4) Clientele effect

The tendency of a firm to attract a set of investors who like its dividend policy

고객효과는 현실적으로 다양한 배당수준이 존재하는 현상을 설명하는 이론이다. 즉, 세율이 높은 주주들은 저배당주를 선호하며, 세율이 낮은 주주들은 고배당주를 선호하기 때문에 투자자들이 자신의 선호에 따라서 서로 다른 배당수준의 주식에 투자한다.

(5) Signaling effect

The theory that investors regard dividend changes as signals of management' earnings forecasts.

정보의 비대칭성 때문에 경영자는 기업의 미래수익성 등 재무정보를 일반투자자에게 전달하는 수단으로 배당정책을 이용할 수 있다. 배당의 증가는 기업이 좋은 투자안을 갖고 있거나 현금동원 능력이 충분하다는 등의 정보를 투자자에게 전달하는 신호가 있다는 것이다.

(6) Residual dividend theory

A model in which the dividend paid is set equal to net income minus the amount of retained earnings necessary to finance the firm' optimal capital budget.

잔여배당이론은 배당정책은 투자정책과 자본조달정책에 따라 결정된다는 이론이다. 즉, 기업이 사전에 선정한 목표부채비율에 따라 순이익 중 재투자를 위한 유보이익을 결정한 후 순이익에서 유보이익을 차감한 잔액에 대해 배당을 지급한다.

Example 5-16

AT&T has a target capital structure that consists of 70 percent debt and 30 percent equity. The company anticipates that its capital budget for the upcoming year will be $3,000,000. If Axel reports net income of $2,000,000 and it follows a residual dividend payout policy, what will be its dividend payout ratio?

Solution

투자금액 $3,000,000 중에서 30%는 자본으로 조달하여야 하므로 $900,000는 net income 중에서 유보를 하여야 한다. 따라서 배당 가능한 금액은 net income $2,000,000 중에서 $900,000을 차감한 $1,100000이며 따라서 배당성향은 $1,100,000 ÷ $2,000,000 = 55% 가 된다.

Example 5-17

Which of the following statements about dividends is true?

a. Dividend irrelevance means that investors prefer dividends to capital gain.
b. If a firm follows a residual dividend policy, then a sudden increase in the number of profitable projects is likely to reduce the firm's dividend payout.
c. The tax preference theory suggests that a firm can increase its stock price by increasing its dividend payout ratio.
d. The bird-in-the-hand theory implies that firms can reduce their cost of equity capital by reducing their dividend payout ratios.

Solution

a. 무관련이론은 주주들은 배당소득과 자본이득을 무차별하게 판단한다는 이론이다.
b. 수익성이 좋은 투자의 증가는 내부유보를 증가시키므로 배당성향은 감소한다는 이론이다.
c. 배당성향을 증가하면 주주들의 세금이 증가하여 주주의 부가 감소하므로 주가는 하락한다는 이론이다.
d. 배당성향을 증가하면 불확실성이 감소하여 주가가 오른다는 이론이다.

정답 : b

3 Payment Procedures

(1) Declaration date

The date the board of directors approves payment

(2) Holder-of-record date

The date on which the shareholders of record are designated.

(3) Ex-dividend date

The cut-off date for receiving the dividend. It is usually two business days prior to the record date.

(4) Payment date

The date the dividend checks are mailed out.

"On November 8, 20X1, the directors of Nike Company met and declared the regular quarterly dividend of 50 cents per share, payable to holders of record at the close of business on December 8, payment to be made on January 3, 20X2."

- Declaration date : November 8

- Dividend goes with stock if it is bought on or before : December 5

- Ex-dividend date. Buyer does not receive the dividend : December 6

- Holder-of-record date : December 8

- Payment date : January 3

4 Stock Repurchase

(1) Types of stock repurchases

자사주 매입은 기업이 발행한 주식을 다시 매입하는 것으로 자사주 매입의 목적은 다음과 같다.

1) situations where the firm has cash available for distribution to its stockholders, and it distributes this cash by repurchasing shares rather than by paying cash dividends.

2) situations where the firm concludes that its capital structure is too heavily weighted with equity, and it then sells debt and uses the proceeds to buy back its stock.

3) situations where the firm has issued options to employees and it then uses open market repurchases to obtain stock for use when the options are exercised.

(2) Advantages of stock repurchases

1) Enhanced EPS

If some of the outstanding stock is repurchased, fewer shares will remain outstanding and the earnings per share on the remaining shares will increase.

2) Signaling

A repurchase announcement may be viewed as a positive signal by investors because repurchases are often motivated by managements' belief that their firms'shares are undervalued.

3) Flexibility

Managements dislike cutting cash dividends because of the negative signal a cut gives. Hence, if the excess cash flow is expected to be temporary, management may prefer to make the distribution as a share repurchase rather than to declare an increased cash dividend that cannot be maintained.

4) Changes in capital structure

Repurchases can be used to produce large-scale changes in capital structure.

5) Offsetting dilution from employee stock options

Companies can use repurchase shares when employees exercise their options. This avoids having to issue new shares and the resulting dilution of EPS.

6) Reduced take-over threat

Share repurchase helps to reduce threat of a hostile takeover as it makes it difficult for predator company to gain control.

Example 5-18

Nike Company has net income of $2,000,000 and it has 1,000,000 shares of common stock outstanding. The company' stock currently trades at $32 a share. Nike is considering a plan in which it will use available cash of $1,600,000 to repurchase its shares in the open market. What will be its stock price and EPS following the repurchase?

Solution

Repurchase shares = $1,600,000 \div $32 = 50,000$ shares
Price per share after the repurchase
$= (1,000,000 \times $32 - $1,600,000) \div 950,000$ shares $= 32
EPS after the repurchase $= $2,000,000 \div 950,000$ shares $= 2.11
Total wealth from the ownership of one share $= 32

5 Special Dividends

(1) Stock Dividend

A dividend paid in the form of additional shares of stock rather than in cash. The total number of shares is increased, so earnings and price per share all decline.

주식배당은 배당을 현금으로 지급하는 대신 신주를 발행하여 지급하는 것으로 재무적 효과는 유보이익의 감소와 납입자본의 증가로 나타나게 되는데 자기자본가치에는 아무런 영향을 주지 못한다. 그러나 발행주식수가 증가하므로, 주가와 EPS는 감소한다.

(2) Stock split

An action taken by a firm to increase the number of shares outstanding, such as doubling the number of shares outstanding by giving each stockholder two new shares for each one formerly held. The total number of shares is increased, so earnings and price per share all decline.

주식분할이란 주당 액면가를 낮춤으로써 1주를 여러 주식으로 분할하는 것을 말한다. 자기자본가치에는 아무런 영향을 주지 못하며, 발행주식수가 증가하므로, 주가와 EPS는 감소한다.

(3) Reverse split

An action taken by a firm to decrease the number of shares outstanding. The total number of shares is decreased, so earnings and price per share all increase.

주식병합이란 주당 액면가를 높임으로써 발행주식수를 감소시키는 것을 말한다. 자기자본가치에는 아무런 영향을 주지 못하며, 발행주식수가 감소하므로, 주가와 EPS는 증가한다.

Example 5-19

Nike Company has net income of $2,000,000 and it has 1,000,000 shares of common stock outstanding. The company' stock currently trades at $32 a share. Nike is considering the following actions. What will be its stock price and EPS following the actions?
Action 1 : 20% stock dividends
Action 2 : a 2-for-1 stock split
Action 3 : a 1-for-2 reverse split

Solution

(1) 20% stock dividends

Post−dividend price= $(1,000,000 \times \$32) \div 1,200,000$ shares = $26.67

Post−dividend EPS = $\$2,000,000 \div 1,200,000$ shares = $1.67

Total wealth from the ownership of one share = $26.67 \times 1.20 = \$32$

(2) 2−for−1 stock split

Post−split price= $(1,000,000 \times \$32) \div 2,000,000$ shares = $16.0

Post−split EPS = $\$2,000,000 \div 2,000,000$ shares = $1.0

Total wealth from the ownership of one share = $16 \times 2 = \$32$

(3) 1−for−2 reverse split

Post−split price= $(1,000,000 \times \$32) \div 500,000$ shares = $64.0

Post−split EPS = $\$2,000,000 \div 500,000$ shares = $4.0

Total wealth from the ownership of one share = $64 \div 2 = \$32$

현금배당, 자사주 매입 및 특수 배당의 재무비율 효과를 정리하면 다음과 같다.

	Cash dividend	Stock repurchase	Stock dividend	Stock split	Reverse split
Outstanding shares	No effect	Decrease	Increase	Increase	Decrease
EPS	No effect	Increase	Decrease	Decrease	Increase
Stock price	Decrease	No effect	Decrease	Decrease	Increase
Par value per share	No effect	No effect	No effect	Decrease	Increase
Debt to equity	Increase	Increase	No effect	No effect	No effect
Shareholder's wealth	No effect	No effect	No effect	No effect	No effect

06 ⟫ Multiple Choice

01. Stanford Company leased some special-purpose equipment from Vincent Inc. under a long-term lease that was treated as an operating lease by Stanford. After the financial statements for the year had been issued, it was discovered that the lease should have been treated as a capital lease by Stanford. All of the following measures relating to Stanford would be affected by this discovery except the

a. debt/equity ratio.   b. accounts receivable turnover.

c. interest coverage ratio.   d. net income percentage.

02. Which one of the following is a debt instrument that generally has a maturity of ten year more? (CMA)

a. A bond.   b. A note.

c. A chattel mortgage.   d. A financial lease.

03. Preferred stock may be retired through the use of any one of the following except a (CMA)

a. conversion.   b. call provision.

c. refunding.   d. sinking fund.

04. Which one of the following best describes the record date as it pertains to common stock? (CMA)

    a. Four business days prior to the payment of a dividend.

    b. The 52-week high for a stock published in the Wall Street Journal.

    c. The date that is chosen to determine the ownership of shares.

    d. The date on which a prospectus is declared effective by the Securities and Exchange Commission.

05. All of the following are characteristics of preferred stock except that (CMA)

    a. it may be callable at the option of the corporation.

    b. it may be converted into common stock.

    c. its dividends are tax deductible to the issuer.

    d. it usually has no voting rights.

06. Which one of the following describes a disadvantage to a firm that issues preferred stock? (CMA)

    a. Preferred stock dividends are legal obligations of the corporation.

    b. Preferred stock typically has no maturity date.

    c. Preferred stock is usually sold on a higher yield basis than bonds.

    d. Most preferred stock is owned by corporate investors.

07. The call provision in some bond indentures allows (CMA)

    a. the issuer to exercise an option to redeem the bonds.

    b. the bondholder to exchange the bond, at no additional cost, for common shares.

    c. the bondholder to redeem the bond early by paying a call premium.

    d. the issuer to pay a premium in order to prevent bondholders from redeeming bonds.

08. Protective clauses set forth in an indenture are known as (CMA)

    a. provisions.   b. requirements.

    c. addenda.   d. covenants.

09. Which one of the following situations would prompt a firm to issue debt, as opposed to equity, the next time it raises external capital? (CMA)

    a. High break even point.

    b. Significant percentage of assets under capital lease.

    c. Low fixed-charge coverage.

    d. High effective tax rate.

10. James Hemming, the chief financial officer of a midwestern machine parts manufacturer, is considering splitting the company's stock, which is currently selling at $80.00 per share. The stock currently pays a $1.00 per share dividend. If the split is two-for-one, Mr. Hemming may expect the post split price to be (CMA)

    a. exactly $40.00, regardless of dividend policy.

    b. greater than $40.00, if the dividend is changed to $0.45 per new share.

    c. greater than $40.00, if the dividend is changed to $0.55 per new share.

    d. less than $40.00, regardless of dividend policy.

11. Mason Inc. is considering four alternative opportunities. Required investment outlays and expected rates of return for these investments are given below.

Project	Investment Cost	IRR
A	$200,000	12.5
B	$350,000	14.2
C	$570,000	16.5
D	$390,000	10.6

The investments will be financed through 40% debt and 60% common equity. Internally generated funds totaling $1,000,000 are available for reinvestment. If the cost of capital is 11%, and Mason strictly follows the residual dividend policy, how much in dividends would the company likely pay? (CMA)

a. $120,000.

b. $328,000.

c. $430,000.

d. $650,000.

12. When determining the amount of dividends to be declared, the most important factor to consider is the (CMA)

a. expectations of the shareholders.

b. future planned uses of retained earnings.

c. impact of inflation on replacement costs.

d. future planned uses of cash.

13. Frasier Products has been growing at a rate of 10% per year and expects this growth to continue and produce earnings per share of $4.00 next year. The firm has a dividend payout ratio of 35% and a beta value of 1.25. If the risk-free rate is 7% and the return on the market is 15%, what is the expected current market value of Frasier's common stock? (CMA)

a. $14.00

b. $16.00

c. $20.00

d. $28.00

14. Cox Company has sold 1,000 shares of $100 par, 8% preferred stock at an issue price of $92 per share. Stock issue costs were $5 per share. Cox pays taxes at the rate of 40%. What is Cox's cost of preferred stock capital? (CMA)

a. 8.00%   b. 8.25%

c. 8.70%   d. 9.20%.

15. In calculating the component costs of long-term funds, the appropriate cost of retained earnings, ignoring flotation costs, is equal to (CMA)

a. the cost of common stock.

b. the same as the cost of preferred stock.

c. the weighted average cost of capital for the firm.

d. zero, or no cost.

16. The capital structure of four corporations is as follows.

	Corporation			
	Sterling	Cooper	Warwick	Pane
Short-term debt	10%	10%	15%	10%
Long-term debt	40%	35%	30%	30%
Preferred stock	30%	30%	30%	30%
Common equity	20%	25%	25%	30%

Which corporation is the most highly leveraged? (CMA)

a. Sterling   b. Cooper

c. Warwick   d. Pane.

17. Which of the following, when considered individually, would generally have the effect of increasing a firm's cost of capital? (CMA)

I. The firm reduces its operating leverage.
II. The corporate tax rate is increased.
III. The firm pays off its only outstanding debt.
IV. The Treasury Bond yield increases.

a. I and III   b. I and IV

c. III and IV   d. I, III and IV.

18. Angela Company's capital structure consists entirely of long-term debt and common equity. The cost of capital for each component is shown below.

Long-term debt 8%

Common equity 15%

Angela pays taxes at a rate of 40%. If Angela's weighted average cost of capital is 10.41%, what proportion of the company's capital structure is in the form of long-term debt? (CMA)

a. 34%   b. 45%   c. 55%   d. 66%.

19. A summary of the Income Statement of Sahara Company is shown below.

Sales	$15,000,000
Cost of sales	9,000,000
Operating expenses	3,000,000
Interest expense	800,000
Taxes	880,000
Net income	$1,320,000

Based on the above information, Sahara's degree of financial leverage is (CMA)

a. 0.96   b. 1.36

c. 1.61   d. 2.27.

20. A degree of operating leverage of 3 at 5,000 units means that a (CMA)

    a. 3% change in earnings before interest and taxes will cause a 3% change in sales.

    b. 3% change in sales will cause a 3% change in earnings before interest and taxes.

    c. 1% change in sales will cause a 3% change in earnings before interest and taxes.

    d.1% change in earnings before interest and taxes will cause a 3% change in sales.

21. The use of debt in the capital structure of a firm (CMA)

    a. increases its financial leverage.

    b. increases its operating leverage.

    c. decreases its financial leverage.

    d. decreases its operating leverage.

22. A financial analyst with Mineral Inc. calculated the company's degree of financial leverage as 1.5. If net income before interest increases by 5%, earnings to shareholders will increase by (CMA)

    a. 1.50%   b. 3.33%

    c. 5.00%   d. 7.50%.

23. Which one of the following statements concerning the effects of leverage on earnings before interest and taxes (EBIT) and earnings per share (EPS) is correct? (CMA)

    a. For a firm using debt financing, a decrease in EBIT will result in a proportionally larger decrease in EPS.

    b. A decrease in the financial leverage of a firm will increase the beta value of the firm.

    c. If Firm A has a higher degree of operating leverage than Firm B, and Firm A offsets this by using less financial leverage, then both firms will have the same variability in EBIT.

    d. Financial leverage affects both EPS and EBIT, while operating leverage only effects EBIT.

24. Firms with high degrees of financial leverage would be best characterized as having (CMA)

    a. high debt-to-equity ratios.

    b. zero coupon bonds in their capital structures.

    c. low current ratios.

    d. high fixed-charge coverage.

25. Donovan Corporation recently declared and issued a 50% stock dividend. This transaction will reduce the company's (CMA)

    a. current ratio.   b. book value per common share.

    c. debt-to-equity ratio.   d. return on operating assets.

26. Which of the following are characteristics of Eurobonds?

    a. Are always denominated in Eurodollars.

    b. Are always sold in some country other than the one in whose currency the bond is denominated.

    c. Are sold outside the country of the borrower but are denominated in the currency of the county in which the issue is sold.

    d. Are generally issued as registered bonds.

Items 27 and 30 are based on the following :

A new company requires $1 million of financing and is considering two arrangements as shown in the table below:

Arrangement	Equity Raised	Debt Financing	Before-Tax Cost of Debt
#1	$700,000	$300,000	8% per annum
#2	$300,000	$700,000	10% per annum

In the first year of operations, the company is expected to have sales revenues of $500,000, cost of sales of $200,000, and general and administrative expenses of $100,000. The tax rate is 30%, and there are no other items on the income statement. All earnings are paid out as dividends at year-end.

---

27. If the cost of equity is 12%, the weighted-average cost of capital under arrangement #1, to the nearest full percentage point, would be

a. 8%

b. 10%

c. 11%

d. 12%

28. Which of the following statements comparing the two financing arrangements is true?

a. The company will have a higher expected gross margin under arrangement #1

b. The company will have a higher degree of operating leverage under arrangement #2

c. The company will have a higher interest expense under arrangement #1

d. The company will have a higher expected tax rate expense under arrangement#1

29. The return on equity will be \<List A\> and the debt ratio will be \<List B\> under Arrangement #2 as compared with Arrangement #1.

	List A	List B
a.	Higher	Higher
b.	Higher	Lower
c.	Lower	Higher
d.	Lower	Lower

30. Under financing arrangement #2, the degree of financial leverage (DFL), rounded to two decimal places, would be

a. 1.09

b. 1.14

c. 1.32

d. 1.54

Items 31 and 32 are based on the following information :

Management of Russell Corporation is considering the following two potential capital structures for a newly acquired business.

Alternative 1	
Long-term debt, 6% interest	$3,000,000
Common equity	$3,000,000
Cost of common equity, 10%	
Marginal tax rate, 15%	
Alternative 2	
Long-term debt, 7% interest	$5,000,000
Common equity	$1,000,000
Cost of common equity, 12%	
Marginal tax rate, 15%	

31. Which of the following statements is not true if management decides to accept Alternative 1?

    a. Alternative 1 is the more conservative capital structure.

    b. Alternative 1 provides the greatest amount of financial leverage.

    c. Net income will be less variable under Alternative 1.

    d. Total interest expense will be less under Alternative 1.

32. Which of the alternatives has the lowest weighted average cost of capital and how much is the differential?

    a. Alternative 1 by 1.5%

    b. Alternative 2 by 0.59%

    c. Alternative 1 by 0.167%

    d. The alternatives have equal WACC.

33. When calculating the cost of capital, the cost assigned to retained earnings should bea. zero.

    b. lower than the cost of external common equity.

    c. equal to the cost of external common equity.

    d. higher than the cost of external common equity.

34. Which one of the following statements accurately compares bond financing alternatives?

    a. A bond with a call provision typically has a lower yield to maturity than a similar bond without a call provision.

    b. A convertible bond must be converted to common stock prior to its maturity.

    c. A call provision is usually considered detrimental to the investor.

    d. A sinking fund prohibits the firm from redeeming a bond issue prior to its final maturity.

35. XYZ Corp. has 1,000 shares outstanding and retained earnings of $25,000. Theoretically, what should be the price of its stock, currently selling for $50 per share, if a 20% stock dividend is declared?

a. Price should increase to $60 per share.

b. Price should decrease to $40 per share

c. Price should decrease to $41.67 per share

d. Nothing;price should remain at $50

36. Which one of the following factors might cause a firm to increase the debt in its financial structure?

a. An increase in the corporate income tax rate

b. Increased economic uncertainty

c. An increase in the federal funds rate

d. An increase in the price-earnings ratio

37. In practice, dividends

a. usually exhibit greater stability than earnings

b. fluctuate more widely than earnings

c. tend to be a lower percentage of earnings for mature firms.

d. are usually set as a fixed percentage of earnings.

38. Residco Inc. expects net income of $800,000 for the next fiscal year. Its targeted and current capital structure is 40% debt and 60% common equity. The director of capital budgeting has determined that the optimal capital spending for the next year is $1.2 million. If Residco follows a strict residual dividend policy, what is the expected dividend payout ratio for the next year?

a. 90.0%   b. 66.7%

c. 40.0%   d. 10.0%

39. The purchase of treasury stock with a firm's surplus cash

    a. increases a firm's assets.

    b. increases a firm's financial leverage.

    c. increases a firm's interest coverage ratio.

    d. dilutes a firm's earnings per share.

40. The benefits of debt financing over equity financing are likely to be highest in which of the following situations?

    a. High marginal tax rates and few noninterest tax benefits.

    b. Low marginal tax rates and few noninterest tax benefits.

    c. High marginal tax rates and many noninterest tax benefits.

    d. Low marginal tax rates and many noninterest tax benefits.

Solution

1	2	3	4	5	6	7	8	9	10
B	A	C	C	C	C	A	D	D	C
11	12	13	14	15	16	17	18	19	20
B	D	C	D	A	A	C	B	B	C
21	22	23	24	25	26	27	28	29	30
A	D	A	A	B	B	B	D	A	D
31	32	33	34	35	36	37	38	39	40
B	B	B	C	C	A	A	D	B	A

1. 리스 유형은 매출채권 및 재고자산 회전율에 영향을 주지 않는다.

2. 채권은 보통 10년 이상의 만기를 갖는다.

3. Refunding은 차입금 만기시점에서 다른 차입으로 revolving하는 것을 말하므로 만기가 존재하지 않는 우선주와는 무관하다.

4. Record dare는 배당의 소유자를 결정하는 일자를 말한다.

5. 이자비용은 법인세 절세효과가 있지만 배당금은 절세효과가 없다.

6. 자본비용의 크기는 보통주 〉우선주 〉채권으로 결정된다.

7. Call provision은 발행자가 중도상환 할 수 있는 권리를 말하며, 이러한 권리가 채권에 포함되면 채권가격은 하락하며 채권 수익률은 상승한다.

8. 채권 약정서에 기재되는 조항을 covenant 라고 한다.

9. 이자비용은 법인세 절세효과가 있기 때문에 법인세율이 높을수록 equity보다는 debt로 자금을 조달하는 것이 유리하다.

10. 2:1로 주식분할을 하면 주가는 1/2수준인 $40가 되며, DPS 〈 $0.50으로 예상되면 주가 〈 $40으로 예상되며, DPS 〉 $0.50으로 예상되면 주가 〉 $40으로 예상된다.

11. IRR 〉 k : 투자안 A, B, C

    투자금액 = \$200,000 + \$350,000 + \$570,000 = \$1,120,000

    투자금액 중 equity = \$1,120,000 × 60% = \$672,000, 잔여배당액 = \$1,000,000 − \$672,000 = \$328,000

12. 배당의 결정 요인 중 가장 중요한 요소는 투자계획이다.

13. CAPM을 이용하면 k = 0.07 + (0.15 − 0.07) × 1.25 = 0.17

    DDM을 이용하면 P0 = \$4 × 0.35 ÷ (0.17 − 0.10) = \$20

14. DDM을 이용하면 k = \$8 ÷ (\$92 − \$5) = 9.195%

15. 이익잉여금의 자본비용은 cost of equity를 적용한다.

16. Debt의 구성 비율이 가장 큰 자본구조는 Sterling Corporation이다.

17. I. Business risk 감소 → Risk premium의 감소 → WACC의 감소

    II. 법인세율의 증가 → 절세효과의 증가 → WACC의 감소

    III. 단일 부채의 감소 → 타인자본의 저렴효과 감소 → WACC의 증가

    IV. 무위험이자율의 증가 → WACC의 증가

18. WACC = 8% × (1 − 0.4) × w + 15% × (1 − w)에서 w = 0.45

19. EBIT = 15M − 9M − 3M = \$3,000,000

    EBT = \$3,000,000 − \$800,000 = \$2,200,000

    DFL = 3M ÷ 2.2M = 1.36

20. DOL은 매출변화율에 대한 EBIT의 변화율(탄력성)을 의미한다.

21. 부채가 증가하면 Operating leverage에는 영향이 없으며 Financial leverage는 증가

22. DFL = EPS 변화율 ÷ EBIT 변화율

    EPS 변화율 = DFL × EBIT 변화율 = 1.5 × 5% = 7.5%

23. a. 부채기업은 EPS 변화율 〉 EBIT 변화율

    b. 재무레버리지가 감소하면 재무위험의 감소로 베타도 감소한다.

c.d. DFL은 EPS, DOL은 EBIT, DTL은 EPS와 EBIT에 영향을 준다.

24. 재무레버리지는 부채사용 정도를 의미한다.

25. 주식배당은 주식수의 증가로 EPS & BPS 모두 감소한다.

26. 유로본드는 현지통화가 아닌 다른 통화로 결제되는 해외채권을 의미한다.

27. WACC = 8% × (1 - 0.3) × 0.3 + 12% × 0.7 = 10%

28. a. 부채사용은 매출총이익과는 무관하다.
    b. 부채사용은 영업이익 및 DOL과는 무관하다.
    c. 부채사용은 이자비용을 증가시킨다.
    d. 부채사용은 법인세 비용을 감소시킨다.

29. 레버리지가 크면 ROE와 부채비율 모두 더 크다.

30. EBIT = 500,000 − 200,000 − 100,000 = 200,000
    EBT = 200,000 − 700,000 × 10% = 130,000
    DFL = 200,000 ÷ 130,000 = 1.538

31. #1은 #2보다 레버리지가 작은 보수적인 방법이며, 이익의 변동성이 작은 방법이다.

32. WACC#1 = 0.06 × (1 − 0.15) × 3/6 + 0.10 × 3/6 = 0.0755
    WACC#2 = 0.07 × (1 − 0.15) × 5/6 + 0.12 × 1/6 = 0.0696

33. 외부자기자본비용은 신주발행비가 발생하므로 내부자기자본비용보다 더 크다.

34. Call provision은 투자자에게는 불리하고 발행자에게 유리한 조항이다.

35. 1,000 shares × $50 = 1,200 shares × Price

36. 법인세율이 증가하면 절세효과 때문에 레버리지가 증가한다. 경제가 불확실하거나 PER가 높으면 레버리지가 감소한다.

37. 배당정책을 통하여 이익보다는 안정적으로 주주에게 배당을 지급한다.

38. Dividend = NI − Investment

    = $800,000 − $1,200,000 × 60% = $80,000

39. 자사주를 매입하면 자산과 자본이 감소, EPS는 증가, 부채비율은 증가한다.

40. 타인자본은 절세효과가 있기 때문에 세율이 높을수록, 다른 세금혜택이 적을수록 유용하다.

07 ▶ Tasked-Based Simulation

◥ Problem−1

KIM Corporation has a target capital structure of 40 percent debt and 60 percent common equity, with no preferred stock. Its before-tax cost of debt is 12 percent, and its marginal tax rate is 40 percent. The current stock price is $22.50. The last dividend was $2.00, and it is expected to grow at a constant rate of 7 percent.

Required

What is its cost of common equity and its WACC?

◥ Problem−2

KIM's capital structure consists solely of debt and common equity. It can issue debt at before-tax cost of debt of 11%, and its common stock currently pays a $2 dividend per share. The stock's price is currently $24.75; its dividend is expected to grow at a constant rate of 7 percent per year; its tax rate is 35 percent; and its WACC is 13.95 percent.

Required

What percentage of the company's capital structure consists of debt?

Problem-3

KIM produces premium stereo headphones that sell for $28.80 per set, and this year's sales are expected to be 450,000 units. Variable production costs for the expected sales under present production methods are estimated at $10,200,000, and fixed production (operating) costs at present are $1,560,000. KIM has $4,800,000 of debt outstanding at an interest rate of 8 percent. There are 240,000 shares of common stock outstanding, and there is no preferred stock. The dividend payout ratio is 70 percent, and KIM is in the 40 percent federal plus- state tax bracket. The company is considering investing $7,200,000 in new equipment. Sales would not increase, but variable costs per unit would decline by 20 percent. Also, fixed operating costs would increase from $1,560,000 to $1,800,000. KIM could raise the required capital by borrowing $7,200,000 at 10 percent or by selling 240,000 additional shares at $30 per share.

Required

What would be KIM's EPS (1) under the old production process, (2) under the new process if it uses debt, and (3) under the new process if it uses common stock?

Problem-4

Adams Corporation is considering four average-risk projects with the following costs and rates of return:

Project	Cost	Expected Rate of Return
1	$2,000	16.00%
2	3,000	15.00
3	5,000	13.75
4	2,000	12.50

The company estimates that it can issue debt at a rate of 10%, and its tax rate is 30percent. It can issue preferred stock that pays a constant dividend of $5 per year at $49 per share. Also, its common stock currently sells for $36 per share, the next expected dividend is $3.50, and the dividend is expected to grow at a constant rate of 6 percent per year. The target capital structure consists of 75 percent common stock, 15 percent debt, and 10 percent preferred stock.

Required

1. What is Adams' WACC?

2. Which projects should Adams accept?

Problem-5

Two textile companies, KIM Manufacturing and Jordan Mills, began operations with identical balance sheets. A year later, both required additional manufacturing capacity at a cost of $200,000. KIM obtained a 5-year, $200,000 loan at an 8 percent interest rate from its bank. Jordan, on the other hand, decided to lease the required $200,000 capacity from National Leasing for 5 years; an 8 percent return was built into the lease. The balance sheet for each company, before the asset increases, is as follows:

Debt	$200,000
Equity	200,000
Total assets	$400,000

Required

1. Show the balance sheet of each firm after the asset increase, and calculate each firm's new debt ratio. (Assume Jordan's lease is operating lease.)

2. Show how Jordan's balance sheet would have looked immediately after the financing if it was capital lease.

3. Would the rate of return (1) on assets and (2) on equity be affected by the choice of financing? How?

Problem-6

An investor has two bonds in his or her portfolio, Bond A and Bond B. Each matures in 4 years, has a face value of $1,000, and has a yield to maturity of 9.6 percent. Bond A pays a 10 percent annual coupon, while Bond B is a zero coupon bond.

Required

Assuming that the yield to maturity of each bond remains at 9.6 percent over the next 4 years, calculate the price of the bonds at the following years to maturity and fill in the following table:

Years to Maturity	Price of Bond A	Price of Bond B
4		
3		
2		
1		
0		

Firms HL and LL are identical except for their leverage ratios and the interest rates they pay on debt. Each has $20 million in assets, $4 million of EBIT, and is in the 40 percent federal-plus-state tax bracket. Firm HL, however, has a debt ratio (D/A) of 50 percent and pays 12 percent interest on its debt, whereas LL has a 30 percentdebt ratio and pays only 10 percent interest on its debt.

Required

1. Calculate the rate of return on equity (ROE) for each firm.

2. Observing that HL has a higher ROE, LL' treasurer is thinking of raising the debt ratio from 30 to 60 percent, even though that would increase LL' interest rate on all debt to 15 percent. Calculate the new ROE for LL.

Problem-8

GE Inc., a producer of turbine generators, is in this situation:
EBIT= $4 million; tax rate =35%; debt outstanding= $2 million;
cost of debt =10%; cost of equity= 15%;
shares of stock outstanding=600,000; book value per share =$10.
Because GE's product market is stable and the company expects no growth, all earnings are paid out as dividends. The debt consists of perpetual bonds.

Required

1. What are GE' earnings per share (EPS) and its price per share?

2. What is GE' weighted average cost of capital (WACC)?

3. GE can increase its debt by $8 million, to a total of $10 million, using the new debt to buy back and retire some of its shares at the current price. Its interest rate on debt will be 12 percent (it will have to call and refund the old debt), and its cost of equity will rise from 15 to 17 percent. EBIT will remain constant. Should GE change its capital structure?

4. If GE did not have to refund the $2 million of old debt, how would this affect things? Assume that the new and the still outstanding debt are equally risky, with rd 12%, but that the coupon rate on the old debt is 10 percent.

5. What is GE' TIE coverage ratio under the original situation and under the conditions in part 3 of this question?

Problem-9

LG Electronics Inc. produces stereo components that sell at P $100 per unit. LG' fixed costs are $200,000; variable costs are $50 per unit; 5,000 components are produced and sold each year; EBIT is currently $50,000; and LG' assets (all equity financed) are $500,000. LG can change its production process by adding $400,000 to assets and $50,000 to fixed operating costs.

This change would (1) reduce variable costs per unit by $10 and (2) increase output by 2,000 units, but (3) the sales price on all units would have to be lowered to $95 to permit sales of the additional output. LG has tax loss carry-forwards that cause its tax rate to be zero, it uses no debt, and its average cost of capital is 10 percent.

Required

1. Should LG make the change?

2. Would LG' breakeven point increase or decrease if it made the change?

3. Suppose LG were unable to raise additional equity financing and had to borrow the $400,000 at an interest rate of 10 percent to make the investment. Use the Du Pont equation to find the expected ROA of the investment. Should LG make the change if debt financing must be used?

Problem-10

1. If a firm repurchases its stock in the open market, the shareholders who tender the stock are subject to capital gains taxes.

2. If you own 100 shares in a company' stock and the company' stock splits 2-for-1, you will own 200 shares in the company following the split.

3. Some dividend reinvestment plans increase the amount of equity capital available to the firm.

4. The Tax Code encourages companies to pay a large percentage of their net income in the form of dividends.

5. If your company has established a clientele of investors who prefer large dividends, the company is unlikely to adopt a residual dividend policy.

6. If a firm follows a residual dividend policy, holding all else constant, its dividend pay-out will tend to rise whenever the firm' investment opportunities improve.

Required

Indicate whether the following statements are true or false.

Problem-11

After a 5-for-1 stock split, the Starbucks Company paid a dividend of $0.75 per new share, which represents a 9 percent increase over last year' pre-split dividend.

Required

What was last year' dividend per share?

Problem-12

Beta Industries has net income of $2,000,000 and it has 1,000,000 shares of common stock outstanding. The company' stock currently trades at $32 a share. Beta is considering a plan in which it will use available cash to repurchase 20 percent of its shares in the open market. The repurchase is expected to have no effect on either net income or the company' P/E ratio.

Required

What will be its stock price following the stock repurchase?

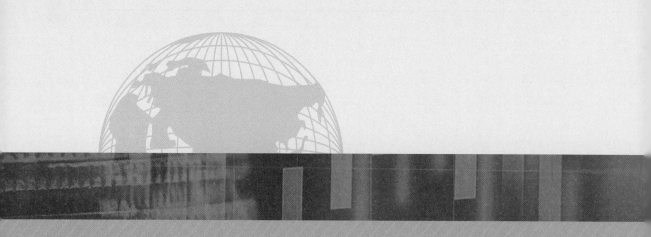

Financial Management For the **US CPA** Exam

Chapter 06

Capital Budgeting

Volume
8

Chapter

6

Capital Budgeting

---

01 》 Basics of Capital Budgeting

1 Definition of Capital Budgeting

The process of planning expenditures on assets whose cash flows are expected to extend beyond one year.

자본예산이란 투자의 효과가 1년 이상 장기간에 걸쳐 나타나는 실물투자결정에 관련된 계획을 수립하는 것을 의미한다. 자본예산의 내용은 투자안으로부터 기대되는 현금흐름을 측정하고 이의 경제성을 평가하여 투자안의 수행 여부를 판단하는 것으로 화폐의 시간가치를 고려하여 현금흐름을 측정하여야 한다. 하지만 1년 이내의 영업활동에 대한 단기적 의사결정인 Master Budgeting에서는 화폐의 시간가치를 고려하지 않는다.

2 Project Classifications

전략적 중요성 등에 따라 투자안은 다음 유형으로 분류될 수 있다.

- Replacement projects
- Expansion into new products or markets
- Safety and environmental projects

다른 투자안과의 상호 관계를 고려하여 세 가지 유형으로 구분된다.

- Mutually exclusive projects

  상호 배타적 투자안은 동일한 작업을 수행하는 여러 가지의 대체적 투자안들 가운데 어느 한 투자안이 채택되면 다른 투자안들이 자동적으로 기각되는 경우이다.

- Independent projects

  어떤 투자안의 현금흐름이 다른 투자안의 채택 또는 기각 결정에 의해 영향을 받지 않는 경우를 말한다. 이 경우 경영자는 서로 다른 업무를 수행하는 여러 투자안들의 일부 또는 전부를 선택할 수 있다.

- Contingent projects

  종속적 투자안은 투자안들이 함께 수행되지 않으면 모두 쓸모가 없게 될 투자안들이다.

3 Capital Budgeting Process

자본예산의 수립과정은 다음과 같이 4단계로 구분된다.

(1) Identify and define the project (투자안의 개발)

(2) Estimating cash flows of projects (투자안의 현금흐름의 추정)

(3) Evaluate the project (투자안의 경제성 평가)

(4) Post-audit (투자안의 재평가)

02 ▷ Estimating Cash Flows

1 Incremental Cash Flow

자본예산의 현금흐름은 증분기준(incremental basis)으로 측정한다. 이와 관련하여 다음의 몇 가지를 주의하여야 한다.

(1) Sunk cost

A cost that has already been incurred and cannot be removed and therefore should not be considered in an investment decision.

매몰원가는 과거의 투자결정에 의해 이미 발생한 비용이므로 현재의 투자의사결정과는 무관하므로 현금유출로 인식하지 않는다.

예 이미 실시된 연구개발비용 또는 시장조사비용,

대체투자시의 구설비(old equipment)의 취득원가 및 장부가액

설비대체의 관련현금흐름을 요약하면 다음과 같다.

	Old equipment	New equipment
Cost	No	Yes
Salvage value	Yes	Yes

(2) Opportunity costs

The most valuable alternative that is given up if a particular investment is undertaken.

기회비용은 다른 용도를 포기함으로써 발생하는 손실이므로 현금유출로 고려하여야 한다.

예 보유중인 토지를 공장건설에 이용한 경우 해당 토지의 시장가격

(3) Side effects

The cash flows of a new project that come at the expense of a firm's existing projects.

부수효과란 한 투자안에 대한 투자결정으로 인해 다른 투자안의 현금흐름에 미치는 영향을 말하는 것으로 부정적인 부수효과를 잠식효과(cannibalization)이라고도 하며 현금유출로 고려하야야 한다. 한다.

예 새로운 제품의 출시로 인하여 기존 제품의 매출 감소

2 Free Cash Flow

자본예산에서 투자안 평가를 위한 현금흐름은 실물시장에서 기업에 귀속되는 잉여현금흐름(free cash flow)으로 영업현금흐름, 자본적 지출 및 순운전자본의 변동에 따른 현금흐름을 모두 반영하여야 한다.

(1) Inflation effects

투자안의 미래현금흐름을 할인하여 주는 할인율이 인플레이션을 반영한 명목이자율이므로 현금흐름도 인플레이션을 반영한 명목현금흐름을 사용하여야 한다.

Discount rate : Nominal discount rate

FCF : Nominal CF

(2) Financing costs (Interest and dividends)

이자비용과 배당금은 기업이 자본제공자에게 지급하는 자본비용으로 실제적인 현금유출을 가져오기는 하지만 이러한 자본사용의 대가는 미래현금흐름을 할인하여 주는 할인율에 반영하여야 한다. 따라서 영업현금흐름은 이자비용과 배당을 지급하기 전의 영업이익(EBIT)를 기준으로 계산한다.

(3) Tax

법인세는 명백한 현금유출이기 때문에 법인세를 반영한 영업현금흐름을 계산하여야 한다.

(4) Depreciation

감가상각비는 실제 현금유출이 아니기 때문에 투자안의 현금흐름에는 반영되지 않으나, 감가상각비의 법인세 감세효과(tax shield effect)는 현금유입으로 반영한다.

(5) Operating cash flow (OCF)

잉여현금흐름(free cash flow)의 영업현금흐름(OCF)는 앞에서 기술한 이자비용과 배당, 법인세 및 감가상각비의 원칙을 반영하면 다음과 같다.

$$OCF = EBITDA \times (1 - T) + Depreciation \times T$$
$$= EBIT \times (1 - T) + Depreciation$$

T = marginal tax rate

- depreciation tax shield (=Depreciation $\times$ T)

The tax saving that results from the depreciation deduction, calculated as depreciation multiplied by the corporate tax rate.

- MACRS (Modified Accelerated Cost Recovery System)

A depreciation method under U.S. tax law allowing for the accelerated write-off of

property under various classifications. Under MACRS, every asset is assigned to a particular class. An asset's class establishes its life for tax purposes. Once an asset's tax life is determined, the depreciation for each year is computed by multiplying the cost of the asset by a fixed percentage.

(6) Changes in working capital

새로운 투자의사결정은 고정자산에 대한 투자뿐만 아니라 유동자산이나 유동부채와 같은 운전자본에 대한 투자를 필요로 한다. 신규투자가 가져오는 추가적은 순운전자본의 변화액은 추가적인 투자금액으로 인식하여야 한다. 즉, 순운전자본의 증가액은 현금유출의 증가이며, 순운전자본의 감소액은 현금유입의 증가이다. 그러나 주의할 것은 순운전자본의 변동액은 그 개념상 기업의 영업활동주기에 따라 투자와 회수가 반복된다는 것이다. 즉, 기초의 순운전자본 증가액만큼의 투자는 기말에 회수된다.

$$\text{working capital} = \text{non-cash current asset} - \text{non-debt current liability}$$
$$\triangle \text{working capital} > 0 \rightarrow \text{cash outflow}$$
$$\triangle \text{working capital} < 0 \rightarrow \text{cash inflow}$$

(7) Salvage value after tax

투자에서 회수되는 잔존가치(SV)와 법인세법의 장부가액(BV)이 다르게 될 경우, 설비의 매각손실이나 매각이익이 발생하게 되고 그에 따른 세금효과를 고려하여야 한다.

$$\text{Sale of fixed asset after tax} = \text{SV} - (\text{SV} - \text{BV}) \times \text{T}$$

where : SV = pre-tax cash proceeds from sale of fixed asset
        BV = book value of the fixed asset

(8) FCF (Free cash flow)

실물시장에서의 영업현금흐름, 자본적 지출 및 순운전자본의 변동에 따른 현금흐름을 모두 반영한 기업에 귀속되는 잉여현금흐름(free cash flow)은 다음과 같다.

$$\text{FCF} = \text{영업활동 현금흐름} - \text{자본적지출} - \text{순운전자본지출}$$
$$= \text{OCF} - \text{Capital Expenditure(CAPEX)} - \triangle \text{Working Capital}$$

3 Estimating Cash Flows

(1) Initial investment outlay (t = 0)

1) Capital expenditure (CAPEX)

2) Changes in working capital

3) Sale of old fixed asset after tax $= SV - (SV - BV) \times T$

(2) Operating cash flow(OCF) (t = 1~n)

$$OCF = \triangle EBITDA \times (1 - T) + \triangle Depreciation \times T$$
$$= \triangle EBIT \times (1 - T) + \triangle Depreciation$$

(3) Terminal cash flow (t = n)

1) Sale of new fixed asset after tax $= SV - (SV - BV) \times T$

2) Changes in working capital

Example 6-1

Netflix Company is trying to estimate the first-year net operating cash flow (at Year 1) for a proposed project. The financial staff has collected the following information on the project:

- Sales revenues : $10 million
- Operating costs (excluding depreciation) 7 million
- Depreciation 2 million
- Interest expense 0.7 million

The company has a 40 percent tax rate, and its WACC is 10 percent.

(1) What is the project' operating cash flow for the first year (t=1)?

(2) If this project would cannibalize other projects by $1 million of cash flow before taxes per year, how would this change your answer to part (1)?

(3) Ignore part (2). If the tax rate dropped to 30 percent, how would that change your answer to part (1)?

Solution

(1) EBITDA = $10 − 7 = $3,   EBIT = $3 − 2 = $1

Operating cash flow = $3 × (1− 0.4) + 2 × 0.4

$$= $1 × (1− 0.4) + 2 = $2.6$$

이자비용은 영업현금흐름이 아니며 NPV 계산과정에서 할인율에 반영한다.

(2) △EBITDA = $3 − 1 = $2

Operating cash flow = $2 × (1− 0.4) + 2 × 0.4 = $2

(3) Operating cash flow = $3 × (1− 0.3) + 2 × 0.3 = $2.7

Example 6-2

Arca Airline is now in the final year of a project. The equipment originally cost $20 million, of which 80 percent has been depreciated. Arca Airline can sell the used equipment today for $5 million, and its tax rate is 40 percent. What is the equipment' after-tax net salvage value?

Solution

Book value of equipment = $20 × 20% = $4
Sale of fixed asset after tax = $5 − ($5 − $4) × 0.4 = $4.6

Example 6-3

Which of the following statements is most correct?

a. An increase in net operating WC is treated as negative initial CF
b. In calculating yearly CF, you must subtract out interest paid.
c. The analysis should focus on accounting income rather than cash flow
d. The timing of CF is not a major factor in the analysis of CF

Solution

a. 순운전자본의 증가는 기업현금흐름의 유출액이다.
b. 이자비용과 배당금은 현금흐름에 반영하지 않는다.
c. 회계적 이익보다는 현금흐름을 기초로 한다.
d. 현재가치의 결정에서 현금흐름의 시기는 중요한 요소이다.

정답 : a

Example 6-4

Tesla Company , is considering the acquisition of a new machine. The machine can be purchase for $90,000 ; It will cost $6,000 to transport to plant and $9,000 to install.
It is estimated that the machine will last 10 years, and it is expected to have an estimated salvage value of $5,000.
Over its 10-year life, the machine is expected to produce 1,000 units per year with a selling price of $500 and combined material and labor costs of $450 per unit. Annual fixed cost (excluding depreciation) will increase by $10,000. Federal tax regulations permit machines of this type to be depreciated using the straight-line method over 5 years with no estimated salvage value.
The company' WACC is 10 percent, and its tax rate is 40 percent. What is the net cash flow of the project and NPV that Tesla should use in a capital budgeting analysis?

- Present value of $1 received after 5 years discounted at 10% : 0.621
- Present value of an ordinary annuity of $1 for 5 years at 10% : 3.791

Solution

(1) Initial investment outlay (t = 0)

Capital expenditure = $-(\$90,000 + 6,000 + 9,000) = -\$105,000$

(2) Operating cash flow (t = 1~10)

투자기간은 10년이지만 감가상각비의 절세효과는 5년 동안만 존재한다.

Annual EBITDA = 1,000개 $\times$ ($500 − $450) − 10,000= $40,000

Annual depreciation = $105,000 / 5년 = $21,000

t = 1 ~ 5 : OCF = $40,000$\times$0.6 + $21,000$\times$0.4 = $32,400

t = 6 ~ 10 : OCF = $40,000$\times$0.6 = $24,000

(3) Terminal cash flow (t=10)

Sale of fixed asset after tax = $5,000 − ($5,000 − 0)$\times$0.4 = $3,000

$\therefore$ NPV = −105,000 + 32,400$\times$3.791 + 24,000$\times$3.791$\times$0.621

       + 3,000$\times$0.621$\times$0.621 = $75,486

Example 6-5

Maxgo Company is considering replacing its current computer system. The new system would cost Maxgo $60,000 to have it installed and operational. It would have an expected useful life of 4 years and an estimated salvage value of $12,000. The system would be depreciated on a straight-line basis for financial statement reporting purposes and use the MACRS depreciation method for income tax reporting purposes. Assume that the percentages of depreciation for MACRS are 25%, 40%, 20%, and 15% for the four-year life of the new computer.

Maxgo's current computer system has been fully depreciated for both financial system and income tax reporting purposes. It could be used for 4 more years, but not as effectively as the new computer system. The old system currently has an estimated salvage value of $8,000. It is estimated that the new system will save $15,000 per year in operating costs. Working capital would increase by $3,000 if the new system is purchased, but it would be recovered at the end of the project' 4-year life. Maxgo expects to have an effective income tax rate of 30 percent for the next four years. What is the net cash flow of the project that the firm should use in a capital budgeting analysis?

Solution

(1) Initial investment outlay ($t = 0$)

   1) Capital expenditure $= -\$60,000$

   2) Sale of old fixed asset after tax $= \$8,000 - (8,000 - 0) \times 0.3 = \$5,600$

   3) Changes in working capital $= -\$3,000$

      Initial Investment Outlay $= -60,000 + 5,600 - 3,000 = -\$57,400$

(2) Operating cash flow ($t = 1 \sim n$)

   $\triangle$EBITDA $= \$0 - (-\$15,000) = \$15,000$

   $OCF_1 = \$15,000 \times 0.7 + \$60,000 \times 0.25 \times 0.3 = \$15,000$

   $OCF_2 = \$15,000 \times 0.7 + \$60,000 \times 0.40 \times 0.3 = \$17,700$

   $OCF_3 = \$15,000 \times 0.7 + \$60,000 \times 0.20 \times 0.3 = \$14,100$

   $OCF_4 = \$15,000 \times 0.7 + \$60,000 \times 0.15 \times 0.3 = \$13,200$

(3) Terminal cash flow (t = 4)

　1) Sale of new fixed asset after tax = $12,000 - (12,000 - 0) \times 0.3 = \$8,400$

　2) Changes in working capital = \$3,000

　　Terminal cash flow = $8,400 + 3,000 = \$11,400$

03 ▶ Evaluating the Projects

1 Introduction

고려대상이 되는 투자안으로부터 예상되는 현금흐름을 측정하고 나면 이 투자안을 선택할 것인지 또는 기각할 것인지의 여부를 결정해야 한다. 이 같은 결정과정을 투자안의 경제성을 평가한다고 하는데, 이에 적용되는 기법으로는 회수기간(Payback Period)법, 회계적 이익률(ARR)법, 순현가법(NPV), 내부수익률(IRR)법, 수익성지수(PI)법등이 있다.

이 중 회수기간법과 회계적 이익률법은 내용이 단순하여 이해하기는 쉽지만 화폐의 시간가치를 고려하지 않은 방법이다. 이에 반해 순현가법, 내부수익률법 및 수익성지수법은 화폐의 시간적 가치를 고려하여 경제성을 평가하는 방법으로 DCF법 (discount cashflow method)이라고 한다.

동일한 현금흐름에 대해서도 이 다섯 가지 분석방법이 서로 다른 결과를 보일 수가 있는데 이 경우 화폐의 시간적 가치를 고려하는 방법이 좋은 방법이고 그 중에서도 순현가법(NPV)이 가장 우월한 방법이다. 다음 예제를 바탕으로 이러한 평가방법을 비교하기로 한다.

Expected net cash flows from project A&B

Year	Project A	Project B
0	(2,000)	(2,000)
1	1,000	200
2	800	600
3	600	800
4	200	1,200

Assume that the firm's cost of capital is 10%.

2 Payback Period

(1) Payback period

The length of time required for an investment to generate cash flows sufficient to recover its initial cost. The payback period is a kind of "break-even" measure. The shorter the payback, the better.

회수기간이란 투자안을 수행하기 위해 수행초기에 지출된 투자비용을 회수하는데 걸리는 기간을 말한다.

	Year	0	1	2	3	4
Project A	Cash flows	−2,000	1,000	800	600	200
	Cumulative CF	−2,000	−1,000	−200	400	600
Project B	Cash flows	−2,000	200	600	800	1,200
	Cumulative CF	−2,000	−1,800	−1,200	−400	800

Payback period (A) = 2년 + 200 ÷ 600 = 2.33년

Payback period (B) = 3년 + 400 ÷ 1,200 = 3.33년

(2) Decision rule

1) Independent projects

payback ⟨ the benchmark payback → accept the project

payback ⟩ the benchmark payback → reject the project

2) Mutually exclusive projects

Choose the project with the shortest payback

(3) Advantages

- Easy to understand
- It provides a measure of liquidity and riskiness.

  회수기간은 투자안의 위험에 대한 대략적인 지표가 된다.

(4) Disadvantages

- It ignores cash flows beyond the payback period
- It ignores the time value of money
- Uses an arbitrary benchmark cutoff rate.

(5) Discounted payback period

The length of time required for an investment's discounted cash flows to equal its initial cost.

할인회수기간은 매기의 현금흐름을 할인하여 현재가치를 계산한 후에 이 현재가치의 합계가 투자원금을 충당하는 회수시간이다.

	Year	0	1	2	3	4
	Cash flows	−2,000	1,000	800	600	200
Project A	Discounted CF	−2,000	910	661	451	136
	Cumulative CF	−2,000	−1,090	−429	22	158
	Cash flows	−2,000	200	600	800	1,200
Project B	Discounted CF	−2,000	182	496	601	820
	Cumulative CF	−2,000	−1,818	−1,322	−721	99

Payback period (A) = 2년 + 429 ÷ 451 = 2.95년

Payback period (B) = 3년 + 721 ÷ 820 = 3.88년

☞ Payback period ﹤ Discounted payback period

Advantages

- Easy to understand
- It provides a measure of liquidity and riskiness.
- It includes time value of money

Disadvantages

- It ignores cash flows beyond the payback period
- Uses an arbitrary benchmark cutoff rate.

3 Accounting Rate of Return (ARR)

(1) Average accounting return

An investment's average net income divided by its average book value.

투자에 따른 연평균순이익을 연평균투자액으로 나누어 계산한 회계적 이익률을 의사결정에 이용하는 방법이다.

$$ARR = \frac{\text{Annual net income}}{\text{Average investment book value}}$$

회계적 이익률법은 현금흐름이 아닌 회계적 이익을 이용하고 있기 때문에 감가상각의 영향을 받는다. 즉, 자본예산의 평가방법 중에서 유일하게 감가상각을 반영하고 있는 방법이다.

(2) Decision rule

1) Independent projects

ARR $>$ the benchmark ARR $\rightarrow$ accept the project

ARR $<$ the benchmark ARR $\rightarrow$ reject the project

2) Mutually exclusive projects

Choose the project with the highest ARR as long as its ARR is higher than the benchmark ARR

(3) Advantages

- Easy to calculate.

- Needed information will usually be available.

(4) Disadvantages

- It ignores the time value of money.

- Based on accounting values, not cash flows.

- Uses an arbitrary benchmark cutoff rate.

4 Net Present Value (NPV)

(1) NPV

The difference between the present value of cash inflows and the present value of cash outflows over a period of time.

순현가는 투자안의 수행으로 예상되는 미래현금유입을 적절한 할인율로 할인하여 사출한 현재가치에서 투자소요액을 차감한 값을 말한다.

$$NPV = \text{PV of cash inflows} - \text{PV of cash outflow}$$

$$= -CF_0 + \frac{CF_1}{1+k} + \frac{CF_2}{(1+k)^2} + \frac{CF_3}{(1+k)^3} + \ldots + \frac{CF_n}{(1+k)^n}$$

$$= \sum_{t=0}^{n} \frac{CF_t}{(1+k)^t}$$

k = Hurdle rate = minimum rate of return = required rate of return = Cost of capital (WACC)

$$NPV_A = -2{,}000 + \frac{1{,}000}{1.1} + \frac{800}{(1.1)^2} + \frac{600}{(1.1)^3} + \frac{200}{(1.1)^4} = \$158$$

$$NPV_B = -2{,}000 + \frac{200}{1.1} + \frac{600}{(1.1)^2} + \frac{800}{(1.1)^3} + \frac{1{,}200}{(1.1)^4} = \$99$$

❖ **Spreadsheet Solution**

[EXCEL] [재무] NPV

A1 = −2,000, A2 = 1,000, A3 = 800, A4 = 600, A5 = 200

NPV(10%, A2:A5) + A1 = +158

* NPV는 투자시점의 현금유출을 인식하지 않는다.

(2) Decision rule

1) Independent projects

NPV $\rangle$ 0 → accept the project

NPV $\langle$ 0 → reject the project

2) Mutually exclusive projects

Choose the project with the highest NPV

(3) NPV profile (순현가곡선)

A graphical representation of the relationship between an investment's NPVs and various discount rates.

[Figure 6-1] 의 순현가곡선은 각각 다른 수준의 할인율을 적용하면서 NPV값의 변화를 보여준다. 이 그림을 통해서 할인율의 각 수준에 따른 NPV값을 알 수 있으며, 투자안의 내부수익률을 구할 수 있다. 이 곡선의 기울기가 가파를수록 할인율 변화에 대해 투자안 NPV가 더욱 크게 변화함을 의미한다.

Example

This investment costs $100 and has a cash flow of $60 per year for two years.

t = 0	t = 1	t = 2
−$100	+$60	+$60

R=0% → NPV = +20

R=5% → NPV = +11.56

R=10% → NPV = +4.13

R=15% → NPV = −2.46

R=20% → NPV = −8.33

[Figure 6-1]

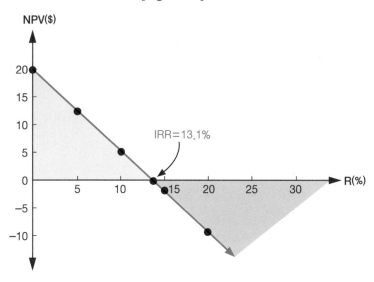

5 Internal Rate of Return (IRR)

(1) IRR

The discount rate that makes the NPV of an investment zero. IRR must be calculated either through trial-and-error or using software programmed.

내부수익률은 투자로 인하여 발생하는 현금유입의 현재가치와 현금유출의 현재가치를 일치시켜 주는 할인율이다. 즉, 순현가(NPV)=0이 되는 할인율이다.

$$CF_0 = \frac{CF_1}{1+IRR} + \frac{CF_2}{(1+IRR)^2} + \frac{CF_3}{(1+IRR)^3} + ... + \frac{CF_n}{(1+IRR)^n}$$

$$NPV = 0 = \sum_{t=0}^{n} \frac{CF_t}{(1+IRR)^t}$$

$$2,000 = \frac{1,000}{1+IRR} + \frac{800}{(1+IRR)^2} + \frac{600}{(1+IRR)^3} + \frac{200}{(1+IRR)^4} \rightarrow IRR_A = 14.5\%$$

$$2,000 = \frac{200}{1+IRR} + \frac{600}{(1+IRR)^2} + \frac{800}{(1+IRR)^3} + \frac{1,200}{(1+IRR)^4} \rightarrow IRR_B = 11.8\%$$

❖ **Spreadsheet Solution**

[EXCEL] [재무] IRR

A1 = −2,000, A2 = 1,000, A3 = 800, A4 = 600, A5 = 200

IRR(A1:A5) = 14.5%

* IRR은 투자시점부터 현금흐름을 인식한다.

(2) Decision rule

1) Independent projects

IRR $>$ k → accept the project

IRR $<$ k → reject the project

2) Mutually exclusive projects

Choose the project with the highest IRR

(3) NPV & IRR

IRR $>$ k → NPV $>$ 0

IRR = k → NPV = 0

IRR $<$ k → NPV $<$ 0

(4) Advantages

- It includes time value of money

- It shows the return on the original money invested.

- We can't estimate the NPV unless we know the appropriate discount rate, but we can still estimate the IRR.

(5) Disadvantages

- May result in multiple answers or not deal with non-conventional cash flows.

- IRR assumes reinvestment of interim cash flows in projects with equal rates of return.

- May lead to incorrect decisions in comparisons of mutually exclusive investments.

6 Profitability Index (PI)

(1) PI

The present value of an investment's future cash flows divided by its initial cost.

수익성지수란 현금유입의 현재가치를 현금유출의 현재가치로 나눈 값으로, 투자자금 $1에 대한 현금유입의 현재가치의 크기를 말한다.

$$PI = \text{PV of cash inflows} \div \text{PV of cash outflow}$$
$$= 1 + \frac{NPV}{CF_0}$$

$$PI_A = \frac{2,158}{2,000} = 1.079 \qquad PI_B = \frac{2,099}{2,000} = 1.0495$$

(2) Decision rule

1) Independent projects

$PI > 1 \rightarrow$ accept the project

$PI < 1 \rightarrow$ reject the project

2) Mutually exclusive projects

Choose the project with the highest PI

(3) NPV & IRR & PI

$$IRR > k \rightarrow NPV > 0 \rightarrow PI > 1$$
$$IRR = k \rightarrow NPV = 0 \rightarrow PI = 1$$
$$IRR < k \rightarrow NPV < 0 \rightarrow PI < 1$$

(4) Advantages

- It includes time value of money
- May be useful when available investment funds are limited.

(5) Disadvantages

- May lead to incorrect decisions in comparisons of mutually exclusive investments.
- An estimate about the cost of capital is required so as to calculate the PI.

7 NPV vs IRR

순현가법과 내부수익률법은 두 방법 모두 화폐의 시간가치를 고려하는 방법으로 투자안의 경제성 분석에 가장 많이 이용되는 분석방법들이다. 하지만 순현가법이 내부수익률보다 더 우수한 평가방법인데 그에 대한 자세한 내용을 살펴본다.

(1) Independent projects

독립적인 단일 투자안을 평가하는 경우 NPV법과 IRR법의 두 가지 평가결과는 같다.

$$IRR > k \rightarrow NPV > 0 \rightarrow Accept$$
$$IRR < k \rightarrow NPV < 0 \rightarrow Reject$$

(2) Mutually exclusive projects

상호 배타적인 투자안의 경우 NPV법과 IRR법은 평가결과가 서로 다르게 나타날 수 있다.

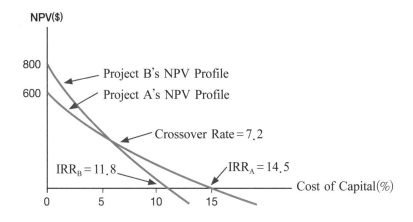

Discount Rate	NPV_A	NPV_B
0%	600.00	800.00
5%	360.84	413.00
10%	157.64	98.36
15%	(16.66)	(160.28)

[Figure 6-2] NPV profile

NPV profile에서 두 투자안의 NPV를 같게 만드는 할인율을 crossover rate이라고 한다. 할인율이 crossover rate보다 큰 구간에서는 NPV법이나 IRR법에 따르더라도 모두 투자안 A를 선택한다. 그러나 할인율이 crossover rate보다 작은 구간에서는 NPV법에 따르면 투자안 B를 선택하지만 IRR법에 따르면 투자안 A를 선택한다.

	k < crossover rate	k > crossover rate
IRR method	Project A	
NPV method	Project B	Project A

이와 같이 상호배타적인 투자안의 경우 NPV profile이 교차할 때에는 NPV와 IRR의 의사결정이 상이하게 된다. NPV profile이 교차하는 이유는 다음과 같다.

- Timing differences exist, where most of the cash flows from one project come in early while most of those from the other project come in later.

- Project size differences exist, where the amount invested in one project is larger than the other.

(3) Multiple IRR problem

- Normal cash flows

  a project has one or more cash outflows followed by a series of cash inflows.

- Non-normal cash flows

  a cash outflow occurs sometime after the inflows have commenced, meaning that the signs of the cash flows change more than once.

- Multiple IRRs

  If a project has nonnormal cash flows, it can have two or more IRRs.

Example

Suppose a firm is considering the development of a strip mine. The mine will cost $16 million, then it will produce a cash flow of $100 million at the end of Year 1, and then, at the end of Year 2, the firm must spend $100 million to restore the land to its original condition.

$$16 + \frac{100}{(1+IRR)^2} = \frac{100}{(1+IRR)^1} \rightarrow \text{IRR=20\%, IRR=400\%}$$

(4) Reinvestment rate assumption

The NPV method implicitly assumes that the reinvestment rate is the cost of capital, whereas the IRR method assumes that the reinvestment rate is the IRR itself.

NPV법은 투자안으로부터 유입되는 현금이 자본비용과 동일한 수익률로 재투자된다고 가정하고, IRR법은 내부수익률로 재투자된다고 가정한다. 하지만 시장에서 공통적으로 평가하는 자본비용수준의 수익률로 재투자된다고 보는 것이 합리적이며 현실적이다.

(5) Modified IRR (MIRR)

The discount rate at which the present value of a project' cost is equal to the present value of its terminal value, where the terminal value is found as the sum of the future values of the cash inflows, compounded at the firm' cost of capital.

투자안의 재투자수익률로서 자본비용을 사용해서 구한 내부수익률을 수정된 내부수익률(MIRR)이라고 한다.

투자안 A의 MIRR을 계산해 보면 다음과 같다.

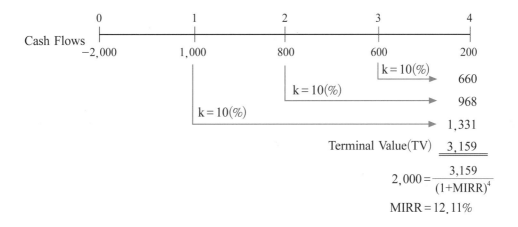

[Figure 6-3] MIRR

Example 6-6

Assume a project has a normal cash flow pattern, which of the following statements is most correct?

a. All else equal. IRR increases as the cost of capital declines
b. All else equal. NPV increases as the cost of capital declines
c. All else equal. MIRR increases as the cost of capital declines
d. All else equal. PI decreases as the cost of capital declines

Solution

k 감소 → NPV, PI : 증가
k 감소 → MIRR 감소
k 감소 → IRR, payback period : no effect

정답 : b

8 Unequal lives

투자수명이 서로 다른 투자안들을 NPV법으로 비교하는 경우 각 투자안들이 투자수명이 종료된 후에도 각각 똑같은 투자안을 다시 수행할 기회가 있다고 가정하여 다음과 같이 평가한다.

	Project C	Project D
NPV	+$184	+$205
Useful life	3	4
Discount rate	10%	

(1) Replacement Chain (Common Life)

각 투자안의 종료시점을 일치시키는 최소공배수에 해당하는 기간까지 반복투자한다고 가정하여 총 NPV를 비교하는 방법이다.

각 투자안의 최소공배수는 12년이므로 투자안 C는 4회, 투자안 D는 3회 반복투자를 가정하여 총 NPV를 구하면 다음과 같다.

투자안 C : $NPV = 184 + \dfrac{184}{1.1^3} + \dfrac{184}{1.1^6} + \dfrac{184}{1.1^9} = \$505$

투자안 D : $NPV = 205 + \dfrac{205}{1.1^4} + \dfrac{205}{1.1^8} = \$441$

∴ 총 NPV의 값이 투자안 C가 크기 때문에 C를 선택한다.

(2) Equivalent Annual Annuities (EAA)

각 투자안의 NPV를 매년의 일정한 현금흐름인 연금액을 EAA라고 하며 이 금액이 큰 투자안을 선택한다.

각 투자안의 EAA를 구하면 다음과 같다

투자안 C : $184 = \displaystyle\sum_{t=1}^{3} \dfrac{EAA}{1.10^t} \rightarrow EAA = \$74$

투자안 D : $205 = \displaystyle\sum_{t=1}^{4} \dfrac{EAA}{1.10^t} \rightarrow EAA = \$65$

∴ EAA의 값이 투자안 C가 크기 때문에 C를 선택한다.

9 Capital rationing

Capital rationing is the situation in which a firm can raise only a specified, limited amount of capital regardless of how many good projects it has.

Capital rationing is essentially a management approach to allocating available funds across multiple investment opportunities. The combination of projects with the highest total net present value (NPV) is accepted by the company.

Example 6-7

	Project A	Project B	Project C	Project D
Initial cost	200,000	253,000	190,000	210,000
NPV	3,770	27,827	29,333	(7,854)
IRR	12.7%	17.6%	17.2%	10.6%
PI	1.02	1.13	1.14	0.96

Cost of capital = 12%
Limited capital = $500,000
Which projects will the firm choose during the year?

Solution

투자안 D는 NPV〈0이므로 투자대상에서 제외
NPV(A+B) = 3,770 + 27,827 = $31,597
NPV(B+C) = 27,827 + 29,333= $57,160
NPV(A+C) = 3,770 + 29,333 = $33,103

→ 주어진 예산한도에서는 투자안 B와 C에 투자한다.

10 Real Options

(1) Traditional capital budgeting

- NPV = present value of expected cash flows by risk adjusted interest rate
- Static investment decision
- Ignore option value

(2) Real options

- Assume that once management makes initial investment, it has an option to take a number of future actions that will change the value of the investment

  실물옵션은 실물투자와 관련해서 옵션 특성이 포함된 경우 옵션의 가치를 평가해서 투자안의 경제성을 평가하는 것이다.

- Project value = NPV + Option value
- Dynamic investment decision
- Managerial option or strategic option

(3) Types of real option

1) Expansion option

the project can be expanded if demand turns out to be stronger than expected.

2) Abandonment option

the project can be shut down if its cash flows are low.

3) Timing option

the project can be delayed until more information about demand and/or costs can be obtained.

11 Economic Value Added

(1) Economic Value Added (EVA)

경제적 부가가치(EVA)는 세후 영업이익(NOPAT : net operating profit after taxes)에서 투자자본의 자본비용을 차감하여 산출하며, 투자자본의 자본비용은 타인자본비용과 자기자본비용을 모두 포함한다. 따라서 EVA는 자본비용을 공제한 후의 잔여이익으로서 경제적 이익(EP : economic profit) 또는 초과이익(excess earnings)이라고도 하는데, 다음과 같은 식으로 측정한다.

$$EVA = NOPAT - \text{Total cost of capital}$$

$NOPAT = EBIT \times (1 - t)$

$\text{Total cost of capital} = \text{Invested capital} \times WACC$

$\text{Invested capital} = \text{Assets} - \text{Operating Liabilities}$

(2) Market Value Added (MVA)

시장부가가치(MVA)는 경제적 부가가치(EVA)를 자본비용으로 할인한 현재가치이다.

$$MVA = \sum_{t=1}^{n} \frac{EVA_t}{(1+WACC)^t}$$

Economic Thinking

코카콜라는 1980년대 들어 라이벌인 펩시사와의 경쟁에서 시장점유율 등 기업 경쟁력이 악화되면서 새로운 경영관리기법인 EVA를 1987년부터 도입하기 시작하였다. 자본비용을 상회하는 수익률을 올리는 프로젝트에 집중 투자하고 저수익 사업부문에서는 과감히 철수함으로써 기업 가치를 증대시키는 전략을 사용한 것이다. 또한 EVA를 이용하여 영업 이익률의 개선, 집중 구매에 의한 경비 절감 및 운전자본의 삭감과 같은 효율성의 향상을 가져왔다. 이러한 노력의 결과 평균자본비용을 16%에서 12%로 낮추고, 52개 생산부문을 40개로 축소하여 집중 생산하도록 하는 방식을 채택했다. 결과적으로 코카콜라사의 EVA는 1987년에 490 달러에서 95년에는 2,172 달러로 상승하였고, 주가도 같은 기간 동안 9.53 달러에서 74.25 달러로 상승하였다.

Example 6-8

Eastman Kodak Co. reported these data at year-end :

Pre-tax operating income	$4,000,000
Current assets	4,000,000
Long-term assets	16,000,000
Current liabilities	2,000,000
Long-term liabilities	5,000,000

The long-term debt has an interest rate of 8%, and its fair value equaled its book value at year-end. The fair value of the equity capital is $2 million greater than its book value. The firm's income tax rate is 25%, and its cost of equity capital is 10%.
What is the firm's EVA?

Solution

$\text{NOPAT} = \text{EBIT} \times (1 - t) = \$4,000,000 \times 0.75 = \$3,000,000$

$\text{Invested capital} = \$4,000,000 + \$16,000,000 - \$2,000,000 = \$18,000,000$

$\text{Book value of equity} = \$20,000,000 - \$7,000,000 = \$13,000,000$

$\text{Fair value of equity} = \$13,000,000 + \$2,000,000 = \$15,000,000$

$\text{Fair value of LT debt} = \$5,000,000$

$\text{WACC} = 8\% \times (1-0.25) \times 5/20 + 10\% \times 15/20 \quad \text{WACC} = 9\%$

$\text{EVA} = \$3,000,000 - (\$18,000,000 \times 9\%) = \$1,380,000$

04 ⟩⟩ Considering Risk in Capital Budgeting

1 Risk-Adjusted Discount Rate

(1) Project risk

Discount rate is increased when evaluating riskier projects—the greater the risk, the higher the discount rate used in the analysis.

- Average-risk projects are discounted at the firm's WACC.
- Higher-risk projects are discounted at a rate above the firm's WACC.
- Lower-risk projects are discounted at a rate below the firm's WACC.

(2) Conservative project (low beta)

If a company incorrectly uses the firm's WACC to calculate the NPV

→ overstate the discount rate, underestimate NPV

(3) Aggressive project (high beta)

If a company incorrectly uses the firm's WACC to calculate the NPV

→ understate the discount rate, overestimate NPV

2 Scenario Analysis

A risk analysis technique in which "bad" and "good" sets of financial circumstances are compared with a most likely, or base-case, situation.

- Base-Case Scenario

  An analysis in which all of the input variables are set at their most likely values.

- Worst-Case Scenario

  An analysis in which all of the input variables are set at their worst reasonably forecasted values.

- Best-Case Scenario

  An analysis in which all of the input variables are set at their best reasonably forecasted values.

3 Sensitivity Analysis

A risk analysis technique that shows how much NPV will change in response to a given change in an input variable, other things held constant. Sensitivity analysis begins with a base-case situation. The base-case NPV is the NPV when sales and other input variables are set equal to their most likely values.

- Input variables

  Sales prices, Variable cost per unit, Sales growth, Units sold, Fixed cost, WACC

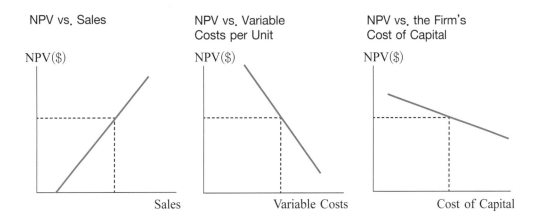

[Figure 6-4] Sensitivity Analysis

4 **Simulation Analysis** (Monte Carlo Simulation)

A risk analysis technique that uses a computer software to simulate future events and thus to estimate the probability and riskiness of a project.

05 ▷ Multiple Choice

01. The following methods are used to evaluate capital investment projects. Which one of the following correctly identifies the methods that utilize discounted cash flow (DCF) techniques? (CMA)

	IRR	ARR	Payback	NPV
a.	Yes	Yes	No	No
b.	No	No	Yes	Yes
c.	Yes	No	Yes	No
d.	Yes	No	No	Yes

02. Which one of the following methods for evaluating capital projects is the least useful from an investment analysis point of view? (CMA)

a. Accounting rate of return.

b. Internal rate of return.

c. Net present value.

d. Payback.

03. Capital investment projects include proposals for all of the following except (CMA)

a. the acquisition of government mandated pollution control equipment.

b. the expansion of existing product offerings.

c. additional research and development facilities.

d. refinancing existing working capital agreements.

04. Cora Lewis is performing an analysis to determine if her firm should invest in new equipment to produce a product recently developed by her firm. The option would be to abandon the product. She uses the net present value (NPV) method and discounts at the firm's cost of capital. Lewis is contemplating how to handle the following items.

I. The book value of warehouse space currently used by another division.

II. Interest payments on debt to finance the equipment.

III. Increased levels of accounts payable and inventory.

IV. R&D spent in prior years and treated as a deferred asset for book and tax purposes.

Which of the above items are relevant for Lewis to consider in determining the cash flows for her NPV calculation? (CMA)

a. I, II, III and IV.   b. II and III only.

c. IV only.   d. III and IV only.

05. Calvin Inc. is considering the purchase of a new state-of-art machine to replace its hand-operated machine. Calvin's effective tax rate is 40%, and its cost of capital is 12%. Data regarding the existing and new machines are presented below.

	Existing Machine	New Machine
Original cost	$50,000	$90,000
Installation costs	0	4,000
Freight and insurance	0	6,000
Expected end salvage value	0	0
Depreciation method	straight-line	straight-line
Expected useful life	10 years	5 years

The existing machine has been in service for seven years and could be sold currently for $25,000. Calvin expects to realize a before-tax annual reduction in labor costs of $30,000 if the new machine is purchased and placed in service. If the new machine is purchased, the incremental cash flows for the fifth year would amount to (CMA)

a. $18,000   b. $24,000

c. $26,000   d. $30,000.

06. Colvern Corporation is considering the acquisition of a new computer-aided machine tool to replace an existing, outdated model. Relevant information includes the following.

Projected annual cash savings $28,400
Annual depreciation - new machine $16,000
Annual depreciation - old machine $1,600
Income tax rate 40%
Annual after-tax cash flows for the project would amount to (CMA)

a. $5,600   b. $7,440

c. $17,040   d. $22,800.

07. A multi-period project has a positive net present value. Which of the following statements is correct regarding its required rate of return?

a. Less than the company's weighted average cost of capital

b. Less than the project's internal rate of return

c. Greater than the company's weighted average cost of capital

d. Greater than the project's internal rate of return

08. Which of the following statements is true regarding the payback method?

a. It does not consider the time value of money.

b. It is the time required to recover the investment and earn a profit.

c. It is a measure of how profitable one investment project is compared to another.

d. The salvage value of old equipment is ignored in the event of equipment replacement.

09. Which of the following capital budgeting techniques would allow management to justify investing in a project that could not be justified currently by using techniques that focus on expected cash flows?

a. Real options.

b. NPV

c. ARR

d. IRR

10. Whatney Co. is considering the acquisition of a new, more efficient press. The cost of the press is $360,000, and the press has an estimated six-year life with zero salvage value. Whatney uses straight-line depreciation for both financial reporting and income tax reporting purposes and has a 40 percent corporate income tax rate. In evaluating equipment acquisitions of this type, Whatney uses a goal of a four-year payback period. To meet Whatney's desired payback period, the press must produce a minimum annual before-tax, operating cash savings of :

a. $90,000

b. $110,000

c. $114,000

d. $150,000

11. In capital budgeting, which of the following items is included in the payback model calculation?

a. The total amount of the initial outlay for the project.

b. The present value of the future cash flows of the project.

c. The present value of the estimated salvage value of the project.

d. The amount of depreciation over the life of the project.

12. In estimating "after-tax incremental cash flows", under discounted cash flow analyses for capital project evaluations, which one of the following options reflects the items that should be included in the analyses? (CMA)

	Sunk Costs	Project related changes in net working capital	Estimated impacts of inflation
a.	No	No	Yes
b.	No	Yes	Yes
c.	No	Yes	No
d.	Yes	No	No

13. If the present value of expected cash inflows from a project equals the present value of expected cash outflows, the discount rate is the (CMA)

a. payback rate.

b. internal rate of return.

c. accounting rate of return.

d. net present value rate.

14. In discounted cash flow techniques, which one of the following alternatives best reflects the items to be incorporated in the initial net cash investment? (CMA)

	Capitalized expenditures (e.g., shipping costs)	Changes in net working capital	Net proceeds from sale of old asset in a replacement decision	Impact of spontaneous changes in current liabilities
a.	No	Yes	Yes	Yes.
b.	Yes	No	No	No.
c.	No	Yes	No	No.
d.	Yes	Yes	Yes	Yes.

15. Sarah Birdsong has prepared a net present value (NPV) analysis for a 15-year equipment modernization program. Her initial calculations include a series of depreciation tax savings, which are then discounted. Birdsong is now considering the incorporation of inflation into the NPV analysis. If the depreciation tax savings were based on original equipment cost, which of the following options correctly shows how she should handle the program's cash operating costs and the firm's required rate return, respectively? (CMA)

	Cash Operating Costs	Required Rate of Return
a.	Adjust for inflation	Adjust for inflation.
b.	Adjust for inflation	Do not adjust for inflation.
c.	Do not adjust for inflation	Adjust for inflation.
d.	Do not adjust for inflation	Do not adjust for inflation.

16. Bell Delivery Co. is financing a new truck with a loan of $30,000, to be repaid in five annual installments of $7,900 at the end of each year. What is the approximate annual interest rate Bell is paying? (CMA)

a. 4%.   b. 5%.

c. 10%.   d. 16%.

17. All of the following are methods used to evaluate investments for capital budgeting decisions except (CMA)

a. accounting rate of return.

b. internal rate of return.

c. excess present value (profitability) index.

d. required rate of return.

18. For a given investment project, the interest rate at which the present value of the cash inflows equals the present value of the cash outflows is called the (CMA)

a. hurdle rate.

b. payback rate.

c. internal rate of return.

d. cost of capital.

19. The net present value of an investment project represents the (CMA)

a. total actual cash inflows minus the total actual cash outflows.

b. excess of the discounted cash inflows over the discounted cash outflows.

c. total after-tax cash flow including the tax shield from depreciation.

d. cumulative accounting profit over the life of the project.

20. Jenson Copying Company is planning to buy a coping machine costing $25,310. The net present values (NPV) of this investment, at various discount rates, are as follows.

Discount Rate	NPV
4%	$2,440
6%	$1,420
8%	$ 460
10%	($ 440)

Jenson's approximate internal rate of return on this investment is (CMA)

a. 6%

b. 8%

c. 9%

d. 10%.

21. Molar Inc. is evaluating three independent projects for the expansion of different product lines. The Finance Department has performed an extensive analysis of each project and the chief financial officer has indicated that there is no capital rationing in effect. Which of the following statements are correct? (CMA)

I. Reject any project with a payback period which is shorter than the company standard.

II. The project with the highest internal rate of return (IRR) exceeding the hurdle rate should be selected and the others rejected.

III. All projects with positive net present values should be selected.

IV. Molar should reject any projects with negative IRRs.

a. I, II and IV only   b. I, II, III and IV

c. II and III only   d. III and IV only

22. Foggy Products is evaluating two mutually exclusive projects, one requiring a $4 million initial outlay and the other a $6 million outlay. The Finance Department has performed an extensive analysis of each project. The chief financial officer has indicated that there is no capital rationing in effect. Which of the following statements is correct? (CMA)

I. Both projects should be rejected if their payback periods are longer than the company standard.

II. The project with the highest Internal Rate of Return (IRR) should be selected (assuming both IRRs exceed the hurdle rate).

III. The project with the highest positive net present value should be selected.

IV. Select the project with the smaller initial investment, regardless of which evaluation method is used.

a. I, II, and IV only.   b. I, II and III only.

c. I and III only.   d. II and III only.

23. An investment decision is acceptable if the (CMA)

a. net present value is greater than or equal to $0.

b. present value of cash inflows is less than the present value of cash outflows.

c. present value of cash outflows is greater than or equal to $0.

d. present value of cash inflows is greater than or equal to $0.

24. Winston Corporation is subject to a 30% effective income tax rate and uses the net present value method to evaluate capital budgeting proposals. Harry Ralston, the capital budget manager, desires to improve the appeal of a marginally attractive proposal. To accomplish his goal, which one of the following actions should be recommended to Ralston? (CMA)

a. Postpone a fully-deductible major overhaul from year 4 to year 5.

b. Decrease the project's estimated terminal salvage value.

c. Immediately pay the proposal's marketing program in its entirety rather than pay in five equal installments.

d. Adjust the project's discount rate to reflect movement of the project from a "low risk" category to an "average risk" category.

25. Which of the following is not a shortcoming of the Internal Rate of Return (IRR) method? (CMA)

a. IRR assumes that funds generated from a project will be reinvested at an interest rate equal to the project's IRR.

b. IRR does not take into account the difference in the scale of investment alternatives.

c. IRR is easier to visualize and interpret than net present value (NPV).

d. Sign changes in the cash flow stream can generate more than one IRR.

26. Which one of the following capital budgeting techniques would result in the same project selection as the net present value method? (CMA)

    a. Discounted Payback   b. Internal Rate of Return

    c. Profitability Index   d. Accounting Rate of Return

27. A company is in the process of evaluating a major product line expansion. Using a 14% discount rate, the firm has calculated the present value of both the project's cash inflows and cash outflows to be $15.8 million. The company will likely evaluate this project further by (CMA)

    a. taking a closer look at the expansion's contribution margin.

    b. comparing the internal rate of return versus the accounting rate of return.

    c. comparing the internal rate of return versus the company's cost of capital.

    d. comparing the internal rate of return versus the company's cost of capital and hurdle rate.

28. Despite its shortcomings, the traditional payback period continues to be a popular method to evaluate investments because, in part, it (CMA)

    a. provides some insight into the risk associated with a project.

    b. ignores the time value of money.

    c. focuses on income rather than cash flow.

    d. furnishes information about an investment's lifetime performance

29. Which one of the following is not a shortcoming of the payback method? (CMA)

    a. It offers no consideration of cash flows beyond the expiration of the payback period.

    b. It ignores the time value of money.

    c. It offers no indication of a project's liquidity.

    d. It encourages establishing a short payback period.

30. In evaluating independent capital investment projects, the best reason for a firm to accept such projects is a(n) (CMA)

    a. accounting rate of return greater than zero.

    b. initial investment greater than the present value of cash inflows.

    c. profitability index greater that one.

    d. internal rate of return greater than the accounting rate of return.

31. Carbide Inc. has the following investment opportunities. Required investment outlays and the profitability index for each of these investments are as follows.

Project	Investment Cost	Profitability Index
I	$300,000	0.5
II	450,000	1.4
III	650,000	1.8
IV	750,000	1.6

Carbide's budget ceiling for initial outlays during the present period is $1,500,000. The proposed projects are independent of each other. Which project or projects would you recommend that Carbide accept? (CMA)

    a. III   b. III and IV

    c. I, II, and IV   d. I, III, and IV

Item 32 and 33 are based on the following information :

A firm, with an 18% cost of capital, is considering the following projects (on 1/1/20X4) :

	Jan. 1, 20X4 Cash outflow	Dec.31, 20X8, Cash inflow	Project Internal rate of return
Project A	$3,500,000	$7,400,000	?
Project B	4,000,000	9,950,000	?

32. Using the net present value method, Project A's net present value is

    a. $316,920   b. $0

    c. $265,460   d. $316,920

33. Project B's internal rate of return is closest to

    a. 15%   b. 18%

    c. 20%   d. 22%

34. Tam Co. is negotiating for the purchase of equipment that would cost $100,000, with the expectation that $20,000 per year could be saved in after-tax cash costs if the equipment were acquired. The equipment's estimated useful life is ten years, with no residual value, and it would be depreciated by the straight-line method. Tam's prede-termined minimum desired rate of return is 12%. The present value of an annuity of 1 at 12% for ten periods is 5.65. The present value of 1 due in ten periods at 12% is .322. In estimating the internal rate of return, the factors in the table of present values of an annuity should be taken from the columns closest to

    a. 0.65   b. 1.30

    c. 5.00   d. 5.65

35. Assume that KIMCPA is considering investing in a project with the following data :

Initial investment	$500,000
Additional investment in working capital	10,000
Cash flows before income taxes for years 1 through 5	140,000
Yearly tax depreciation	90,000
Terminal value of investment	50,000
Cost of capital	10%
Present value of $1 received after 5 years discounted at 10%	.621
Present value of an ordinary annuity of $1 for 5 years at 10%	3.791
Marginal tax rate	30%
Investment life	5 years

Assume that all cash flows come at the end of the year. What is the net present value of the investment?

a. $175,000

b. $58,000

c. $1,135

d. $12,340

Item 36 and 39 are based on the following information :

An organization has four investment proposals with the following costs and expected cash inflows :

Project	Cost	End of Year 1	End of year 2	End of year 3
A	Unknown	$10,000	$10,000	$10,000
B	$20,000	5,000	10,000	15,000
C	25,000	15,000	10,000	5,000
D	30,000	20,000	Unknown	20,000

36. If Project A has an internal rate of return (IRR) of 15%, then it has a cost of

a. $8,696   b. $22,832

c. $24,869   d. $27,232

37. If the discount rate is 10%, the net present value (NPV) of Project B is

a. $4,079   b. $6,789

c. $9,869   d. $39,204

38. The payback period of Project C is

a. 0 year   b. 1 year

c. 2 years   d. 3 years.

39. If the discount rate is 5% and the discounted payback period of Project D is exactly two years, then the year two cash inflow for Project D is

a. $5,890   b. $10,000

c. $12,075   d. $14,301

Solution

1	2	3	4	5	6	7	8	9	10
D	A	D	D	C	D	B	A	A	B

11	12	13	14	15	16	17	18	19	20
A	B	B	D	A	C	D	C	B	C

21	22	23	24	25	26	27	28	29	30
D	B	A	A	C	C	D	A	C	C

31	32	33	34	35	36	37	38	39	
B	C	C	C	C	B	A	C	C	

1. DCF models : IRR, NPV, PI, Discounted payback method

   Undiscounted models: ARR, Payback method

2. ARR은 현금흐름과 현재가치를 고려하지 못하는 단점 때문에 장기투자 의사결정에는 부적합하다.

3. 자본예산은 1년 이상의 투자결정이며, 순운전자본은 1년 미만의 의사결정이다.

4. I. 창고의 장부가액은 sunk cost이므로 증분현금흐름에 반영하지 않는다.

   II. 이자비용은 NPV의 현금흐름이 아닌 할인율에 반영한다.

5. 5년 후의 현금흐름

   $OCF = EBITDA \times (1-T) + Depreciation \times T$

   $= \$30,000 \times (1 - 0.4) + (\$100,000 \div 5 \text{ years}) \times 0.4 = \$26,000$

6. $OCF = EBITDA \times (1-T) + \triangle Depreciation \times T$

   $= \$28,400 \times (1-0.4) + (\$16,000 - \$1,600) \times 0.4 = \$22,800$

7. $NPV \rangle 0 \rightarrow IRR \rangle WACC$

   $WACC = \text{hurdle rate} = \text{required rate of return}$

8. Payback method는 수익성이 아닌 안정성 지표로서 현재가치를 고려하지 않는다.

9. Real option에서는 NPV 〈 0이더라고 옵션의 가치가 더 크면 채택할 수 있다.

10. OCF = 360,000 ÷ 4 years = $90,000

    $90,0000 = EBITDA × 0.6 + 60,000 × 0.4 → EBITDA = $110,000

11. b. Payback method는 현재가치를 고려하지 않는다.

    c. Payback method는 현재가치를 고려하지 않는다.

    d. Payback method는 회계적 이익이 아닌 현금흐름을 고려하기 때문에 감가상각비를 고려하지 않는다.

12. 할인율을 명목이자율을 사용하므로 현금흐름도 인플레이션을 반영한 명목현금흐름을 사용한다.

13. IRR은 현금유입의 현재가치와 현금유출의 현재가치를 동일하게 하는 이자율이다.

14. 투자시점의 현금흐름은 자본적지출액, 순운전자본의 변동, 기존자산의 처분 등을 모두 고려하여야 한다.

15. 할인율을 명목이자율을 사용하므로 현금흐름도 인플레이션을 반영한 명목현금흐름을 사용한다.

16. $30,000 ÷ $7,900 = 3.7974

    PVIFA (R%, 5) = 3.7974 → R=10%

17. Required rate of return은 자본비용으로 자본예산기법이 아닌 NPV의 할인율이다.

18. IRR은 현금유입의 현재가치와 현금유출의 현재가치를 동일하게 하는 이자율이다.

19. NPV = 현금유입의 현재가치 − 현금유출의 현재가치

20. IRR은 NPV=0으로 만드는 할인율이므로 8%와 10%사이의 값이다.

21. 상호 독립적인 투자안의 의사결정이므로

    NPV 〉 0, IRR 〉 k, Payback 〈 benchmark period로 의사결정을 한다.

22. 상호 배타적인 투자안의 의사결정이므로

    가장 큰 NPV & IRR, 가장 짧은 Payback의 투자안을 선택한다.

23. 투자안의 선택기준 : NPV 〉 0, IRR 〉 k, PI 〉 1

24. a. 현금유출시점 증가 → 현금유출의 현재가치 감소 → NPV 증가

　　b. 현금유입액 감소 → 현금유입의 현재가치 감소 → NPV 감소

　　c. 현금유입액 감소 → 현금유입의 현재가치 감소 → NPV 감소

　　d. 할인율 증가 → 현금유입의 현재가치 감소 → NPV 감소

25. 그림으로 분석하기에는 NPV가 더 용이하다.

26. NPV = 현금유입의 현재가치 − 현금유출의 현재가치

　　PI = 현금유입의 현재가치 ÷ 현금유출의 현재가치

　　일반적으로 NPV와 PI는 동일한 결과를 갖는다.

27. IRR = 14%이므로 hurdle rate와 비교하여 의사결정을 한다.

28. Payback method은 간편하고 투자안의 위험을 평가하는 장점이 있다.

29. Payback method은 현재가치를 무시하며, 회수기간 이후의 현금흐름을 고려하지 못하는 단점이 있다.

30. 상호 독립적인 투자안의 의사결정은 NPV 〉 0, IRR 〉 k, PI 〉 1

31. Capital rationing : PI가 높은 순서대로 결정 → III 〉 IV 〉 II

32. PVIF (18%, 5) = 0.43711

　　NPV = −3,500,000 + 7,400,000 × 0.43711 = (−)263,386

33. 4,000 ÷ 9,950 = 0.4020

　　PVIFA (R%, 5) = 0.4020 → R=20% → IRR = 20%

34. 100,000 ÷ 20,000 = 5

　　PVIFA (R%, 5) = 5 → R=15% → IRR = 15%

35. OCF = EBITDA × (1 − T) + Depreciation × T

　　　　 = 140,000 × 0.7 + 90,000 × 0.3 = 125,000

　　NPV = −$510,000 + $125,000 × 3.791 + 60,000 × 0.621 = $1,135

36. PVIFA (15%, 3) = 2.2832 → $10,000 × 2.2832 = $22,832

37. NPV = −20,000 + 5,000 × 0.9091 + 10,000 × 0.8264 + 15,000 × 0.7513
    = $4,079

38. 25,000 = 15,000 + 10,000 → Payback period = 2년

39. 30,000 = 20,000 × 0.9524 + CF × 0.9070에서 CF = 12,074

06 ❯ Tasked-Based Simulation

Problem-1

A firm has two mutually exclusive investment projects to evaluate.
The projects have the following cash flows:

Time	Project X	Project Y
0	($100,000)	($70,000)
1	30,000	30,000
2	50,000	30,000
3	70,000	30,000
4	-	30,000
5	-	10,000

Projects X and Y are equally risky and may be repeated indefinitely.

Required

If the firm"s WACC is 12 percent, what is the EAA of the project that adds the most value to the firm? (Round your final answer to the nearest whole dollar.)

Problem-2

KIM is evaluating a capital budgeting project that should last for 4 years. The project requires $800,000 of equipment. He is unsure what depreciation method to use in his analysis, straight-line or the 3-year MACRS accelerated method. Under straight-line depreciation, the cost of the equipment would be depreciated evenly over its 4-year life (ignore the half-year convention for the straight-line method). The applicable MACRS depreciation rates are 33, 45, 15, and 7 percent. The company"s WACC is 10 percent, and its tax rate is 40 percent.

Required

1. What would the depreciation expense be each year under each method?
2. Which depreciation method would produce the higher NPV, and how much higher would it be?

Problem-3

A firm with a 14 percent WACC is evaluating two projects for this year's capital budget. After-tax cash flows, including depreciation, are as follows:

Time	Project X	Project Y
0	($6,000)	($18,000)
1	2,000	5,600
2	2,000	5,600
3	2,000	5,600
4	2,000	5,600
5	2,000	5,600

Required

1. Calculate NPV, IRR, MIRR, payback, and discounted payback for each project.
2. Assuming the projects are independent, which one or ones would you recommend?
3. If the projects are mutually exclusive, which would you recommend?
4. Notice that the projects have the same cash flow timing pattern. Why is there a conflict between NPV and IRR?
5. If the discount rate is zero, what is the NPV? If the discount rate is infinite, what is the NPV? At what discount rate is the NPV just equal to zero?
6. Over what range of discount rates would you choose Project X? Project Y? At what discount rate would you be indifferent between these two projects?

KIM Corporation's income statement (dollars are in thousands) is given here:

Accounts	Amount
Sales	$14,000,000
Operating costs excluding depreciation	7,000,000
EBITDA	$ 7,000,000
Depreciation	3,000,000
Earnings before interest and taxes (EBIT)	$ 4,000,000
Interest expense	1,500,000
Earnings before taxes (EBT)	$ 2,500,000
Income taxes (40%)	1,000,000
Net income	$ 1,500,000

Its total operating capital is $20 billion, and its total after-tax dollar cost of operating capital is $2 billion. During the year, KIM invested $1.3 billion in net operating capital.

1. What is its NOPAT?
2. What is its operating cash flow?
3. What is its free cash flow?

KIM is forecasting the following income statement:

Accounts	Amount
Sales	$8,000,000
Operating costs excluding depreciation	4,400,000
EBITDA	$3,600,000
Depreciation	800,000
Earnings before interest and taxes (EBIT)	$2,800,000
Interest expense	600,000
Earnings before taxes (EBT)	$2,200,000
Income taxes (40%)	880,000
Net income	$1,320,000

The CEO would like to see higher sales and a forecasted net income of $2,500,000. Assume that operating costs (excluding depreciation and amortization) are 55 percent of sales, and depreciation and amortization and interest expenses will increase by 10 percent. The tax rate, which is 40 percent, will remain the same.

What level of sales would generate $2,500,000 in net income?

Problem-6

You must evaluate a proposal to buy a new milling machine. The base price is $108,000, and shipping and installation costs would add another $12,500. The machine falls into the MACRS 3-year class, and it would be sold after 3 years for $65,000. The applicable depreciation rates are 33, 45, 15, and 7 percent. The machine would require a $5,500 increase in working capital (increased inventory less increased accounts payable)but it would be recovered at the end of the project' 3-year life. There would be no effect on revenues, but pre-tax labor costs would decline by $44,000 per year. The marginal tax rate is 35 percent, and the WACC is 12 percent. Also, the firm spent $5,000 last year investigating the feasibility of using the machine.

Required

1. What is the net cost of the machine for capital budgeting purposes, that is, the Year 0 project cash flow?
2. What are the net operating cash flows during Years 1, 2, and 3?
3. What is the terminal year cash flow?
4. Should the machine be purchased? Explain your answer.

Problem-7

Kell Inc. is analyzing an investment for a new product expected to have annual sales of 100,000 units for the next 5 years and then be discontinued. New equipment will be purchased for $1,200,000 and cost $300,000 to install. The equipment will be depreciated on a straight-line basis over 5 years for financial reporting purposes and 3 years for tax purposes. At the end of the fifth year, it will cost $100,000 to remove the equipment, which can be sold for $300,000. Additional working capital of $400,000 will be required immediately and needed for the life of the product. The product will sell for $80, with direct labor and material costs of $65 per unit. Annual indirect costs will increase by $500,000. (CMA)

Required

If the tax rate is 40 percent and the discount rate is 12 percent, what is the NPV of this project?

Skytop Industries is analyzing a capital investment project using discounted cash flow (DCF) analysis. The new equipment will cost $250,000. Installation and transportation costs aggregating $25,000 will be capitalized. A five year MACRS depreciation schedule (20%, 32%, 19.2%, 11.52%, 11.52%, 5.76%) with the half-year convention will be employed.

Existing equipment will be sold immediately after installation of the new equipment. The existing equipment has a tax basis of $100,000 and an estimated market value of $80,000. Skytop estimates that the new equipment's capacity will generate additional receivables and inventory of $30,000, while payables will increase by $15,000. Annual incremental pre-tax cash inflows are estimated at $75,000. (CMA)

Required

If the tax rate is 40 percent and the discount rate is 8 percent, what is the NPV of this project?

Problem-9

Holmes Manufacturing is considering a new machine that costs $250,000 and would reduce pre-tax manufacturing costs by $90,000 annually. Holmes would use the 3-year MACRS method to depreciate the machine, and management thinks the machine would have a value of $23,000 at the end of its 5-year operating life. The applicable depreciation rates are 33, 45, 15, and 7 percent. Working capital would increase by $25,000 initially, but it would be recovered at the end of the project' 5-year life. Holmes' marginal tax rate is 40 percent, and a 10 percent WACC is appropriate for the project.

Required

1. Calculate the project' NPV, IRR, MIRR, and payback.
2. Assume management is unsure about the $90,000 cost savings—his figure could deviate by as much as plus or minus 20 percent. What would the NPV be under each of these situations?

Problem-10

As a financial analyst, you must evaluate a proposed project to produce printer cartridges. The equipment would cost $55,000, plus $10,000 for installation. Annual sales would be 4,000 units at a price of $50 per cartridge, and the project' life would be 3 years. Current assets would increase by $5,000 and payables by $3,000. At the end of 3 years the equipment could be sold for $10,000. Depreciation would be based on the MACRS 3-year class, so the applicable rates would be 33, 45, 15, and 7 percent. Variable costs would be 70 percent of sales revenues, fixed costs excluding depreciation would be $30,000 per year, the marginal tax rate is 40 percent, and the corporate WACC is 11 percent.

Required

1. If the project is of average risk, what is its NPV, and should it be accepted?

2. Suppose management is uncertain about the exact unit sales. What would the project' NPV be if unit sales turned out to be 20 percent below forecast, but other inputs were as forecasted? Would this change the decision?

3. The CFO asks you to do a scenario analysis using these inputs:

	Probability	Unit Sales	VC%
Best case	0.25	4,800	65%
Base case	0.50	4,000	70%
Worst case	0.25	3,200	75%

Other variables are unchanged. What are the expected NPV and its standard deviation?

Problem-11

Huang Industries is considering a proposed project whose estimated NPV is $12 million. This estimate assumes that economic conditions will be "average." However, the CFO realizes that conditions could be better or worse, so she performed a scenario analysis and obtained these results:

Economic Scenario	Probability of Outcome	NPV($ million)
Recession	0.05	(70)
Below average	0.20	(25)
Average	0.50	12
Above average	0.20	20
Boom	0.05	30

Required

Calculate the project' expected NPV, standard deviation, and coefficient of variation.

Problem-12

Kore Industries is analyzing a capital investment proposal for new equipment to produce a product over the next eight years. The analyst is attempting to determine the appropriate "end-of-life" cash flows for the analysis. At the end of eight years, the equipment must be removed from the plant and will have a net book value of zero, a tax basis of $75,000 and scrap salvage value of $10,000. Kore's effective tax rate is 40 percent.

Required

What is the terminal year cash flow?

Financial Management For the **US CPA** Exam

Chapter 07

Financial Risk Management

Volume
8

Chapter 7

Financial Risk Management

01 ▷▷ Derivatives

1 Derivatives

- A derivative is a financial instrument or contract whose value depends on the value of another asset, typically referred to as the underlying asset or simply "the underlying".

- Common types of derivative contracts include options, forwards, futures and swaps.

- Underlying assets are equities or equity indices, fixed-income securities, currencies, commodities, credit events and even other types of derivatives.

Derivatives	Underlying assets	Underlying prices
Options	Stock	Stock prices
Forwards	Bond	Interest rates
Futures	Foreign currency	Foreign exchange rates
Swaps	Commodity	Commodity prices

- Derivative contracts are typically used by investors for the purpose of speculating, or hedging against the future market value of an underlying asset.

2 Forwards

(1) Forward contract (선도계약)

A contract under which one party agrees to buy an underlying asset at a specified price on a specified future date and the other party agrees to make the sale.

미래 일정 시점에 약정된 가격에 의해 계약상의 특정 대상을 사거나 팔기로 계약 당사자 간에 합의한 거래.

e.g.) "Company A contracts to buy 500 bushels of wheat from Company B for delivery in one year at $3 per bushel."

One party to a forward contract can win only at the expense of the other, so a forward contract is a zero-sum game.

(2) Buyer of a forward contract (Long position)

The buyer of a forward contract has the obligation to take delivery and pay for the good. The buyer of a forward contract benefits if prices increase because the buyer will have locked in a lower price.

Price	$2	$2.5	$3	$3.5	$4
P/L	-500	-250	0	+250	+500

(3) Seller of a forward contract (Short position)

The seller has the obligation to make delivery and accept payment. The buyer of a forward contract benefits if prices fall because a higher selling price has been locked in.

Price	$2	$2.5	$3	$3.5	$4
P/L	+500	+250	0	-250	-500

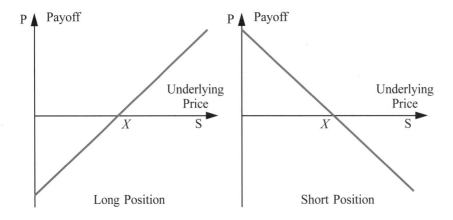

[Figure 7-1] Payoff on forward contracts

(4) Credit Risk

Since a forward contract is not exchange traded, there is credit risk in a forward contract.

(5) Settlement

A forward contract can be settled in two ways: delivery or cash settlement. In case of a cash settled forward contract, the party for whom the contract has a negative value will pay the amount of negative value to the party with the positive value.

(6) Hedge strategy

- Long hedge : Buying forward contracts to protect against price increases
- Short hedge : Selling forward contracts to protect against price decreases
- Cross-hedging : Hedging an asset with contracts written on a closely related, but not identical, asset.
- Basis risk : the risk associated with imperfect hedging.

Example 7-1

For the following scenarios, describe a hedging strategy using forwards contracts.

(1) A large Texas oil producer would like to hedge against adverse movements in the price of oil, since this is the firm's primary source of revenue.

(2) A textile manufacturer wanted to hedge against adverse movements in cotton prices.

(3) A U.S. company exports its goods to Japan.

(4) A company has a large bond issue maturing in one year. When it matures, the company will float a new issue. Current interest rates are attractive, and the company is concerned that rates next year will be higher.

Solution

(1) Short hedge—oil
(2) Long hedge—cotton
(3) Short hedge—yen
(4) Short hedge—bond

3 Futures

(1) Futures contract

Standardized contracts that are traded on exchanges and are market-to-market daily, but where physical delivery of the underlying asset is virtually never taken.

수량 · 규격 · 품질 등이 표준화되어 있는 특정 대상에 대하여 현재 시점에서 결정된 가격에 의해 미래 일정 시점에 인도 · 인수할 것을 약정한 계약으로서 조직화된 시장에서 정해진 방법으로 거래되는 것

(2) Comparison forwards with futures

	Forwards	Futures
Exchanges(Clearing house)	No	Yes
Standardization	No	Yes
Market-to-market	No	Yes
Physical delivery	Yes	No
Default risk	Yes	No

Example 7-2

Suppose Golden Grain Farms (GGF) expects to harvest 50,000 bushels of wheat in September. GGF is concerned about the possibility of price fluctuations between now and September. The futures price for September wheat is $2 per bushel, and the relevant contract calls for 5,000 bushels. What action should GGF take to lock in the $2 price? Suppose the price of wheat actually turns out to be $3 or $1.

Solution

(1) Each contract calls for delivery of 5,000 bushels, so GGF needs to sell 10 futures contracts.

(2) If wheat prices actually turn out to be $3, then GGF will receive $150,000 for its crop, but it will have a loss of $50,000 on its futures position when it closes that position because the contracts require it to sell 50,000 bushels of wheat at $2, when the going price is $3. He thus nets $100,000 overall.

(3) If wheat prices turn out to be $1 per bushel, then the crop will be worth only $50,000. However, GGF will have a profit of $50,000 on its futures position, so GGF again nets $100,000.

4 Option

(1) Option contract

A contract which allows (do not require) the holder to buy or sell an underlying asset at a specified price on a specified future date or during a specified period of time.

(2) Differences between an option contract and a forward contract

- With a forward contract, both parties are obligated to transact. With an option, the transaction occurs only if the owner of the option chooses to exercise it.

- Whereas no money changes hands when a forward contract is created, the buyer of an option contract gains a valuable right and must pay the seller for that right. The price of the option is frequently called the option premium.

	Futures	Options
Obligation of buyer	Yes	No (Right)
Degree of P/L	Unlimited	Limited
Advance payment	No	Yes (Premiums)

(3) Terminology

- Striking price (= Exercise price)

    The price that must be paid for an underlying asset when an option is exercised.

- Call option

    An option to buy the underlying asset at a striking price.

- Put option

    An option to sell the underlying asset at a striking price.

- American option

    An option to exercise during a specified period of time.

- European option

  An option to exercise at a specified date.

- Option buyer (= investor, holder)

  일정한 금액 (option premium)을 주고 옵션을 매입한 사람

- Option seller (= issuer, writer)

  일정한 금액 (option premium)을 받고 옵션을 매도한 사람

(4) Option position

1) Buyer of a call option

has the right to buy the underlying asset by paying the strike price.

2) Seller of a call option

is obligated to deliver the asset and accept the strike price if the option is exercised.

3) Buyer of a put option

has the right to sell the underlying asset and receive the strike price.

4) Seller of a put option

is obligated to accept the asset and pay the strike price if the option is exercised.

(5) Moneyness

옵션의 행사에 따른 손익은 만기의 기초자산의 시장가격(x)와 행사가격(a)과의 관계에서 결정된다. 옵션을 행사하면 이익이 생기는 경우를 내가격(ITM: in the money)이라고 하며, 손실을 보게 되는 경우를 외가격(OTM: out of the money)이라고 한다. 그리고 기초자산의 가격과 행사가격이 같아서 옵션행사로 손익이 발생하지 않는 경우를 등가격(ATM: at the money)이라고 한다. 콜옵션과 풋옵션의 경우 이러한 관계는 다음과 같이 나타난다.

	call option	put option
ITM (in the money)	x > a	x < a
ATM (at the money)	x = a	x = a
OTM (out of the money)	x < a	x > a

x : Underlying price   a : Exercise price

(6) Call option payoff

Profit/Loss from a long call

= Cash flow at expiration - Initial cash flow

Initial cash flow = call option premium

Cash flow at expiration = Max (0, x − a)

Example 7-3

A call option with a strike price of $50. Compute cash flow at expiration of call option for the stock prices of $55, $50, and $45. And compute profit or loss of call option if the call premium is $3.

Solution

	Cash flow at expiration	Profit/Loss
Stock price = $55	Max [0, 55 − 50] = $5	$5 − $3 = $2
Stock price = $50	Max [0, 50 − 50] = $0	$0 − $3 = △$3
Stock price = $45	Max [0, 45 − 50] = $0	$0 − $3 = △$3

break even stock price = $53

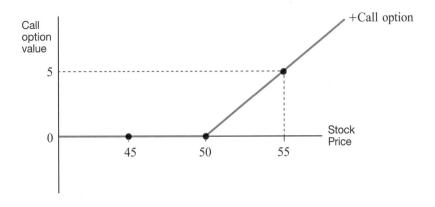

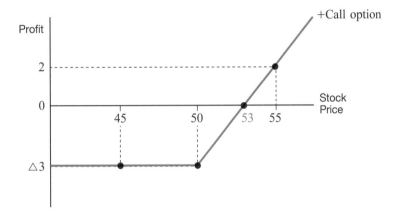

[Figure 7-2] call option payoff

Profit/Loss from a short call

= Initial cash flow − Cash flow at expiration

= − Profit/Loss from a long call

(7) Put option payoff

> Profit/Loss from a long put
> = Cash flow at expiration − Initial cash flow

Initial cash flow = put option premium

Cash flow at expiration = Max $(0, a - x)$

Example 7-4

A put option with a strike price of $50. Compute cash flow at expiration of put option for the stock prices of $55, $50, and $45. And compute profit or loss of put option if the put premium is $3.

Solution

	Cash flow at expiration	Profit/Loss
Stock price = $55	Max [0, 50 − 55] = $0	$0 − $3 = △$3
Stock price = $50	Max [0, 50 − 50] = $0	$0 − $3 = △$3
Stock price = $45	Max [0, 50 − 45] = $5	$5 − $3 = $2

break even stock price = $47

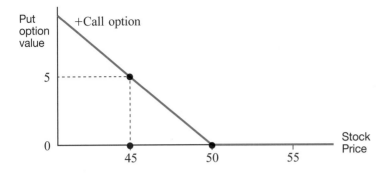

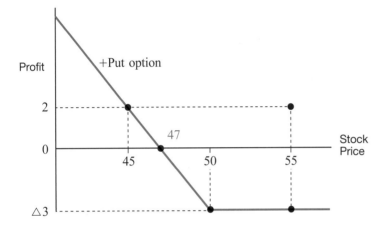

[Figure 7-3] put option payoff

Profit/Loss from a short put

= Initial cash flow − Cash flow at expiration

= − Profit/Loss from a long put

Example 7–5

For the following scenarios, describe a hedging strategy using option contracts.

(1) A large Texas oil producer would like to hedge against adverse movements in the price of oil, since this is the firm's primary source of revenue.

(2) A textile manufacturer wanted to hedge against adverse movements in cotton prices.

(3) A U.S. company exports its goods to Japan.

(4) A company has a large bond issue maturing in one year. When it matures, the company will float a new issue. Current interest rates are attractive, and the company is concerned that rates next year will be higher.

Solution

(1) Buy put option—oil
(2) Buy call option—cotton
(3) Buy put option—yen
(4) Buy put option—bond

Example 7-6

Microsoft	Strike price	Expira-tion	Calls		Puts	
			Vol.	Last	Vol.	Last
125	120	Feb	85	8.10	40	0.55
125	120	Mar	61	9.60	22	1.50
125	120	Apr	22	11.45	11	2.70

(1) Suppose you buy 10 contracts of the February 120 call option. How much will you pay, ignoring commissions?

(2) In part (1), suppose that Microsoft stock is selling for $140 per share on the expiration date. How much is your options investment worth? What is your net gain? What is the break-even price, that is, the terminal stock price that results in a zero profit?

(3) Suppose you buy 10 contracts of the April 120 put option. What is your maximum gain? On the expiration date, Microsoft is selling for $114 per share. How much is your options investment worth? What is your net gain?

(4) In part (3), suppose you sell 10 of the April 120 put contracts. What is your net gain or loss if Microsoft is selling for $113 at expiration? For $132? What is the break-even price, that is, the terminal stock price that results in a zero profit?

Solution

(1) Initial cash flow = $10 \times \$8.10 = \$81$

(2) Cash flow at expiration = $10 \times \max(0, \$140 - \$120) = \$200$
Profit/Loss from a long call = $\$200 - \$81 = \$119$
Break-even price = $120 + 8.10 = \$128.10$

(3) Maximum gain = $10 \times \$120 - 10 \times \$2.70 = \$1,173$
Cash flow at expiration = $10 \times \max(0, \$120 - \$114) = \$60$
Profit/Loss from a long put = $\$60 - 10 \times \$2.70 = \$33$

(4) Profit/Loss from a long put $= 10 \times \max(0, 120 - 113) - 10 \times \$2.70 = \$43$

Profit/Loss from a short put $= -\$43$

Profit/Loss from a long put $= 10 \times \max(0, 120 - 132) - 10 \times \$2.70 = -\$27$

Profit/Loss from a short put $= +\$27$

Break-even price $= 120 - 2.70 = \$117.3$

(8) Option value (Option premium)

옵션의 가치는 내재가치와 시간가치로 구성이 된다.

$$\text{Option premium} = \text{Intrinsic value} + \text{Time value}$$

1) Intrinsic value (내재가치)

옵션의 내재가치는 현재 그 해당 옵션의 권리를 행사한다고 할 때에 얻을 수 있는 가치와 0의 값 중 큰 값을 의미한다. 예를 들면 현재주가가 $107인 경우 행사가격이 $100인 콜옵션의 내재가치는 $7이지만 행사가격이 $100인 풋옵션의 내재가치는 $0이다.

2) Time value (시간가치)

옵션의 시간가치는 옵션을 보유할 때 주가가 자신에게 유리한 방향으로 변동할 가능성에 대한 가치로서 그 크기는 옵션의 실제가격에서 내재가치를 차감한 값으로 측정한다. 예를 들면 현재주가가 $107인 경우 행사가격이 $100인 콜옵션의 현재가격이 $10라면 시간가치는 $3이며 행사가격이 $100인 풋옵션의 현재가격이 $2라면 시간가치는 $2이다.

(9) Option pricing model (OPM)

옵션의 이론가격을 산출하는 모형을 OPM이라고 한다.

1) Binominal model

주가변동이 이항분포를 따른다고 가정하여 옵션의 이론가격을 결정하는 모형이다.

2) Black-Scholes model (1973)

The Black-Scholes formula was the first widely used model for option pricing.

It's used to calculate the theoretical value of European-style options using current stock prices, expected dividends, the option's strike price, expected interest rates, time to expiration and expected volatility.

3) Factors that affect the value of an option

Factors	Call option	Put option
Current stock price	+	−
Exercise price	−	+
Expiration date	+	+
Volatility of stock price	+	+
Risk−free interest	+	−
Expected dividends	−	+

The higher the stock's market price, the higher will be the call option price.

The higher the strike price, the lower will be the call option price.

The longer the option period, the higher will be the call option price.

Example 7-7

The exercise price on one of Flanagan Company' options is $15, its exercise value (intrinsic value) is $22, and its premium (time value) is $5. What are the option' market value and the price of the stock?

Solution

Option value = Intrinsic value + Time value = 22 + 5 = $27

Intrinsic value = max (0, stock price − $15) = $22 → stock price = $37

Example 7-8

Which of the following events are likely to decrease the market value of a call option on a common stock?

a. An increase in the stock' price.
b. An increase in the volatility of the stock price.
c. An increase in the risk-free rate.
d. A decrease in the time until the option.

Solution

다음 변수가 증가하면 콜옵션의 가격은 증가한다.
current stock prices, expected interest rates, time to expiration and expected volatility.

정답 : d

• Quadruple witching day

the third Friday of every March, June, September and December. On these days, market index futures, market index options, stock options and stock futures expire, usually resulting in increased volatility. (second Thursday of every March, June, September and December in Korea)

• CBOT (Chicago Board of Trade)

시카고거래소(CBOT)는 1848년에 설립된 세계 최대의 선물거래소로 전 세계 곡물선물거래의 80%이상을 차지하고 있다. 세계 최초의 현대적 상품 거래소로 평가를 받고 있으며, 뉴욕 증권 거래소(NYSE : New York Stock Exchange)와 함께 세계 금융시장을 주도하는 가장 중요한 시장 가운데 하나이다.

19세기 중반 대규모 운하가 개통되면서 시카고는 미국 중서부 곡창지대의 중심지이자 곡물의 집산지로 떠올랐다. 당시 곡물은 그해 날씨와 곡물의 수확시기에 따라 가격이 큰 폭으로 변동했다. 이 같은 가격 변동의 피해를 줄이기 위해 상인들은 미래의 곡물 가격을 미리 정해놓고 수확시기 한참 전에 거래를 확정하는 방식을 도입했다. 이 제도가 활성화되면서 시카고거래소는 단번에 세계 곡물 거래를 주도하는 중심지로 떠올랐다. 1975년에는 미국 정부 보증 주택저당채권을 대상으로 세계 최초로 금리 선물거래를 시작했다.

• CME (Chicago Mercantile Exchange)

시카고상품거래소(CME) 는 시카고에 있는 세계 제2위의 선물거래소로 미국 전체 선물 및 옵션 거래량의 약 37%를 거래하고 있다. CME는 1874년 계란, 버터, 닭 등을 거래하던 농산물 거래상인들에 의하여 설립되었다. 1919년 소, 돼지 등의 농축산물을 상장 거래하였고, 1972년 통화선물거래를 개시함으로써 최초로 금융선물거래를 시작한 거래소이다. 2007년에는 CME는 CBOT를 합병했다.

5 Swap

An agreement between two or more parties to exchange cash flows over a period in the future. (A type of forward contract)

	Forward	Futures	Option	Swap
장내거래		✓	✓	
장외거래	✓		✓	✓

☞ 장외거래는 채무불이행위험이 발생하며, 장내거래는 채무불이행위험이 없다.

(1) Currency Swap (CS, 통화스왑)

Two companies agree to exchange a specific amount of one currency for a specific amount of another at specific dates in the future.

일정 기간 동안 두 당사자가 서로 다른 통화의 이자와 원금을 교환하는 계약

(2) Interest Rate Swap (IRS, 금리스왑)

An interest rate swap is a forward contract in which one stream of future interest payments is exchanged for another based on a specified principal amount. Interest rate swaps usually involve the exchange of a fixed interest rate for a floating rate

일정 기간 동안 두 당사자가 고정금리이자(fixed interest)와 변동금리이자(floating interest)를 교환하는 계약

Company S has a 20-year, $1,000 million floating-rate (LIBOR) bond outstanding, while Company F has a $1,000 million, 20-year, fixed-rate (5%) issue outstanding. Each company has an obligation to make a stream of interest payments.

Suppose Company S has stable cash flows, and it wants to lock in its cost of debt. Company F has cash flows that fluctuate with the economy and Company F has concluded that it would be better off with variable rate debt.

If the companies swapped their payment obligations, Company S would now have to make fixed payments and Company F would have a floating stream.

Company S

LIBOR	4%	4.5%	5%	5.5%	6%
Bond interest	-40	-45	-50	-55	-60
Swap interest inflow	+40	+45	+50	+55	+60
Swap interest outflow	-50	-50	-50	-50	-50

Company F

LIBOR	4%	4.5%	5%	5.5%	6%
Bond interest	-50	-50	-50	-50	-50
Swap interest inflow	+50	+50	+50	+50	+50
Swap interest outflow	-40	-45	-50	-55	-60

(3) Zero-coupon model (swap valuation method)

An interest rate swap valuation method that views a swap as a series of cash flows for each of which is applied a zero coupon rate (spot rate).

The present value for each cash flow is determined using a spot rate. The sum of all present values is the value of the swap.

02 ▷ Hedging Accounting

1 Derivatives (US GAAP)

(1) Derivatives

A derivative instrument is a financial instrument or other contract with all of the following characteristics.

파생상품은 다음의 요건을 모두 충족하는 금융상품 또는 유사한 계약을 말한다.

1) The contract has both of the following terms.

- One or more underlyings

- One or more notional amounts or payment provisions or both.

  기초변수 및 계약단위의 수량(또는 지급규정)이 있어야 한다.

2) The contract requires no initial net investment or an initial net investment that is smaller than would be required for other types of contracts that would be expected to have a similar response to changes in market factors.

   최초 계약시 순투자금액을 필요로 하지 않거나 시장가격변동에 유사한 영향을 받는 다른 유형의 거래보다 적은 순투자금액을 필요로 해야 한다.

3) Net settlement : The contract can be settled net.
   차액결제가 가능해야 한다.

(2) Underlying (기초변수)

파생상품의 가치를 결정하는 기초변수의 사례는 다음과 같다.

1) A security price or security price index

2) A commodity price

3) An interest rate

4) A credit rating

5) An exchange rate

6) A climatic or geological condition

(3) Notional amount (계약단위의 수량)

A notional amount is a number of currency units, shares, bushels, pounds, or other units specified in the contract.

2 Accounting for Derivatives

(1) Classification

파생상품은 보유목적에 따라 다음과 같이 분류한다.

- Non-hedge derivatives
- Fair value hedge derivatives
- Cash flow hedge derivatives
- Hedge of a net investment in a foreign operation

(2) Non-hedge derivatives

단기매매목적이거나 위험회피요건을 충족하지 못한 경우에 적용되며 공정가치의 변동으로 인한 평가손익은 당기손익에 보고한다.

Example 7-9

On 11/1/20X1, AIFA purchased an at-the-money call option for $9,000 to purchase 100,000 gallons at $15 per gallon on 2/1/20X2. AIFA designates the derivatives as speculation. The market price of fuel and time value of the call option follow:

	11/1/20X1	12/31/20X1	2/1/20X2
fuel	15	13	14
call option-time value	9,000	3,000	0

11/1/20X1	Call option(Asset) Cash	9,000	9,000
12/31/20X1	Loss on call option Call option(Asset)	6,000	6,000
2/1/20X2	Loss on call option Call option(Asset)	3,000	3,000
Settlement	No entry		

Example 7-10

On 11/1/20X1, AIFA issued an at-the-money call option for $9,000 to purchase 100,000 gallons at $15 per gallon on 2/1/20X2. AIFA designates the derivatives as speculation. The market price of fuel and time value of the call option follow:

	11/1/20X1	12/31/20X1	2/1/20X2
fuel	15	13	14
call option-time value	9,000	3,000	0

11/1/20X1	Cash	9,000	
	Call option(Liability)		9,000
12/31/20X1	Call option(Liability)	6,000	
	Gain on call option		6,000
2/1/20X2	Call option(Liability)	3,000	
	Gain on call option		3,000
Settlement	No entry		

3 Hedging Accounting

(1) Fair Value Hedge

A hedge of the exposure to changes in the fair value of a recognized asset or liability that are attributable to a particular risk

공정가치위험회피는 특정위험으로 인한 자산 또는 부채의 공정가치변동위험을 상계하기 위하여 파생상품 등을 이용하는 것이다.

- Determine the fair value of both your hedged item and hedging instrument at the reporting date.
- Recognize any change in fair value (gain or loss) on the hedging instrument in current earnings.
- Recognize any change in fair value (gain or loss) on the hedged item in current earnings.

위험회피수단의 평가손익을 해당 회계연도에 당기손익으로 처리하며, 특정위험으로 인한 위험회피대상항목의 평가손익은 전액을 해당 회계연도에 당기손익으로 처리한다.

Example 7-11

On 11/1/20X1, KIMCPA purchased one share of MS for $500 as an FVTNI investment and purchased an at-the-money put option for $30. The put option gives KIMCPA the rights to sell one share of MS at $500 and option expires on 1/31/20X2. KIMCPA designates the hedge as fair value hedge. The market value of the stock and time value of put option follow:

	11/1/20X1	12/31/20X1	1/31/20X2
Investment-FVTNI	500	430	400
Put option-time value	30	10	0

11/1/20X1	Investment-FVTNI	500	
	Put option (Asset)	30	
	Cash		530
12/31/20X1	Unrealized loss on FVTNI	70	
	Investment-FVTNI		70
	Put option (Asset)	50*	
	Unrealized gain on put option		50
1/31/20X2	Unrealized loss on FVTNI	30	
	Investment-FVTNI		30
	Put option (Asset)	20	
	Unrealized gain on put option		20
Settlement	Cash	100	
	Put option (Asset)		100

(2) Cash Flow Hedge

A hedge of the exposure to variability in the cash flows of a recognized asset or liability, or of a forecasted transaction, that is attributable to a particular risk.

인식된 자산이나 부채에서 발생한 미래현금흐름의 변동 또는 발생가능성이 매우 높은 예상거래의 현금흐름 변동에 대한 위험회피이다.

- Determine the fair value of both your hedged item and hedging instrument at the reporting date.

- The effective portion of the gain or loss on a derivative instrument designated as a cash flow hedge is reported in other comprehensive income, and the ineffective portion is reported in earnings.

위험회피수단의 손익 중 위험회피에 효과적인 부분은 기타포괄손익으로 인식하며, 비효과적인 부분은 당기손익으로 인식하며 현금흐름 위험회피대상항목의 평가손익은 인식하지 않는다.

- If the effectiveness of a hedging relationship with an option is assessed based on changes in the option's intrinsic value, the changes in the option's time value would be recognized in earnings.

(3) Interest rate swap

1) Fair value hedge

이자율 변동으로 인한 고정금리 채무상품의 공정가치 변동위험을 회피하기 위하여 고정금리조건 채무상품을 변동금리조건 채무상품으로 전환하는 경우

- Fixed- rate borrowing
  → interest rate swap as a floating-rate payer

- Fixed- rate lending
  → interest rate swap as a fixed-rate payer

2) Cash flow hedge

이자율 변동으로 인한 미래이자의 변동성을 제거하기 위하여 변동금리조건 채무상품을 고정금리조건 채무상품으로 전환하는 경우

- Floating-rate borrowing
  → interest rate swap as a fixed-rate payer

- Floating-rate lending
  → interest rate swap as a floating-rate payer

03 ▷▷ Multiple Choice

01. Buying a wheat futures contract to protect against price fluctuation of wheat would be classified as a (CMA)

a. fair value hedge.   b. cash flow hedge.

c. foreign currency hedge.   d. swap.

02. An American importer expects to pay a British supplier 500,000 British pounds in three months. Which of the following hedges is best for the importer to fix the price in dollars?

a. Buying British pound call options

b. Buying British pound put options

c. Selling British pound put options

d. Selling British pound call options

03. An American importer of English clothing has contracted to pay an amount fixed in British pounds three months from now. If the importer worried that the US dollar might depreciate sharply against the British pound in the interim, it would be well advised to

a. buy pounds in the forward exchange market.

b. sell pounds in the forward exchange market.

c. buy dollars in the futures market.

d. sell dollars in the futures market.

04. An automobile company that uses the future market to set the price of steel to protect a profit against price increases is an example of

a. a short hedge.

b. a long hedge.

c. selling futures to protect the company from loss.

d. selling futures to protect against price declines.

05. A firm is planning to issue a callable bond with an 8% coupon rate and 10 years to maturity. A straight bond with a similar rate is priced at $1,000. If the value of the issuer's call option is estimated to be $50, what is the value of the callable bond?

a. $1,000   b. $950

c. $1,050   d. $900

06. How much must the stock be worth at expiration in order for a call holder to break even if the exercise price was $60 and the call premium was $3?

a. $57.00   b. $60.00

c. $61.50   d. $63.00

07. How much must the stock be worth at expiration in order for a put holder to break even if the exercise price was $60 and the put premium was $3?

a. $57.00   b. $60.00

c. $61.50   d. $63.00

08. A number of variables impact the value of options. These variables include all but which of the following :

a. Time to maturity.

b. Volatility of stock price per period.

c. Book value of common stock.

d. Exercise price.

09. What is a characteristic of a forward?

a. Traded on an exchange

b. Negotiated with a counter-party

c. Covers a stream of future payments

d. Must be settled daily

10. What is a characteristic of a swap?

a. Traded on an exchange

b. Only interest rates can be the underlying

c. Covers a stream of future payments

d. Must be settled daily

11. What is a characteristic of a future?

a. Gives the holder the right but not the obligation to buy or sell

b. Negotiated with a counter-party

c. Covers a stream of future payments

d. Must be settled daily

12. What is a characteristic of an option?

    a. Gives the holder the right but not the obligation to buy or sell

    b. Negotiated with a counter-party

    c. Covers a stream of future payments

    d. Must be settled daily

13. Which is true about the seller of a put option?

    a. They have the right to buy the underlying

    b. They have the right to sell the underlying

    c. They have the obligation to buy the underlying

    d. They have the obligation to sell the underlying

14. Which is true about the holder of a call option?

    a. They have the right to buy the underlying

    b. They have the right to sell the underlying

    c. They have the obligation to buy the underlying

    d. They have the obligation to sell the underlying

15. Which is true about the seller of a call option?

    a. They have the right to buy the underlying

    b. They have the right to sell the underlying

    c. They have the obligation to buy the underlying

    d. They have the obligation to sell the underlying

16. Which is true about the holder of a put option?

a. They have the right to buy the underlying

b. They have the right to sell the underlying

c. They have the obligation to buy the underlying

d. They have the obligation to sell the underlying

Solution

1	2	3	4	5	6	7	8	9	10
B	A	A	B	B	D	A	C	B	C

11	12	13	14	15	16
D	A	C	A	D	B

1. 예상거래의 위험의 제거 : 현금흐름 위험회피
   인식된 자산 또는 부채의 위험의 제거 : 공정가치 위험회피

2. 수출기업 : short hedge or buy put options
   수입기업 : long hedge or buy call options

3. 수출기업 : short hedge or buy put options
   수입기업 : long hedge or buy call options

4. 철강 회사의 철강가격 : short hedge or buy put options
   자동차 회사의 철강가격 : long hedge or buy call options

5. Callable bond = straight bond − value of call option = $1,000 − $50 = $950
   Puttable bond = straight bond + value of put option = $1,000 + $50 = $1,050

6. Break-even of call option = exercise price + call premium = $60 + $3 = $63

7. Break-even of put option = exercise price − put premium = $60 − $3 = $57

8. The Black-Scholes formula was option pricing using current stock prices, expected dividends, the option's strike price, expected interest rates, time to expiration and expected volatility.

9. forward : 장외거래

10. swap : 장외거래, 현금흐름교환, 통화스왑 및 이자율스왑

11. futures : 장내거래

12. option : 옵션 보유자는 매수 또는 매도 권리

13. seller of a put option : 기초자산 매수 의무

14. holder of a call option : 기초자산 매입 권리

15 seller of a call option : 기초자산 매도 의무

14. holder of a put option : 기초자산 매도 권리

04 ▷ Tasked-Based Simulation

Problem-1

KIM is considering an investment in Morgan Communications, whose stock currently sells for $60. A put option on Morgan's stock, with an exercise price of $55, has a market value of $3.06. Meanwhile, a call option on the stock with the same exercise price and time to maturity has a market value of $9.29. The market believes that at the expiration of the options the stock price will be either $70 or $50, with equal probability.

Required

1. What is the premium associated with the put option? The call option?

2. If Morgan's stock price increases to $70, what would be the return to an investor who bought a share of the stock? If the investor bought a call option on the stock? If the investor bought a put option on the stock?

3. If Morgan's stock price decreases to $50, what would be the return to an investor who bought a share of the stock? If the investor bought a call option on the stock? If the investor bought a put option on the stock?

4. If KIM buys 0.6 share of Morgan Communications and sells one call option on the stock, has she created a riskless hedged investment? What is the total value of her portfolio under each scenario?

5. If KIM buys 0.75 share of Morgan Communications and sells one call option on the stock, has she created a riskless hedged investment? What is the total value of her portfolio under each scenario?

Problem-2

You are the vice president of Micro, headquartered in Chicago, Illinois. All shareholders of the firm live in the United States. Earlier this month, you obtained a loan of 5 million Canadian dollars from a bank in Toronto to finance the construction of a new plant in Montreal. At the time the loan was received, the exchange rate was 75 U.S. cents to the Canadian dollar. By the end of the month, it has unexpectedly dropped to 70 cents.

Required

Has your company made a gain or loss as a result, and by how much?

Problem-3

Early in September 20X1, it took 245 Japanese yen to equal $1. Nearly 4 years later, in July 20X5 that exchange rate had fallen to 111 yen to $1. Assume the price of a Japanese-manufactured automobile was $9,000 in September 20X1 and that its price changes were in direct relation to exchange rates.

Required

1. Has the price, in dollars, of the automobile increased or decreased during the 22-year period because of changes in the exchange rate?

2. What would the dollar price of the automobile be in July 20X5, again assuming that the car's price changes only with exchange rates?

Problem-4

On January 2, Year 1, AIFA entered into three options contracts through its brokerage firm, Goldman Sachs. An analyst in the company's derivatives trading department is reviewing the confirmations for the three trades to get the details of the transactions.

	Trade confirmation			
	#1	#2	#3	#4
Underlying	ABC stock	DEF stock	GHI stock	JKL stock
Action	Buy	Sell	Buy	Sell
Option type	Call	Call	Put	Put
Quantity	10 contracts	30 contracts	60 contracts	20 contracts
Underlying shares	500	100	100	400
Term	90 days	60 days	90 days	30 days
Striking price	$22/share	$13/share	$30/share	$30/share
Premium	$3/share	$2.50share	$1.75/share	$2.75/share

Required

1. Use the information in the exhibits above to determine whether AIFA will benefit if the stock prices rise or fall.

	Trade confirmation			
	#1	#2	#3	#4
up				
down				

2. Calculate the profit or loss for the option on the ABC stock
   (1) if the stock goes to $30 at the maturity.
   (2) if the stock goes to $20 at the maturity.

3. Calculate the profit or loss for the option on the DEF stock
   (1) if the stock goes to $20 at the maturity.
   (2) if the stock goes to $10 at the maturity.

4. Calculate the profit or loss for the option on the GHI stock
   (1) if the stock goes to $25 at the maturity.
   (2) if the stock goes to $35 at the maturity.

5. Calculate the profit or loss for the option on the JKL stock
   (1) if the stock goes to $25 at the maturity.
   (2) if the stock goes to $35 at the maturity.

Problem-5

Suppose a financial manager buys call options on 50,000 barrels of oil with an exercise price of $25 per barrel. She simultaneously sells a put option on 50,000 barrels of oil with the same exercise price of $25 per barrel.

Required

Consider her gains and losses if oil prices are $20, $22, $25, $28, and $30.

Financial Management For the **US CPA** Exam

Chapter 08

Working Capital Management

Volume
8

Working Capital Management

01 　 Working Capital Management

1 　 Cash Conversion Cycle (CCC)

(1) Inventory conversion period (=DIO)

The average time required to convert materials into finished goods and then to sell those goods.

Inventory conversion period = Inventory ÷ COGS per day

(2) Receivable collection period (=DSO)

The average time required to convert the firm's receivables into cash.

Receivable collection period = Receivables ÷ Sales per day

(3) Payable deferral period (=DPO)

The average time between material purchase and payment.

Payable deferral period = Payables ÷ COGS (or Purchase) per day

(4) Operating cycle

The time period between the acquisition of inventory and the collection of cash from receivables.

> Operating cycle = Inventory conversion period + Receivable collection period

(5) Cash conversion cycle (=cash cycle)

The time between cash disbursement and cash collection.

> Cash conversion cycle = Operating cycle − Payable deferral period

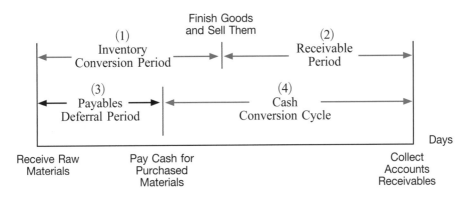

[Figure 8-1] cash conversion cycle

(6) Shortening the cash conversion cycle

The shorter cash conversion cycle, the better working capital management.

- Reducing the inventory conversion period by processing and selling goods more quickly.

- Reducing the receivables collection period by speeding up collections.

- Lengthening the payables deferral period by slowing down the firm's payments.

Example 8-1

Assume that average inventory is $10,000, average receivables balance is $3,000 and average payables balance is $2,500. Also annual sales are $40,000, cost of goods sold is $30,000. Compute the operating cycle and cash conversion cycle.

Solution

Inventory conversion period = $10,000 ÷ ($30,000 / 365) = 122 days
Receivables collection period = $3,000 ÷ ($40,000 / 365) = 27 days
Payables deferral period = $2,500 ÷ ($30,000 / 365) = 30 days
Operating cycle = 122 days + 27 days = 149 days
Cash conversion cycle = 122 days + 27 days − 30 days = 119 days

2 Current Asset Investment Policies

(1) Relaxed current asset investment policy

Relatively large amounts of cash, marketable securities, and inventories are carried, and a liberal credit policy results in a high level of receivables.

(2) Restricted current asset investment policy

Holdings of cash, marketable securities, inventories, and receivables are constrained.

(3) Moderate current asset investment policy

Between the relaxed and restricted policies.

3 Current Asset Financing Policies

(1) Current assets

1) Permanent current asset

Current assets that a firm must carry even at the low point of its cycle.

계절적 요인이나 일시적 요인과 관계없이 영업활동에 따라 일정한 추세로 유지되는 유동자산

2) Temporary current asset

Current assets that fluctuate with seasonal or cyclical variations in sales.

계절적 요인이나 일시적 요인에 의해서 변동성을 보이는 유동자산

(2) Maturities matching (= Moderate policy)

A financing policy that matches asset and liability maturities.

short-term, non-spontaneous debt financing = all temporary current assets

(3) Aggressive approach

short-term, non-spontaneous debt financing

= all temporary current assets and a prat of permanent current assets

(4) Conservative approach

short-term, non-spontaneous debt financing = a part of temporary current assets

[Figure 8-2] current asset financing policies

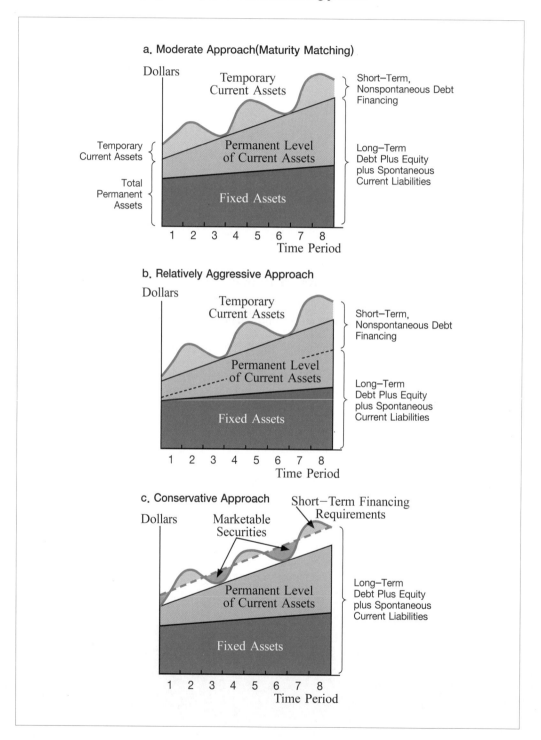

(5) Short-term debt versus long-term debt

1) Interest rate

Because the yield curve is normally upward-sloping, the cost of short-term debt is generally lower than that of long-term debt.

2) Risk

Short-term debt is riskier to the borrowing firm

3) Speed

Short-term loans can generally be negotiated much faster than long-term loans.

4) Flexibility

Short-term debt may offer greater flexibility.

5) Restrictions

Short-term credit agreements generally have fewer restrictions.

02 ⟩ Cash and Marketable Securities

1 Cash Management

(1) Reasons for Holding Cash

1) Transactions balance

A cash balance associated with routine payments and collections (for day-to-day operation)

2) Precautionary balance

A cash balance held in reserve for random, unforseen fluctuations in cash inflows and outflows.

3) Speculative balance

A cash balance that is held to enable the firm to take advantage of any bargain purchases that might arise.

4) Compensating balance

A bank balance that a firm must maintain to compensate the bank for services rendered or for granting a loan.

2 Float Management

(1) Float

The difference between book cash and bank cash, representing the net effect of checks in the process of clearing.

수표지급에서 추후 추심까지의 시간으로 미국에서는 보통 3일에서 5일 걸린다.

Float = Firm's available balance − Firm's book balance
Float $> 0 \rightarrow$ disbursement float $>$ collection float
Float $< 0 \rightarrow$ disbursement float $<$ collection float

Example 8-2

Suppose you have $5,000 on deposit. One day, you write a check for $1,000 to pay for books, and you deposit $2,000. What are your disbursement, collection, and net floats?

Solution

disbursement float = $5,000 − 4,000 = \$1,000$
collection float = $5,000 − 7,000 = -\$2,000$
net float = $1,000 − 2,000 = -\$1,000$

(2) Measuring float

Average daily float = average daily receipts/payments × weighted average delay

Float = Average daily disbursement float − Average daily collection float

Example 8-3

Suppose that each day you writes checks for $5,000 and receives checks for $3,000. If it takes five days for the checks written to clear and only four days for the deposits to clear, what is the float?

Solution

Average daily disbursement float = $5,000 \times 5$ days = $25,000$
Average daily collection float = $3,000 \times 4$ days = $12,000$
float = $25,000 - 12,000 = \$13,000$

(3) Float management

- Shorting collection float

- Extending disbursement float

e.g.) a New York supplier might be paid with checks drawn on a LA bank.

Shorting collection float	Extending disbursement float
Lock-box system Concentration banking Electronic Fund Transfer (EFT)	Zero-balance account Electronic Fund Transfer (EFT)

3 Electronic Fund Transfer (EFT)

Electronic Fund Transfer is a system in which funds are moved electronically between accounts without the use of checks. This system reduces float for both cash collection and cash disbursement.

4 Zero-Balance Account

A disbursement account in which the firm maintains a zero balance, transferring funds in from a master account only as needed to cover checks presented for payment.

Example 8-4

An organization has an opportunity to establish a zero balance account system using four different regional banks. The total amount of the maintenance and transfer fees is estimated to be $6,000 per annum. The organization believes that it will increase the float on its operating disbursements by an average of four days, and its cost of short-term funds is 4.5%. Assuming the organization estimates its average daily operating disbursements to be $40,000 what decision should the organization make regarding this opportunity?

Solution

1) Benefit = $40,000 × 4 days × 4.5% = $7,200
2) Cost = $6,000

Therefore, establish the zero balance account system because it results in estimated net savings of $1,200.

5 Lock-Box System

Special post office boxes set up to intercept and speed up accounts receivable payments.

우체국에 lock-box를 만들어 고객이 수표를 lock-box로 우송시키면, 기업의 거래은행이 이를 수집하여 그 기업의 계좌에 입금시키는 방법이다.

Example 8-5

A firm is evaluating whether to establish a lockbox system. The bank will charge $30,000 per year for the lockbox and the firm will save approximately $8,000 in internal processing costs. The firm estimates that the float will be reduced by three days if the lockbox system is put into place. Assuming that average daily cash receipts are $350,000 and short-term interest rates are 4%, what decision should the firm make regarding the lockbox system?

Solution

- Incremental benefit = $350,000 × 3 days × 4% = $42,000
- Incremental cost = $30,000 − $8,000 = $22,000
- Incremental profit = 42,000 − 22,000 = $20,000

  Establish the lockbox system because the net benefit is $20,000.

6 Concentration Banking

The practice of and procedures for moving cash from multiple banks into the firm's main accounts.

판매 및 입금지역이 널리 퍼져 있는 경우 각 지역별로 집중은행을 두어 각 지역의 지사를 통하여 수금된 것을 집중은행에 예치하도록 하는 기법

Example 8-6

A firm is evaluating whether to establish a concentration banking system. The bank will charge $5,000 per year for maintenance and transfer fees. The firm estimates that the float will be reduced by two days if the concentration banking is put into place. Assuming that average daily receipts are $115,000 and short-term interest rates are 4%, what decision should the firm make regarding the concentration banking system?

Solution

- Incremental benefit = $115,000 × 2 days × 4% = $9,200
- Incremental cost = $5,000
- Incremental profit = 9,200 − 5,000 = $4,200

Establish the concentration banking system because the net benefit is $4,200.

7 Marketable Securities

유가증권의 보유 목적은 주로 현금보유 보다는 더 높은 수익률과 빨리 현금화 할 수 있는 유동성 때문이다. 따라서 유가증권의 가장 중요한 요소는 다음과 같다.

- maturity : interest rate risk
- default risk
- marketability : liquidity risk
- taxability

(1) Treasury bills (T-Bills)

- Issued by federal government
- Short term (3 month 6 month)
- Zero-coupon securities : Issued at discount (할인채)
- No default risk, no liquidity risk, no interest rate risk

(2) Municipal securities

- Issued by states or municipalities
- Exempt from federal taxes
- More default risk than U.S. Treasury issues and are less marketable.

(3) Federal agency securities (공채)

- Issued by government agency
- Slightly higher yield than Treasury securities.
- Examples : Federal Home Loan Bank, Fannie Mae, Freddie Mac, Sallie Mae

(4) Certificate of Deposits (CD ; 양도성예금증서)

- Short-term loans to commercial banks.

  은행이 정기예금에 대하여 발행하는 무기명의 증서로서 예금자는 제3자에게 양도가가능한 정기예금증서이다.

- More default risk than U.S. Treasury issues.

- Secondary market exists

- CD는 treasury증권보다는 default risk가 더 크다.

(5) Commercial paper (CP ; 기업어음)

- Issued by large, high credit rating companies

- Unsecured

- The default risk of commercial paper depends on the financial strength of the issuer.

- Maturity less than one year

- There is no active secondary market.

(6) Repurchase agreements (repos)

- Sales of government securities by a bank or securities dealer with an agreement to repurchase.

- An investor buys some Treasury securities from a bond dealer and simultaneously agrees to sell them back at a later date at a specified higher price.

(7) Money market funds (MMF)

투자신탁회사가 고객들의 자금을 모아 펀드를 구성한 다음 금리가 높은 만기 1년 미만의 기업어음(CP) · 양도성예금증서(CD)등 주로 단기금융상품에 투자하여 얻은 수익을 고객에게 되돌려주는 만기 30일 이내의 초단기금융상품이다.

(8) Equity and Debt securities

Higher risk and higher return than T-securities and other money market instruments.

03 ▷ Accounts Receivables

1 Credit Policy

(1) Credit period

The length of time buyers are given to pay for their purchases.

long credit periods	
Benefits	Costs
increase sales	lengthen the cash conversion cycle increase bad debt

(2) Discount

Price reductions given for early payment.

e.g.) 2/10, n/30 : 2% discount be given if the customer pays within 10 days.

offering discount	
Benefits	Costs
increase sales quantity shorten the cash conversion cycle	lower sales revenues

(3) Credit standards

The required financial strength of acceptable credit customers.

tighter credit standards	
Benefits	Costs
lower bad debt	lose sales

(4) Collection policy

Degree of toughness in enforcing to collect past due accounts.

tough	
Benefits	Costs
collect cash quickly	negative relationship with customers

Example 8-7

ZARA company plans to relax its credit policy. ZARA's variable costs are 70% of sales and its required rate of return is 12%. The company projects that annual sales will increase from $360,000 to $432,000, but the average collection period on receivable will go from 30 days to 40 days. Assuming a 360-day year, what is the company's benefit (loss) from the planned change in credit policy

Solution

(1) Incremental revenue = $432,000 - 360,000 = \$72,000$

(2) Incremental variable costs = $\$72,000 \times 0.7 = \$50,400$

(3) Incremental interest costs

$$= (432,000 \times 0.7 \times 12\% \times 40/360) - (360,000 \times 0.7 \times 12\% \times 30/360)$$

$$= \$1,512$$

$\therefore$ incremental benefit = $72,000 - 50,400 - 1,512 = \$20,088$

2 Monitoring Accounts Receivables

(1) Days sales outstanding (DSO)

$$DSO = Receivables \div Average\ Sales\ per\ day$$

(2) Aging schedules

매출채권 기말잔액이 $20,000이고 신용기간이 60일 인 경우

Aging days	Amount	Percentage
0 – 30 days	$14,000	70%
31 – 60 days	3,000	15%
61 – 90 days	2,000	10%
Over 90days	1,000	5%
Total	$20,000	100%

04 〉 Inventory Management

1 Inventory Costs

(1) Carrying costs (=Holding costs, 재고유지비용)

Carrying costs represent all of the direct and opportunity costs of keeping inventory on hand.

- Storage and tracking costs

- Insurance and taxes

- Losses due to obsolescence, deterioration, or theft

- The opportunity cost of capital on the invested amount

(2) Shortage costs

Shortage costs are costs associated with having inadequate inventory on hand.

shortage costs = ordering costs + stock-out costs

1) Ordering costs (Restocking costs, 주문비용)

필요한 물품을 주문해서 입수될 때까지의 모든 비용

- the costs of placing an order with suppliers : freight costs, inspection costs

- the costs of setting up a production run

2) Stock out costs (Costs related to safety reserves, 재고부족비용)

수요자의 구매요구가 있음에도 불구하고 재고가 부족하여 판매하지 못함으로써 발생되는 모든 손실

- opportunity losses such as lost sales

- loss of customer reputation

(3) Inventory management

1) Trade-off in inventory management

inventory levels ↑ : shortage costs ↓ vs carrying costs ↑

2) The goal of inventory management

minimize the sum of carrying costs and shortage costs.

2 Economic Order Quantity (EOQ)

Economic order quantity (EOQ) is the order quantity that minimizes the total holding costs and ordering costs. (주문비용과 재고유지비가 최소가 되게 하는 1회 주문량)

(1) Total costs (총재고비용)

Total costs = carrying costs + ordering costs

Order size ↑ : ordering cost ↓ vs carrying costs ↑
Order size ↓ : ordering cost ↑ vs carrying costs ↓

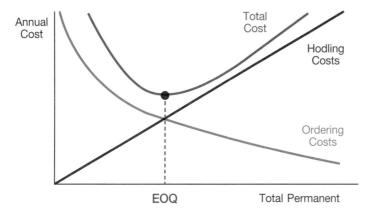

[Figure 8-3] Total cost

(2) EOQ formula

1) Carrying costs

Total carrying costs = Average inventory x Carrying costs per unit

$$= (Q/2) \times C$$

where : Q = restocking quantity each time

2) Ordering costs

Total ordering cost = Fixed cost per order x Number of orders

$$= O \times (D/Q)$$

where : D = Total demand units per year

3) Total costs

Total costs = Total carrying costs + Total ordering cost

$$= (Q/2) \times C + O \times (D/Q)$$

the minimum point where the two lines cross

$$EOQ = \sqrt{\frac{\cdot 2 \times D \times O}{C}}$$

D = demand in units per year, C = carrying costs per unit, O = order cost per order

4) EOQ formula assumption

The EOQ formula is used in situations where demand, ordering, and holding costs remain constant over time.

Example 8-8

NIKE Shoes begins each period with 100 pairs of hiking boots in stock. This stock is depleted each period and reordered. NIKE sells a total of 600 pairs of boots in a year. The restocking cost is $20 per order and the carrying cost per pair of boots per year is $3.

(1) What are the total carrying costs for the hiking boots?
(2) How many times per year does NIKE restock? What are total restocking costs? (3) What size orders should NIKE place to minimize costs? How often will NIKE restock? What are the total costs?

Solution

(1) total carrying costs = $(100 \div 2) \times \$3 = \$150$

(2) number of orders = $600 \div 100 = 6$ times per year

total ordering costs = 6 orders $\times \$20 = \$120$

(3) $EOQ = \sqrt{\dfrac{2 \times 600 \times \$20}{\$3}} = 89.44$ units

number of orders = $600 \div 89.44 = 6.71$ times per year

total carrying costs = $(89.44 \div 2) \times \$3 = \$134.16$

total ordering costs = 6.71 orders $\times \$20 = \$134.16$

total costs = $\$268.33$

3 Reorder Point

(1) Reorder points (발주점)

the times at which the firm will actually place its inventory orders.

(2) Safety stocks (안전재고량)

the minimum level of inventory that a firm keeps on hand.

수요나 공급의 추정 오차에 따른 재고 부족을 방지하기 위해 여분으로 보유

Safety stock ↑ : Stock-out cost ↓ vs carrying costs ↑
Safety stock ↓ : Stock-out cost ↑ vs carrying costs ↓

(3) Lead time

상품의 주문일시와 인도일시 사이에 경과된 시간

Lead time ↓ : inventory levels ↓
Lead time ↑ : inventory levels ↑

(4) Reorder point formula

Reorder point = (Daily demand units × Lead time) + Safety stock

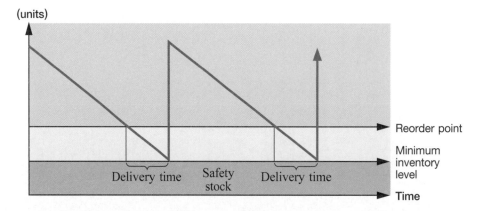

[Figure 8-4] Reorder points and safety stocks

Example 8-9

The following information pertains to wallets that are sold by ABC MART.
Annual sales units : 8,000 units
Weeks per year : 50 weeks
Lead-time : 5 week
Safety stock : 1,200 units
Order quantity : 1,600 units

Solution

Weekly sales = 8,000 ÷ 50 = 160 units
Reorder Point = 160 × 5 + 1,200 = 2,000 units

4 Push System

(1) The push system of inventory control

- Forecasting inventory needs to meet customer demand.

- Produce enough product to meet the forecast demand.

- Sell (=push) the goods to the consumer.

  e.g.) warm jackets get pushed to clothing retailers as summer ends and the fall and
  winter seasons start.

(2) Materials Requirement Planning (MRP)

- Computer-based information system designed to calculate the materials and components
  needed to manufacture a product.

- bill of materials + inventory data + master production schedule (MPS)
  → calculate required materials

- MRP is considered a "push" system

- Manufacturing Resource Planning (MRP II) : 1983

- Enterprise Resource Planning (ERP) : 1990

(3) Advantages

- Economies of scale (규모의 경제)

- Decrease stock out costs

(4) Disadvantages

- Forecasts are often inaccurate

- Increase carrying costs

- High inventories and waste

- Bullwhip effect (채찍효과)

5 Pull System

(1) The pull system of inventory control

- Begins with a customer's order.

- Only produce enough product to meet customer's orders.

(2) Just-in-time (JIT system)

- Keep inventory levels to a minimum by only having enough inventor to meet customer demand.

- JIT is considered a "pull" system

(3) Advantages

- Reduce inventory levels

- Decrease carrying costs

- Decrease bullwhip effect

- Waste reduction

(3) Disadvantages

- Ordering dilemmas, such as a supplier not being able to get a shipment out on time.

- Increase stock out costs and customer dissatisfaction.

- Reduce economies of scale.

6 Just In Time (JIT)

(1) JIT (적기생산방식)

- 1970년대 일본의 도요타(Toyota)자동차가 원가절감을 위하여 만든 생산방식

- Demand-pull system

  제조업체가 부품업체로부터 부품을 필요한 시기에 필요한 수량만큼만 공급받아 재고가 없도록 해주는 재고관리 시스템

- Kanban

  Kanban is a card with an inventory number that's attached to a part. A part is only manufactured or ordered if there is a kanban card for it.

(2) Lean production (Lean)

- A manufacturing method used for eliminating waste within the manufacturing system.

- Reduce the waste generated from uneven workloads and overburden in order to increase value and reduce costs.

- Lean is based on the Toyota Production System (TPS)

- Wastes : unnecessary transportation, excess inventory, waiting, defects

- Continual process improvement (Kaizen)

- Identify value from the customer's perspective

(3) Characteristics of JIT

- Reduce inventory level, ideally to zero

- Reduce production cycle time

- Production flexibility using manufacturing cells

- Solving production problems immediately

- A few reliable, quality-oriented suppliers who inspects goods and makes frequent delivery.

- Back-flush costing

- Increase number of orders

(4) Advantages

- Decrease inventory carrying costs

- Decrease defects

- Increase inventory turnover and productivity

- Quickly move from one product to another.

- Spend less money on raw materials

(5) Achilles point in JIT

The success of the JIT production process relies on steady production, high-quality workmanship, no machine breakdowns, and reliable suppliers.

- Suppliers do not deliver goods promptly

- Poorly trained employees

- Unreliable technology and equipment

- Higher manufacturing costs

7 Supply Chain Management (SCM)

(1) Supply chain management

- the handling of the entire production flow of a good or service, starting from the raw components all the way to delivering the final product to the consumer.

- ERP and CRM help SCM by connecting firm to suppliers and customers.

(2) ERP (Enterprises Resource Planning)

통합적인 컴퓨터 데이터베이스를 구축해 회사의 자금, 회계, 구매, 생산, 판매 등 모든 업무의 흐름을 효율적으로 자동 조절해주는 전산 시스템

(3) CRM (Customer Relationship Management)

고객과 관련된 기업의 내/외부 자료를 분석, 통합하여 고객 특성에 기초한 마케팅 활동을 계획하고, 지원하며, 평가하는 과정.

05 ⟩ Short-Term Financing

1 Accounts Payable (Trade Credit)

(1) Accounts payable

- Normally no interest when paid on time.
- Spontaneous source of financing : A/P
- Non-spontaneous source of financing : short-term debt
- Discount : 2/10, n/30
- Stretching accounts payable : the practice of deliberately paying late.

(2) Nominal annual cost of trade credit if the cash discount is not taken

$$\text{Nominal annual cost} = \frac{\text{Discount \%}}{100\% - \text{Discount \%}} \times \frac{365\ (360)\text{days}}{\text{Total pay period} - \text{Discount period}}$$

Example 8-10

Calculate the nominal annual cost of not taking discount with the following terms

(1) 2/10, n/30 (2) 1/10, n/30 (3) 2/10, n/20 (4) 2/10, n/45 (5) 3/10, n/30

Solution

(1) Nominal annual interest = $(2/98) \times (365/20) = 37.2\%$

(2) Nominal annual interest = $(1/99) \times (365/20) = 18.4\%$

(3) Nominal annual interest = $(2/98) \times (365/10) = 74.5\%$

(4) Nominal annual interest = $(2/98) \times (365/35) = 21.3\%$

(5) Nominal annual interest = $(3/97) \times (365/20) = 56.4\%$

2 Bank Loans

(1) Promissory note

A document specifying the terms and conditions of a loan, including the amount, interest rate, and repayment schedule.

(2) Interest rate

- Interest rate can be either fixed or floating.
- Floating
  indexed to the bank' prime rate, to the T−bill rate, to the LIBOR.
- Bank uses a 360- or 365-day year for purposes of calculating interest.
- The indicated rate is a nominal rate, and the effective annual rate is generally higher.

(3) Compensating balance

A minimum checking account balance that a firm must maintain.

Example 8−11

Dior Company's bank requires a compensating balance of 20% on a $100,000 loan. If the stated interest on the loan is 7%, what is the effective cost of the loan?

Solution

$$\text{Effective interest} = 7\% \times \frac{10}{\$100,000 - \$20,000} = 8.75\%$$

(4) Line of credit

An arrangement in which a bank agrees to lend up to a specified maximum amount of funds during a designated period.

- Revolving credit agreement

A formal, committed line of credit extended by a bank or other lending institution.

(5) Letter of credit

The bank issuing the letter promises to make a loan if certain conditions are met. The letter guarantees payment on a shipment of goods provided that the goods arrive as promised.

3 Commercial Paper (CP)

- Issued by large, high credit rating companies
- Unsecured and large amount
- Maturity less than one year

4 Secured Loan

A loan backed by collateral, often inventories or accounts receivable.

(1) Accounts receivable financing

1) Pledging

provide receivables as collateral to get bank loans

2) Factoring

- Firm sells receivables to finance company

- Finance company accepts receivables and advance funds

- Finance company charge factor fee plus interest rate on the fund

Example 8-12

A company enters into an agreement with a firm who will factor the company's accounts receivable. The factor agrees to buy the company's receivables, which average $100,000 per month and have an average collection period of 30 days. The factor will advance up to 80% of the face value of receivables at an annual rate of 10% and charge a fee of 2% on all receivables purchased. The controller of the company estimates that the company would save $18,000 in collection expenses over the year. Fees and interest are not deducted in advance. Assuming a 360-day year, what is the annual cost of financing?

Solution

Total amount paid to the factor

$= \{\$100,000 \times 80\% \times 10\%\} + \{\$100,000 \times 12 \text{ months} \times 2\%\} = \$32,000$

Net cost $= \$32,000 - \$18,000 = \$14,000$

Annual interest $= \$14,000 \div \$80,000 = 17.5\%$

※ Asset−backed securities (ABS)

a financial security collateralized by a pool of assets such as loans, leases, credit card debt, royalties or receivables.

06 》 Multiple Choice

01. A firm is given payment terms of 3/10, net 90 and forgoes the discount paying on the net due date. Using a 360-day year and ignoring the effects of compounding, what is the effective annual interest rate cost? (CMA)

a. 12.0%   b. 12.4%

c. 13.5%   d. 13.9%.

02. All of the following are reasons for holding cash except for the (CMA)

a. precautionary motive.   b. transactions motive.

c. motive to make a profit.   d. motive to meet future needs.

03. All of the following can be utilized by a firm in managing its cash outflows except (CMA)

a. zero-balance accounts.   b. centralization of payables.

c. controlled disbursement accounts.   d. lock-box system.

04. Clauson Inc. grants credit terms of 1/15, net 30 and projects gross sales for the year of $2,000,000. The credit manager estimates that 40% of customers pay on the 15th day, 40% of the 30th day and 20% on the 45th day. Assuming uniform sales and a 360-day year, what is the projected amount of overdue receivables? (CMA)

a. $50,000   b. $83,333

c. $116,676   d. $400,000

05. The establishment and maintenance of a zero-balance account (ZBA) typically reduces all of the following except (CMA)

a. the cost of cash management.   b. the disbursement float.

c. excess bank balances.   d. management time.

06. Which one of the following instruments would be least appropriate for a corporate treasurer to utilize for temporary investment of cash? (CMA)

a. U.S. Treasury bills   b. Money market mutual funds

c. Commercial paper   d. Municipal bonds

07. Which one of the following statements best characterizes U.S. Treasury bills? (CMA)

a. They have no coupon rate, no interest rate risk, and are issued at par.

b. They have an active secondary market, one to twenty-four month maturities, and monthly interest payments.

c. They have an active secondary market, the interest received is exempt from federal income tax, and there is no interest rate risk.

d. They have no coupon rate, no default risk, and interest received is subject to federal income tax.

08. The Duoplan Company is determining the most appropriate source of short-term funding. Trade credit terms from suppliers are 2/30, net 90. The rate for borrowing at the bank is 12%. The company has also been approached by an investment banker offering to issue Duoplan's commercial paper. The commercial paper would be issued quarterly in increments of $9.1 million with net proceeds of $8.8 million. Which option should the firm select? (CMA)

a. The trade discount, because it provides the lowest cost of funds.

b. Bank borrowing, because it provides the lowest cost of funds.

c. Commercial paper, because it provides the lowest cost of funds.

d. The costs are so similar that the decision is a matter of convenience.

09. Northville Products is changing its credit terms from net 30 to 2/10, net 30. The least likely effect of this change would be a(n) (CMA)

a. increase in sales.

b. shortening of the cash conversion cycle.

c. increase in short-term borrowings.

d. lower number of days sales outstanding.

10. A credit manager considering whether to grant trade credit to a new customer is most likely to place primary emphasis on (CMA)

a. profitability ratios.

b. valuation ratios.

c. growth ratios.

d. liquidity ratios.

11. Locar Corporation had net sales last year of $18,600,000 (of which 20% were installment sales). It also had an average accounts receivable balance of $1,380,000. Credit terms are 2/10, net 30. Based on a 360-day year, Locar's average collection period last year was (CMA)

a. 26.2 days

b. 26.7 days

c. 27.3 days

d. 33.4 days

12. All of the following are carrying costs of inventory except (CMA)

a. storage costs.

b. insurance.

c. shipping costs.

d. opportunity costs.

13. Carnes Industries uses the Economic Order Quantity (EOQ) model as part of its inventory control program. An increase in which one of the following variables would increase the EOQ? (CMA)

a. Carrying cost rate
b. Purchase price per unit
c. Ordering costs
d. Safety stock level

14. Ferndale Distributors is reviewing its inventory policy with respect to safety stocks of its most popular product. Four safety stock levels were analyzed and annual stock-out costs estimated for each level. (CMA)

Safety Stock	Stockout Costs
1,000 units	$3,000
1,250 units	2,000
1,500 units	1,000
1,500 units	0

The cost of this product is $20 per unit, holding costs are 4% per year, and the cost of short-term funds is 10% per year. What is the optimal safety stock level?

a. 1,000 units
b. 1,250 units
c. 1,500 units
d. 2,000 units

15. Which one of the following is not explicitly considered in the standard calculation of Economic Order Quantity (EOQ)? (CMA)

a. Level of sales
b. Fixed ordering costs
c. Carrying costs
d. Quantity discounts

16. Which one of the following statements concerning the economic order quantity (EOQ) is correct? (CMA)

    a. The EOQ results in the minimum ordering cost and minimum carrying cost.
    b. Increasing the EOQ is the best way to avoid stockouts.
    c. The EOQ model assumes constantly increasing usage over the year.
    d. The EOQ model assumes that order delivery times are consistent.

17. Moss Products uses the Economic Order Quantity(EOQ) model as part of its inventory management process. A decrease in which one of the following variables would increase the EOQ? (CMA)

    a. Annual sales   b. Cost per order
    c. Safety stock level   d. Carrying costs

18. Assume that the following inventory values are determined to be appropriate for Louger Company.

    Sales   = 1,000 units
    Carrying costs = 20% of inventory value
    Purchase price = $10 per unit
    Cost per order = $10

    What is the economic order quantity (EOQ) for Louger? (CMA)

    a. 45 units   b. 100 units
    c. 141 units   d. 1,000 units.

19. Of the following, the working capital financing policy that would subject a firm to the greatest level of risk is the one where the firm finances (CMA)

   a. fluctuating current assets with short-term debt.

   b. permanent current assets with long-term debt.

   c. fluctuating current assets with long-term debt.

   d. permanent current assets with short-term debt.

20. Dudley Products is given terms of 2/10, net 45 by its suppliers. If Dudley forgoes the cash discount and instead pays the suppliers 5 days after the net due date, what is the annual interest rate cost (using a 360-day year)? (CMA)

   a. 18.0%   b. 18.4%

   c. 21.0%   d. 24.5%.

Solution

1	2	3	4	5	6	7	8	9	10
D	C	D	A	B	D	D	B	C	D
11	12	13	14	15	16	17	18	19	20
B	C	C	C	D	D	D	B	D	B

1. Trade discount = $(3 \div 97) \times (360/80) = 13.92\%$

2. 현금보유목적은 거래목적, 차입목적, 예방목적, 투자목적으로 구분되며 수익창출이 목적이면 현금보다는 유가증권이 더 바람직하다.

3. Lock−box system은 출금관리가 아닌 입금관리 방법이다.

4. Receivables = DSO × Sales / 360
   = 45 days × $2,000,000 × 20% / 360 = $50,000

5. Zero−balance account (ZBA)는 출금기간을 증가시키는 출금관리 방법이다.

6. 단기 유동성을 요구하는 Marketable Securities가 적합한 상품이며, 지방채는 국채와는 달리 유동성 위험이 있기 때문에 부적절하다.

7. T/B은 무이자 단기채권이며, T/N or T/B는 이자부 장기채권으로 모두 국채이므로 채무불이행 위험은 없지만 지방채와는 달리 이자소득 과세대상이다.

8. 3가지 방안에 대한 k를 계산한 후 가장 낮은 금리로 조달한다.
   Trade discount = $(2 \div 98) \times 360\text{days} / 60\text{days} = 12.25\%$,
   Borrowing = 12%
   CP = $(9.1 - 8.8) \div 8.8 \times 4 = 13.64\%$

9. n/30 → 2/10, n/30으로 변경하면 매출증가, 매출채권 회수기간 감소, cash conversion cycle 감소하여 유동성이 좋아지므로 단기차입은 감소한다.

10. 순운전자본관리의 가장 중요한 요소는 유동성이다.

11. DSO = $1,380,000 ÷ {$18,600,000 / 360 days} = 26.7 days

12. Shipping costs는 저장비용이 아닌 주문비용이다.

13. EOQ 공식에서 D와 O에 비례하지만, C와는 반비례한다.
    또한 Safety stock level과는 무관하다.

14. Total cost를 최소화 하는 안전재고를 구하면 1,500개이다.

Safety stocks	Carrying costs	Stockout costs	Total costs
1000units	$2800	$3000	$5800
1250	3500	2000	5500
1500	4200	1000	5200
2000	5600	0	5600

Carrying costs = safety stock × $20 × 14%

15. EOQ 공식에는 수량할인이 존재하지 않는다는 가정이 필요하다.

16. EOQ의 가정
    1) 연간수요 (D)가 확정적으로 알 수 있다.
    2) Cost per purchase order와 carrying cost per unit는 주문량과 관계없이 일정하다.
    3) Quantity discount가 존재하지 않는다.

17. EOQ 공식에서 D와 O에 비례하지만, C와는 반비례한다.
    또한 Safety stock level과는 무관하다.

18. EOQ $= \sqrt{\dfrac{2 \times 1,000 \times \$10}{\$10 \times 0.2}}$ = 100 units

19. c가 가장 보수적인 방법이고, d가 가장 공격적인 방법이다.

20. Trade discount = (2 ÷ 98) × 360days / 40days = 18.36%

07 Tasked-Based Simulation

Problem-1

Indicate by a (+), (−), or (0) whether each of the following events would probably cause accounts receivable (A/R), sales, and profits to increase, decrease, or be affected in an indeterminate manner:

	A/R	Sales	Profits
(1)			
(2)			
(3)			
(4)			

(1) The firm tightens its credit standards

(2) The terms of trade are changed from 2/10, net 30, to 3/10, net 30.

(3) The terms are changed from 2/10, net 30, to 3/10, net 40.

(4) The credit manager gets tough with past-due accounts.

Problem-2

KIM has $15 million of sales, $2 million of inventories, $3 million of receivables, and $1 million of payables. Its cost of goods sold is 80 percent of sales, and it finances working capital with bank loans at an 8 percent rate.

Required

1. What is KIM's cash conversion cycle (CCC)?

2. If KIM could lower its inventories and receivables by 10 percent each and increase its payables by 10 percent, all without affecting either sales or cost of goods sold, what would the new CCC be, how much cash would be freed up, and how would that affect pre−tax profits?

Problem-3

Cash conversion cycle The Zocco Corporation has an inventory conversion period of 75 days, an average collection period of 38 days, and a payables deferral period of 30 days.

Required

1. What is the length of the cash conversion cycle?

2. If Zocco' annual sales are $3,421,875 and all sales are on credit, what is the investment in accounts receivable?

3. How many times per year does Zocco turn over its inventory?

Problem-4

HARLEY Company sells on terms of 3/10, net 30. Total sales for the year are $912,500; 40 percent of the customers pay on the 10th day and take discounts, while the other 60 percent pay, on average, 40 days after their purchases.

Required

1. What is the days'sales outstanding?

2. What is the average amount of receivables?

3. What is the percentage cost of trade credit to customers who take the discount and to those who do not take it?

4. What would happen to its accounts receivable if HARLEY toughened up on its collection policy with the result that all nondiscount customers paid on the 30th day?

The HONDA Corporation produces motorcycle batteries. HONDA turns out 1,500 batteries a day at a cost of $6 per battery for materials and labor. It takes the firm 22 days to convert raw materials into a battery. HONDA allows its customers 40 days in which to pay for the batteries, and the firm generally pays its suppliers in 30 days.

Required

1. What is the length of HONDA' cash conversion cycle?

2. At a steady state in which HONDA produces 1,500 batteries a day, what amount of working capital must it finance?

3. By what amount could HONDA reduce its working capital financing needs if it was able to stretch its payables deferral period to 35 days?

4. HONDA' management is trying to analyze the effect of a proposed new production process on its working capital investment. The new production process would allow HONDA to decrease its inventory conversion period to 20 days and to increase its daily production to 1,800 batteries. However, the new process would cause the cost of materials and labor to increase to $7. Assuming the change does not affect the average collection period (40 days) or the payables deferral period (30 days), what will be the length of its cash conversion cycle and its working capital financing requirement if the new production process is implemented?

Problem-6

The Ritz-Carlton Corporation is investigating the optimal level of current assets for the coming year. Management expects sales to increase to approximately $2 million as a result of an asset expansion presently being undertaken. Fixed assets total $1 million, and the firm plans to maintain a 60 percent debt ratio. Ritz-Carlton's interest rate is currently 8 percent on both short-term and longer-term debt (which the firm uses in its permanent structure). Three alternatives regarding the projected current asset level are under consideration: (1) a tight policy where current assets would be only 45 percent of projected sales, (2) a moderate policy where current assets would be 50 percent of sales, and (3) a relaxed policy where current assets would be 60 percent of sales. Earnings before interest and taxes should be 12 percent of total sales, and the federal-plus-state tax rate is 40 percent.

Required

1. What is the expected return on equity under each current asset level?

2. In this problem, we assume that expected sales are independent of the current asset policy. Is this a valid assumption?

3. How would the firm' risk be affected by the different policies?

Problem-7

The Hardin-Gehr Corporation (HGC) began operations 5 years ago as a small firm serving customers in the Detroit area. However, its reputation and market area grew quickly, and today HGC has customers all over the United States. Despite its broad customer base, HGC has maintained its headquarters in Detroit, and it keeps its central billing system there. On average, it takes 5 days from the time customers mail in payments until HGC can receive, process, and deposit them. HGC would like to set up a lockbox collection system, which it estimates would reduce the time lag from customer mailing to deposit by 3 days—ringing it down to 2 days. HGC receives an average of $1,400,000 in payments per day.

Required

1. How much free cash would HGC generate if it implemented the lockbox system? Would this be a one-time cash flow or a recurring one, assuming the company ceases to grow? How would growth affect your answer?

2. If HGC has an opportunity cost of 10 percent, how much is the lockbox system worth on an annual basis?

3. What is the maximum monthly charge HGC should pay for the lockbox system?

Problem-8

Your neighbor goes to the post office once a month and picks up two checks, one for $20,000 and one for $4,000. The larger check takes four days to clear after it is deposited; the smaller one takes six days.

Required

1. What is the total float for the month?

2. What is the average daily float?

3. What are the average daily receipts and weighted average delay?

Financial Management For the US CPA Exam

Chapter 09

Business Combinations and Divestitures

Volume
8

Business Combinations and Divestitures

1 Motivations

(1) Synergy

- The condition wherein the whole is greater than the sum of its parts.

- The post-merger value exceeds the sum of the separate companies' pre-merger values.

(2) Diversification

(3) Tax benefits

(4) Purchase of assets below their replacement cost

(5) Personal benefits for managers

(6) Achieving more rapid growth

(7) Increased market power

Example 9-1

Firms A and B are competitors with very similar assets and business risks. Both are all-equity firms with aftertax cash flows of $10 million per year forever, and both have an overall cost of capital of 10 percent. Firm A is thinking of buying Firm B. The aftertax cash flow from the merged firm would be $21 million per year. Does the merger generate synergy?

Solution

Synergy = ($20 ÷ 0.10) − ($21 ÷ 0.10) = $10 million

2 Types of Merger

(1) Horizontal merger

A combination of two firms that produce the same type of good or service.

e.g.) Volkswagen's 2012 acquisition of Porsche

(2) Vertical merger

A merger between a firm and one of its suppliers or customers (supply chain) .

- forward integration : an ice cream manufacturer + a restaurant chain

- backward integration : an ice cream manufacturer + a farm

(3) Conglomerate merger

A merger between two firms completely unrelated.

e.g.) Walt Disney's 1995 acquisition of American Broadcasting Company (ABC)

3 Forms of Integration

(1) Merger (흡수합병)

The complete absorption of one company by another, wherein the acquiring firm retains its identity and the target firm ceases to exist as a separate entity.

(2) Consolidation (신설합병)

A merger in which an entirely new firm is created and both the acquired and target firms cease to exist.

(3) Acquisition of stock (주식인수)

The target company becomes a subsidiary of the acquiring firm.

4 Takeovers

(1) A friendly takeover

A takeover whose terms are approved by the managements of both companies.

(2) A hostile takeover

A takeover in which the target firm's management resists acquisition.

(3) Tender offer

The offer of one firm to buy the stock of another by going directly to the stockholders, frequently (but not always) over the opposition of the target company's management.

회사의 경영권을 획득하거나 강화하기 위하여 불특정 다수인으로부터 주식 등을 집단적으로 장외에서 매수하는 방법

(4) Proxy fight

An attempt to gain control of a firm by soliciting stockholders to vote for a new management team.

다수의 주주로부터 주주총회에서의 의결권 행사 위임장을 확보하는 전략.

(5) White knight

A friendly third party that comes to the rescue of the target company.

매수대상기업의 경영자에게 우호적인 기업 인수자.

(6) Poison pill

A poison pill gives current shareholders the right to purchase additional shares of stock at extremely attractive prices (at a discount to current market value)

신주인수권등을 발행하여 주식수를 희석화시키는 전략

(7) Green mail

A payoff to the potential acquirer to terminate the hostile takeover attempt.

경영권을 담보로 보유주식을 시가보다 비싸게 되파는 행위

(8) Golden parachutes

Compensation agreements between the target and its senior management that give the managers lucrative cash payouts if they leave the target company after a merger.

인수대상 기업이 CEO가 인수로 인하여 임기 전에 사임하게 될 경우를 대비하여 거액의 보수를 받을 권리를 사전에 고용계약에 기재하여 기업의 인수 비용을 높이는 방법.

(9) Crown jewel defense

Selling a subsidiary or major asset to a neutral third party.

(10) Going-private

Transactions in which all publicly owned stock in a firm is replaced with complete equity ownership by a private group.

(11) Leveraged buyouts (LBOs)

Going-private transactions in which a large percentage of the money used to buy the stock is borrowed. Oftentimes, incumbent management is involved.

5 Method of Payment

The two basic methods of payment are a securities offering and a cash offering.
Factors that should be considered.

- Distribution between risk and reward for the acquirer and target shareholders.
- Relative valuations of companies involved.
- Changes in capital structure.

6 Target Company Valuation

(1) Discount cash flow (DCF) analysis

- The DCF approach to valuing a business involves the application of capital budgeting procedures to an entire firm rather than to a single project.
- Pro forma statements that forecast the incremental free cash flows expected to result from the merger.
- A discount rate, or cost of capital, to apply to these projected cash flows.

(2) Market Multiple Method

- A method of valuing a target company that applies a market determined multiple to net income, sales, book value and so forth.
- Market determined multiples : P/E, P/B, P/S, P/CF

Example 9-2

Consider the following information for two all-equity firms, A and B:

	Firm A	Firm B
Shares outstanding	2,000	6,000
Price per share	$40	$30

Firm A estimates that the value of the synergistic benefit from acquiring Firm B is $6,000. Firm B has indicated that it would accept a cash purchase offer of $35 per share. Should Firm A proceed?

Solution

$$NPV = (\$30 \times 6,000 + \$6,000) - (\$35 \times 6,000) = -\$24,000$$

Example 9-3

Consider the following information for two all-equity firms, A and B:

	Firm A	Firm B
Total earnings	$3,000	$1,100
Shares outstanding	600	400
Price per share	$70	$15

Firm A is acquiring Firm B by exchanging 100 of its shares for all the shares in B. What is the cost of the merger if the merged firm is worth $63,000? What will happen to Firm A's EPS? Its P/E ratio?

Solution

(1) Cost of merger =($63,000 ÷ 700 shares) × 100 shares = $9,000

(2) EPS = ($3,000 + $1,100) ÷ 700 shares = $5.86

(3) P/E = $90 ÷ $5.86 = 15.36

02 >> Divestiture

1 Types of Divestiture

Spin-off, split-off, and carve-out are different methods a company can use to divest certain assets, a division, or a subsidiary.

(1) Spin-off

The parent company distributes shares of the subsidiary to its existing shareholders on a pro rata basis. The parent company receives no cash consideration for the spin-off. Existing shareholders benefit by now holding shares of two separate companies after the spin-off.

(2) Split-off

Shareholders in the parent company are offered shares in a subsidiary and exchange some or all of the shares held in the parent company for shares in the subsidiary.

(3) Equity carve-out (ECO)

The parent company sells some or all of the shares in its subsidiary to the public through an initial public offering (IPO). Only part of the shares are offered to the public, so the parent company retains an equity stake in the subsidiary.

(4) Liquidation

A divestiture in which the assets of a division are sold off piecemeal.

2 Reasons of Divestiture

- To settle antitrust suits

- To concentrate on a particular type of activity

- To raise capital

- Division no longer fits into management's long-term strategy

- Lack of profitability

03 ▷ Tasked-Based Simulation

Problem-1

Disney Company is interested in acquiring 21st Century Fox . Assume that the risk-free rate of interest is 5 percent and the market risk premium is 6 percent.

Fox currently expects to pay a year-end dividend of $2.00 a share. Fox's dividend is expected to grow at a constant rate of 5 percent a year, and its beta is 0.9.

Disney estimates that if it acquires Fox, the year-end dividend will remain at $2.00 a share, but synergies will enable the dividend to grow at a constant rate of 7 percent a year (instead of the current 5 percent). Disney also plans to increase the debt ratio of what would be its Fox subsidiary—the effect of this would be to raise Fox's beta to 1.1.

Required

1. What is the current price of Fox's stock?

2. What is the per-share value of Fox to Disney?

3. If Disney were to acquire Fox, what would be the range of possible prices that it could bid for each share of Fox common stock?

Problem-2

Eastman Corp. is analyzing the possible acquisition of Kodak Company. Both firms have no debt. Eastman believes the acquisition will increase its total aftertax annual cash flows by $2.6 million indefinitely. The current market value of Kodak is $102 million, and that of Eastman is $140 million. The appropriate discount rate for the incremental cash flows is 12 percent. Eastman is trying to decide whether it should offer 40 percent of its stock or $110 million in cash to Kodak's shareholders.

Required

1. What is the cost of each alternative?

2. What is the NPV of each alternative?

3. Which alternative should Eastman choose?

Financial Management For the **US CPA** Exam

Chapter 10

Market Influences on Business

Volume
8

01 > The Laws of Demand and Supply

1 Demand

(1) 수요량(quantity demanded)

소비자들이 값을 치르고 구입할 의사와 능력이 있는 재화의 양을 말한다. 수요량을 결정하는 변수에는 여러 가지가 있다. 그 중 가격이 가장 중요한 변수이다.

(2) 수요의 법칙(law of demand)

다른 조건이 같을 때 어느 재화의 가격이 상승하면 그 재화의 수요량은 감소하고, 가격이 하락하면 수요량은 증가한다.

(3) 수요곡선(demand curve)

가격과 수요량의 관계를 보여주는 곡선

경제학의 관행에 따라 가격(P)은 수직축에, 수량(Q)은 수평축에 표시

다른 조건이 불변일 때, 가격이 낮아질수록 수요량이 증가하기 때문에 수요곡선은 우하향

기울기가 마이너스

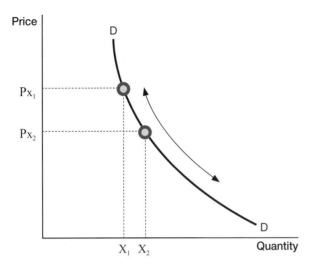

[Figure 10-1]

(4) 수요곡선이 우하향하는 이유

1) 소득효과(income effect)

특정 재화의 가격 인하로 인한 실질소득 증가로 재화 구매량이 변화하는 효과를 의미하며, 재화 간 상대가격 불변을 전제로 한다.

예 콜라 가격이 하락하면 소비자의 구매력이 커져서 콜라와 피자를 더 많이 소비

2) 대체효과(substitution effect)

재화 간 상대가격 변화로 인해 상대적으로 비싸진 재화는 수요량이 감소하고, 상대적으로 저렴해진 재화는 수요량이 증가하는 효과를 의미하며 실질소득 불변을 전제로 한다.

예 콜라 가격이 하락하면 콜라가 상대적으로 싸져서 콜라의 수요량은 증가하지만 피자는 상대적으로 비싸져서 피자의 수요량은 감소

∴ 콜라의 가격이 하락하면 콜라는 소득효과와 대체효과가 같은 방향으로 움직이므로 콜라의 소비는 증가한다. 콜라의 가격이 하락하면 피자는 소득효과와 대체효과가 반대 방향으로 움직이므로 피자의 소비가 어떻게 변할지 알 수 없다.

2 Shift in the Demand Curve

(1) 수요곡선의 이동

1) 수요의 증가(increase in demand)

주어진 가격에서 소비자들이 사고자 하는 재화의 양을 증가시키는 변화가 일어나면 수요곡선이 오른쪽으로 이동한다.

2) 수요의 감소(decrease in demand)

주어진 가격에서 소비자들이 사고자 하는 재화의 양을 감소시키는 변화가 일어나면 수요곡선이 왼쪽으로 이동한다.

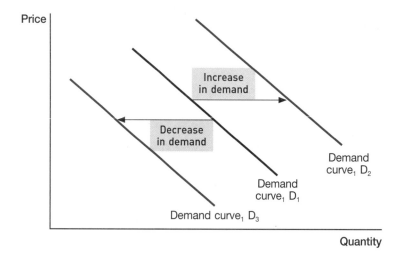

[Figure 10-2] Shift in the Demand Curve

수요곡선을 이동시키는 변수는 매우 많으며, 그 중 다음과 같은 변수들이 가장 중요하다.

> ※ 가격
>
> → 수요곡선상의 이동(movement) (changes in quantity demanded)
>
> ※ 소득, 연관재의 가격, 취향, 미래에 대한 기대, 소비자의 수
>
> → 수요곡선의 이동(shift) (changes in demand)

(2) Income(소득)

1) 정상재(normal good)

소득이 증가(감소)함에 따라 수요가 증가(감소)하는 재화

대부분 재화와 서비스

소득의 증가 → 수요의 증가 → 수요곡선 오른쪽 이동

소득의 감소 → 수요의 감소 → 수요곡선 왼쪽 이동

2) 열등재(inferior good)

소득이 증가(감소)함에 따라 수요가 감소(증가)하는 재화

버스나 지하철 (소득이 증가하면 자가용을 타거나 택시를 타고 버스나 지하철을 덜 이용)

소득의 감소 → 수요의 증가 → 수요곡선 오른쪽 이동

소득의 증가 → 수요의 감소 → 수요곡선 왼쪽 이동

(3) Prices of related goods (연관재의 가격)

1) 대체재(substitutes)

한 재화의 가격이 하락함에 따라 다른 한 재화의 수요가 감소하는 경우

영화 관람권과 영화 스트리밍 서비스, 커피와 차, 기차와 버스, 소고기와 돼지고기

대체재의 가격 상승 → 원래 재화의 수요 증가 → 수요곡선 오른쪽 이동

대체재의 가격 하락 → 원래 재화의 수요 감소 → 수요곡선 왼쪽 이동

2) 보완재(complements)

한 재화(A)의 가격이 하락함에 따라 다른 한 재화(B)의 수요가 증가하는 경우

자동차와 휘발유, 컴퓨터와 소프트웨어, 커피와 쿠키

보완재의 가격 하락 → 원래 재화의 수요 증가 → 수요곡선 오른쪽 이동

보완재의 가격 상승 → 원래 재화의 수요 감소 → 수요곡선 왼쪽 이동

(4) Taste (취향, 소비자의 기호)

인간의 취향은 경제학의 영역을 벗어난 역사적 · 심리적 요인에 따라 결정

아이스크림을 좋아하면 아이스크림을 더 많이 사 먹음

재화의 선호도 증가 → 수요의 증가 → 수요곡선 오른쪽 이동

재화의 선호도 감소 → 수요의 감소 → 수요곡선 왼쪽 이동

(5) Expectations (미래에 대한 기대)

내일 재화의 가격이 하락할 것으로 예상된다면 오늘 재화를 덜 구입

미래 가격이 상승할 것으로 기대 → 해당 재화의 수요 증가 → 수요곡선 오른쪽 이동

미래 가격이 하락할 것으로 기대 → 해당 재화의 수요 감소 → 수요곡선 왼쪽 이동

(6) Number of buyers (소비자의 수)

A와 B만 있는 아이스크림 시장에 C가 들어온다면 아이스크림에 대한 시장 수요량은 모든 가격에서 늘어나서 수요곡선은 오른쪽으로 이동

소비자의 수 증가 → 시장 수요 증가 → 수요곡선 오른쪽 이동

소비자의 수 감소→ 시장 수요 감소 → 수요곡선 왼쪽 이동

Example 10-1

(1) 담뱃갑에 흡연이 건강에 미치는 폐해에 대한 광고가 인쇄된 것을 보고 소비자들이 담배를 덜 피운다면 담배 수요곡선에 어떤 영향을 주는가?
(2) 세금 부과로 인해 담배 가격이 오른다면 담배 수요곡선에 어떤 영향을 주는가?

Solution

(1) Taste의 변화로 담배 수요곡선은 왼쪽으로 이동(shift)한다.
(2) 수요곡선은 이동하지 않고 수요곡선상에서 이동(movement)한다. 동일한 수요곡선 상의 한 점에서 가격이 높고 수요량은 적은 다른 점으로 이동한다.

Example 10-2

A decrease in the price of a complementary good will
A. Shift the demand curve of the joint commodity to the left.
B. Increase the price paid for a substitute good.
C. Shift the supply curve of the joint commodity to the left.
D. Shift the demand curve of the joint commodity to the right.

Solution

보완재의 가격 하락 → 원래 재화의 수요 증가 → 수요곡선 오른쪽 이동
정답 : D

3 Supply

(1) 공급량(quantity supplied)

판매자가 팔 의사와 능력이 있는 수량을 말한다. 공급량을 결정하는 변수에는 여러 가지가 있다. 그 중 가격이 가장 중요한 변수이다.

(2) 공급의 법칙(law of supply)

다른 조건이 불변일 때 어느 재화의 가격이 상승하면 그 재화의 공급량이 증가하고, 가격이 하락하면 공급량이 감소한다.

(3) 공급곡선(supply curve)

가격과 공급량의 관계를 보여주는 곡선

경제학의 관행에 따라 가격(P)은 수직축에, 수량(Q)은 수평축에 표시

다른 변수들이 동일하다면 가격이 높을수록 공급량이 증가하기 때문에 공급곡선은 우상향

기울기가 플러스

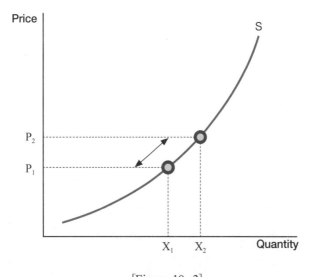

[Figure 10-3]

4 Shift in the Supply Curve

(1) 공급곡선의 이동

1) 공급의 증가(increase in supply)

주어진 가격에서 판매자(생산자)들이 팔고자 하는 재화의 양을 증가시키는 변화가 일어나면 공급곡선이 오른쪽으로 이동한다.

2) 공급의 감소(decrease in supply)

주어진 가격에서 판매자(생산자)들이 팔고자 하는 재화의 양을 감소시키는 변화가 일어나면 공급곡선이 왼쪽으로 이동한다.

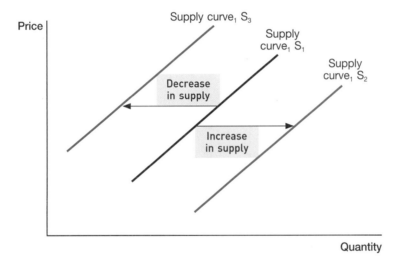

[Figure 10-4] Shift in the Supply Curve

공급곡선을 이동시키는 변수는 매우 많으며, 그 중 다음과 같은 변수들이 가장 중요하다.

※ 가격

→ 공급곡선상의 이동(movement) (changes in quantity supplied)

※ 투입요소가격, 기술, 연관재의 가격, 미래에 대한 기대, 판매자의 수

→ 공급곡선의 이동(shift) (changes in supply)

(2) Input prices (투입요소가격)

재화를 생산하려면 원재료, 기계장치, 매장 건물, 종업원 등 여러 가지 투입요소가 필요하다. 투입요소가격이 상승하면 사업의 채산성이 낮아져 제조업체는 생산량을 줄일 것이다.

투입요소의 가격 하락 → 재화의 공급 증가 → 공급곡선 오른쪽 이동

투입요소의 가격 상승 → 재화의 공급 감소 → 공급곡선 왼쪽 이동

(3) Technology (기술)

생산 자동화가 되면 생산에 투입되는 인력이 절감되어 비용이 낮아지므로 재화의 공급량은 늘어난다.

기술이 진보할 때 → 공급의 증가 → 공급곡선 오른쪽 이동

최신 기술을 사용할 수 없을 때 → 공급의 감소 → 공급곡선 왼쪽 이동

(4) Prices of related goods (연관재의 가격)

1) 대체재(substitutes)

대체재의 가격 하락 → 원래 재화의 공급 증가 → 공급곡선 오른쪽 이동
대체재의 가격 상승 → 원래 재화의 공급 감소 → 공급곡선 왼쪽 이동

2) 보완재(complements)

보완재의 가격 상승 → 원래 재화의 공급 증가 → 공급곡선 오른쪽 이동
보완재의 가격 하락 → 원래 재화의 공급 감소 → 공급곡선 왼쪽 이동

(5) Expectations (미래에 대한 기대)

내일 재화의 가격이 하락할 것으로 예상된다면 오늘 재화를 더 공급

미래 가격이 하락할 것으로 기대 → 해당 재화의 공급 증가 → 공급곡선 오른쪽 이동

미래 가격이 상승할 것으로 기대 → 해당 재화의 공급 감소 → 공급곡선 왼쪽 이동

(6) Number of suppliers (판매자의 수)

판매자의 수 증가 → 시장 공급 증가 → 공급곡선 오른쪽 이동

판매자의 수 감소→ 시장 공급 감소 → 공급곡선 왼쪽 이동

Example 10-3

An improvement in technology that in turn leads to improved worker productivity would most likely result in

A. A shift to the right in the supply curve and a lowering of the price of the output.
B. A shift to the left in the supply curve and a lowering of the price of the output.
C. An increase in the price of the output if demand is unchanged.
D. Wage increases.

Solution

기술 진보(생산성 향상) → 공급의 증가 → 공급곡선 오른쪽 이동 → 균형가격 하락, 균형거래량 증가
급여는 노동시장의 수요와 공급으로 결정되므로 위의 자료로는 알 수 없음

정답 : A

5 Market Equilibrium

(1) 균형(equilibrium)

1) 균형

균형수요량과 공급량을 일치시키는 시장가격에 도달한 상태

2) 균형가격

수요량과 공급량을 일치시키는 가격

3) 균형거래량

균형가격에서 수요량과 공급량

4) 초과공급(excess supply) 혹은 공급과잉(surplus)

공급량이 수요량을 초과하는 상태

공급과잉이 발생하면 팔지 못한 재고가 점점 쌓이고, 판매자들은 가격을 낮출 것이다. 낮아지는 가격은 다시 수요를 증가시키고 공급량을 감소시킨다. 이러한 조정 과정은 가격이 균형가격 수준으로 내려갈 때까지 계속될 것이다.

5) 초과수요(excess demand) 혹은 물량부족(shortage)

수요량이 공급량을 초과하는 상태

물량부족이 있으면 소비자들이 줄을 서서 기다려야 한다. 공급량에 비해 소비자들이 사려는 수요량이 많으므로 판매자들은 판매량이 줄 것을 염려하지 않고 가격을 올릴 수 있다. 가격이 상승함에 따라 수요량이 감소하고 공급량이 증가하여 결국 균형이 회복된다.

6) 수요 · 공급의 법칙(law of demand and supply)

어느 재화의 가격이 그 재화에 대한 수요량과 공급량이 일치하도록 조정되는 현상

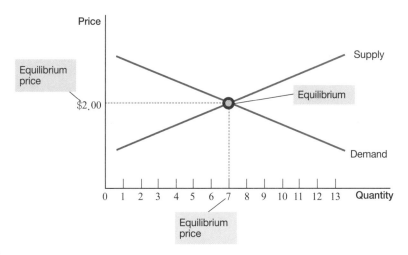

[Figure 10-5] The Equilibrium of Supply and Demand

(2) A change in market equilibrium due to a shift in demand

1) 수요의 증가(increase in demand)

수요곡선을 오른쪽으로 이동

균형가격이 상승하고 균형거래량도 증가

2) 수요의 감소(decrease in demand)

수요곡선을 왼쪽으로 이동

균형가격이 하락하고 균형거래량도 감소

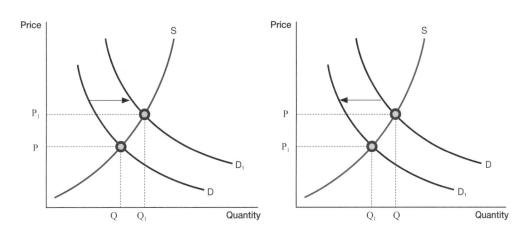

[Figure 10-6] Effects of a Change in Demand on Equilibrium

(3) A change in market equilibrium due to a shift in supply

1) 공급의 증가(increase in supply)

공급곡선을 오른쪽으로 이동

균형가격이 하락하고 균형거래량은 증가

2) 공급의 감소(decrease in supply)

공급곡선을 왼쪽으로 이동

균형가격이 상승하고 균형거래량은 감소

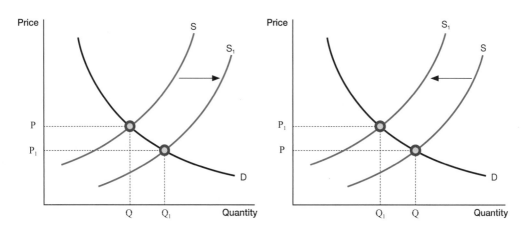

[Figure 10–7] Effects of a Change in Supply on Equilibrium

(4) Shifts in both supply and demand

1) 수요의 증가 & 공급의 증가

균형가격 불분명, 균형거래량 증가

2) 수요의 증가 & 공급의 감소

균형가격 상승, 균형거래량 불분명

3) 수요의 감소 & 공급의 증가

균형가격 하락, 균형거래량 불분명

4) 수요의 감소 & 공급의 감소

균형가격 불분명, 균형거래량 감소

(5) Supply, Demand and Government Policies

1) 가격통제 (controls of prices)

① 가격상한제(price ceiling)

어떤 재화 판매가격의 법정 최고치

예 주택시장의 임대료 규제

시장가격 〈 가격상한 → 실효성 없음

시장가격 〉 가격상한 → 실효성 있음, 물량부족(shortage) → 판매자들은 다수의 잠재적인 고객 중에서 일부를 선별하여 희소한 재화를 배당

② 가격하한제(price floor)

어떤 재화 판매가격의 법정 최저치

예 최저임금제

시장가격 〉 가격하한 → 실효성 없음

시장가격 〈 가격하한 → 실효성 있음, 공급과잉(surplus) → 판매자들이 인종적 유대나 가족관계에 호소하면서 판매

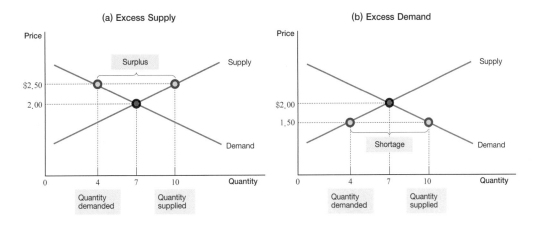

[Figure 10-8] Markets Not in Equilibrium

2) 조세(Taxes)

① Taxes or subsidies on buyers (소비자에 대한 세금 또는 보조금)

ⓐ 소비자에게 부과되는 세금의 감소 또는 보조금의 증가

수요의 증가 → 수요곡선 오른쪽 이동 → 균형가격이 상승하고 균형거래량도 증가

ⓑ 소비자에게 부과되는 세금의 증가 또는 보조금의 감소

수요의 감소 → 수요곡선 왼쪽 이동 → 균형가격이 하락하고 균형거래량도 감소

② Taxes or subsidies on sellers (판매자에 대한 세금 또는 보조금)

ⓐ 판매자에게 부과되는 세금의 감소 또는 보조금의 증가

공급의 증가 → 공급곡선 오른쪽 이동 → 균형가격이 하락하고 균형거래량은 증가

ⓑ 판매자에게 부과되는 세금의 증가 또는 보조금의 감소

공급의 감소 → 공급곡선 왼쪽 이동 → 균형가격이 상승하고 균형거래량은 감소

Example 10-4

An increase in the market supply of beef would result in a(n)

A. Increase in the price of beef.

B. Decrease in the demand for beef.

C. Increase in the price of pork.

D. Increase in the quantity of beef demanded.

Solution

beef market

공급의 증가 → 공급곡선 오른쪽 이동 → 균형가격 하락, 균형거래량 증가

pork market

대체재의 가격 하락 → 수요 감소/공급 증가 → 균형가격 하락, 균형거래량 불분명

정답 : D

Example 10-5

If the federal government regulates a product or service in a competitive market by setting maximum price below the equilibrium price, what is the long-run effect?
A. A surplus.
B. A shortage.
C. A decrease in demand.
D. No effect on the market.

Solution

시장가격 > 가격상한 → 물량부족(shortage)

정답 : B

02 > Elasticity of Demand and Supply

1 The Elasticity of Demand

(1) 수요의 가격탄력성(price elasticity of demand)

1) 수요의 가격탄력성

수요의 가격탄력성이란 어떤 재화의 가격이 변할 때 그 재화의 수요량이 얼마나 변하는지 나타내는 지표로 수요량의 변화율을 가격 변화율로 나눈 수치를 말한다.

$$E_P = \% \text{ changes in quantity demanded} \,/\, \% \text{ changes in price}$$

예를 들어 아이스크림 가격이 10% 인상되었는데, 아이스크림 수요량이 20% 감소한 경우 수요의 가격탄력성은 다음과 같다.

$$E_P = -20\% \,/\, 10\% = -2$$

재화의 수요량은 그 재화의 가격과 반대 방향으로 변하기 때문에 수요의 가격탄력성을 (−)로 표시한다.

그러나 경제학의 관례는 (−)부호를 붙이지 않고 절댓값을 강조하기 위하여 (+)로 표시한다. 이는 가격탄력성이 크다는 것은 수요가 가격 변화에 더 민감하다는 뜻을 강조하기 위함이다. 가격탄력성은 2이므로 수요량의 변화율이 가격 변화율의 2배에 해당한다.

$$E_P = 20\% \,/\, 10\% = 2$$

2) Simple method (Point method)

변화량을 최초값으로 나누어 변화율을 구하는 방법
기준점이 다르면 탄력성의 차이가 발생하는 문제점이 있음

$$\% \text{ changes in quantity demanded} = \frac{Q_2 - Q_1}{Q_1}$$

$$\% \text{ changes in price} = \frac{P_2 - P_1}{P_1}$$

Example 10-6

수요곡선상에 있는 두 점
점 A에서는 가격＝$4, 수요량＝120개
점 B에서는 가격＝$6, 수요량＝80개
수요의 가격탄력성은 simple method로 절댓값으로 계산
(1) 점 A에서 점 B로 변할 때의 수요의 가격탄력성은 얼마인가?
(2) 점 B에서 점 A로 변할 때의 수요의 가격탄력성은 얼마인가?

Solution

(1) 점 A에서 점 B로 변할 때의 수요의 가격탄력성

$$\% \text{ changes in quantity demanded} = \frac{80-120}{120} = 33\%$$

$$\% \text{ changes in price} = \frac{6-4}{4} = 50\%$$

$$E_P = 33\% / 50\% = 0.67$$

(2) 점 B에서 점 A로 변할 때의 수요의 가격탄력성

$$\% \text{ changes in quantity demanded} = \frac{120-80}{80} = 50\%$$

$$\% \text{ changes in price} = \frac{4-6}{6} = 33\%$$

$$E_P = 50\% / 33\% = 1.52$$

3) Midpoint method (Arc method)

변화량을 중간값으로 나누어 변화율을 구하는 방법

$$\% \text{ changes in quantity demanded} = \frac{Q_2 - Q_1}{\dfrac{Q_1 + Q_2}{2}}$$

$$\% \text{ changes in price} = \frac{P_2 - P_1}{\dfrac{P_1 + P_2}{2}}$$

Example 10-7

수요곡선상에 있는 두 점
점 A에서는 가격 = \$4, 수요량 = 120개
점 B에서는 가격 = \$6, 수요량 = 80개
수요의 가격탄력성은 midpoint method로 절댓값으로 계산
(1) 점 A에서 점 B로 변할 때의 수요의 가격탄력성은 얼마인가?
(2) 점 B에서 점 A로 변할 때의 수요의 가격탄력성은 얼마인가?

Solution

(1) 점 A에서 점 B로 변할 때의 수요의 가격탄력성

$$\% \text{ changes in quantity demanded} = \frac{80 - 120}{100} = 40\%$$

$$\% \text{ changes in price} = \frac{6 - 4}{5} = 40\%$$

$$E_p = 40\% \,/\, 40\% = 1$$

(2) 점 B에서 점 A로 변할 때의 수요의 가격탄력성

$$\% \text{ changes in quantity demanded} = \frac{120 - 80}{100} = 40\%$$

$$\% \text{ changes in price} = \frac{4 - 6}{5} = 40\%$$

$$E_p = 40\% \,/\, 40\% = 1$$

4) 수요의 가격탄력성의 표시 (절댓값 기준)

- 비탄력(Inelastic) : 수요의 가격탄력성 $<$ 1
- 탄력적(elastic) : 수요의 가격탄력성 $>$ 1
- 단위 탄력적(unit elastic) : 수요의 가격탄력성 = 1
- 완전 비탄력적(perfectly inelastic) : 수요의 가격탄력성 = 0
- 완전 탄력적(perfectly elastic) : 수요의 가격탄력성 = ∞

5) 수요의 가격탄력성 결정요인

① 필수재와 사치재 (necessities versus luxuries)

필수품에 대한 수요는 비탄력적인 반면, 사치품에 대한 수요는 탄력적이다.

② 밀접한 대체재의 존재 (close substitute)

어느 재화에 밀접한 대체재가 있으면 소비자들은 그 재화 대신 다른 재화를 사용할 수 있으므로 그 재화의 수요는 탄력적이다.

③ 시간 (time horizon)

시간을 길게 잡을수록 수요는 더 탄력적이 된다.

예) 휘발유 가격이 인상될 때 단기적 탄력성보다 장기적 탄력성이 크다.

6) 총수입과 수요의 가격탄력성

총수입(total revenue : TR) = 가격(P) × Q(수량)

현재 가격 = \$4, 수요량 = 120개라고 하면 총수입(TR) = \$4 × 120 = \$480이다.

가격 변화가 총수입(TR)에 미치는 영향은 수요의 탄력성에 달렸다.

① 수요가 비탄력적인 경우

가격이 \$6로 오를 때 수요량이 100개인 경우 총수입(TR) = \$6 × 100개 = \$600이다.

$$\% \text{ changes in quantity demanded} = \frac{100-120}{110} = 18\%$$

$$\% \text{ changes in price} = \frac{6-4}{5} = 40\%$$

$E_P = 18\% / 40\% = 0.45 < 1$

비탄력적인 경우, 가격이 상승할 때 수요량이 가격 상승에 비해 작은 폭으로 감소한다.

② 수요가 탄력적인 경우

가격이 $6로 오를 때 수요량이 60개인 경우 총수입(TR) = $6 x 60개 = $360이다.

$\%$ changes in quantity demanded $= \dfrac{60-120}{90} = 67\%$

$\%$ changes in price $= \dfrac{6-4}{5} = 40\%$

$E_p = 67\% / 40\% = 1.68 > 1$

탄력적인 경우, 가격이 상승할 때 수요량이 가격 상승에 비해 큰 폭으로 감소한다.

※ **수요의 가격탄력성 < 1**

가격과 총수입은 같은 방향으로 변한다.
가격이 상승하면 총수입도 증가하며, 가격이 하락하면 총수입도 감소한다.

※ **수요의 가격탄력성 > 1**

가격과 총수입은 반대 방향으로 변한다.
가격이 상승하면 총수입은 감소하며, 가격이 하락하면 총수입은 증가한다.

※ **수요의 가격탄력성 = 1**

가격이 변해도 총수입은 변하지 않는다.

---

(2) 수요의 소득탄력성(income elasticity of demand)

수요의 소득탄력성이란 소비자의 소득이 변할 때 어떤 재화의 수요량이 얼마나 변하는지 나타내는 지표로 수요량의 변화율을 소득 변화율로 나눈 수치를 말한다.

$$E_I = \% \text{ changes in quantity demanded} / \% \text{ changes in income}$$

1) 정상재(normal good)

정상재는 소득이 상승하면 수요량도 증가하므로 정상재의 소득탄력성은 (+)이다.

2) 열등재(inferior good)

열등재는 소득이 상승하면 수요량도 감소하므로 열등재의 소득탄력성은 (–)이다.

3) 필수재와 사치재 (necessities versus luxuries)

필수재는 소비자들의 소득이 얼마가 되든 어느 정도는 구입하므로 소득탄력성이 낮다.
사치재는 소비자들의 소득이 낮으면 없이도 지낼 수 있는 물건들이므로 소득탄력성이 크다.

(3) 수요의 교차탄력성(cross-price elasticity of demand)

수요의 교차탄력성이란 한 재화의 가격이 변할 때 다른 재화의 수요량이 얼마나 변하는지 나타내는 지표로 한 재화의 수요량의 변화율을 다른 재화의 가격 변화율로 나눈 수치를 말한다.

교차탄력성은 재화 X의 수요량 변화율을 재화 Y의 가격 변화율로 나누어 계산한다.

$$E_C = \% \text{ changes in quantity demanded of good X} / \% \text{ changes in price of good Y}$$

1) 대체재(substitutes)

X와 Y가 대체재인 경우 Y의 가격이 상승하면 사람들은 X를 소비하게 되므로 X의 수요량이 증가한다. Y의 가격과 X의 수요량이 같은 방향으로 변하므로 대체재의 교차탄력성은 (+)가 된다.

2) 보완재(complements)

X와 Y가 보완재인 경우 Y의 가격이 상승하면 X의 수요량이 감소한다. Y의 가격과 X의 수요량이 반대 방향으로 변하므로 보완재의 교차탄력성은 (–)가 된다.

2 The Elasticity of Supply

(1) 공급의 가격탄력성(price elasticity of supply)

1) 공급의 가격탄력성

공급의 가격탄력성이란 어떤 재화의 가격이 변할 때 그 재화의 공급량이 얼마나 변하는지 나타내는 지표로 공급량의 변화율을 가격 변화율로 나눈 수치를 말한다.

$$E_p = \% \text{ changes in quantity supplied} / \% \text{ changes in price}$$

예를 들어 아이스크림 가격이 10% 인상되었는데, 아이스크림 공급량이 8% 증가한 경우 공급의 가격탄력성은 다음과 같다.

$$E_p = 8\% / 10\% = 0.8$$

2) 공급의 가격탄력성의 표시

- 비탄력(inelastic) : 공급의 가격탄력성 < 1
- 탄력적(elastic) : 공급의 가격탄력성 > 1
- 단위 탄력적(unit elastic) : 공급의 가격탄력성 $= 1$
- 완전 비탄력적(perfectly inelastic) : 공급의 가격탄력성 $= 0$
- 완전 탄력적(perfectly elastic) : 공급의 가격탄력성 $= \infty$

3) 공급의 가격탄력성 결정요인

① 생산량을 얼마나 신축적으로 조절할 수 있는지 여부

자동차, TV 등 공산품은 가격이 높아지면 공장 조업시간을 연장하여 생산량을 늘릴 수 있기 때문에 공급이 탄력적이다. 주택을 건설하기 위한 토지는 추가 생산이 불가능하기 때문에 공급이 비탄력적이다.

② 시간 (time horizon)

시간을 길게 잡을수록 공급은 더 탄력적이 된다. 장기적으로는 기업이 공장을 새로 건설하거나 기존의 공장을 폐쇄할 수 있기 때문에 공급량이 가격 변화에 대해 상당히 민감하게 반응한다.

03 ▶ Effects of Inflation

1 Inflation

(1) Terminology

Inflation : increase of the general level of prices in an economy.

Deflation : reduction of the general level of prices in an economy.

Hyperinflation : a very high and typically accelerating inflation.

Disinflation : reduction in the rate of inflation.

(2) 인플레이션율의 측정

1) 소비자물가지수(consumer price index, CPI)

대표적인 소비자가 구입하는 재화와 서비스의 전반적인 비용을 나타내는 지표

2) 인플레이션율(inflation rate)

소비자물가지수의 전년도 대비 상승률

$$\text{Inflation rate in year 2} = \frac{CPI \ in \ year \ 2 - CPI \ in \ year \ 1}{CPI \ in \ year \ 1} \times 100$$

CPI in year 1 = 100

CPI in year 2 = 175

CPI in year 3 = 250

Inflation rate in year 2 = (175−100)/100 x 100 = 75%

Inflation rate in year 3 = (250−175)/175 x 100 = 43%

2 Effect of Inflation on prices

(1) Monetary and non-monetary items

중요한 화폐성 및 비화폐성 항목의 분류는 다음과 같다.

	Monetary	Non-monetary
Assets	Cash Receivables Debt investments Advances to suppliers—no fixed	Inventories PPE Intangible assets Equity investments Advances to suppliers—fixed
Liabilities	Almost	Warranty obligations Advances from customer—fixed
Equity	No	Yes

(2) Purchasing power gain or loss

물가상승시에 구매력 손익은 다음과 같다.

	Monetary	Non-monetary
Assets	purchasing power loss	해당사항 없음
Liabilities	purchasing power gain	

따라서 화폐성 자산과 부채의 크기에 따라 구매력손익은 결정된다.

> monetary assets $>$ monetary liabilities $\Rightarrow$ purchasing power loss
> monetary assets $<$ monetary liabilities $\Rightarrow$ purchasing power gain

3 Effect of Inflation on debt investment

(1) Fixed rate debt investments

Inflation erodes the purchasing power of fixed-coupon payments and the final principal payment, which therefore reduces the present value of the investment.

(2) Floating rate debt investments

A debt whose interest rate is adjusted periodically according to a predetermined formula; it is usually linked to an interest rate index such as LIBOR or SOFR. Inflation erodes the purchasing power of the final principal payment.

※ SOFR (Secured Overnight Financing Rate)

LIBOR의 대체금리로 미국 국채를 담보로 하는 1일물 환매조건부채권(RP) 금리 .

(3) Treasury Inflation-Protected Securities (TIPS)

물가연동채권(TIPS)는 투자 원금에 물가상승률을 반영한 뒤 그에 대한 이자를 지급하는 채권으로, 인플레이션이 일어나더라도 채권의 실질가치를 보전해준다는 점에서 대표적인 인플레이션 헤지 상품으로 꼽힌다.

4 Effect of Inflation on equity investment

Inflation will erode the value of dividend payments. Also, inflation causes production costs to rise, which drives up sales prices. Consumers may purchase fewer goods and services as a result of higher prices, which could lead to revenue, profit, and stock price declines.

5 Effect of Inflation on alternative investment

Alternative investment

주식이나 채권 같은 전통적인 투자 상품이 아닌 다른 대상에 투자하는 방식을 말한다. 대상은 사모펀드, 헤지펀드, 부동산, 벤처기업, 원자재, 선박 등 다양하다.

Alternative investments may be used to effectively hedge against inflation. Real estate tends to increase in value over time and can generate returns that outpace inflation in the long term. Commodities are also used to hedge against inflation, as the value of precious metals, energy, livestock, and agriculture tend to move in line with inflation.

Example 10-8

Company AIFA issues $1,000,000 in 5 percent fixed-rate debt maturing In 10 years. Inflation increases at 2 percent per year. The company pays $50,000 in interest costs each year and at maturity, the company pays the principal of $1,000,000 to its debtholders. What will it will have a real cost?

Solution

$$\text{Real cost of debt} = \frac{FV}{(1 + inf)^n} = \frac{1,000,000}{(1.02)^{10}} = 820,348$$

Example 10–9

Company AIFA is concerned about the potential for rising prices over the next several years. To hedge against inflation, the CFO invests $4,000,000 in TIPS (Treasury Inflation-Protected Securities) paying interest at 1.50 percent and maturing in three years. After one year, inflation rises 2.50 percent. What amount will be the next year's interest payments?

Solution

The new face value of the security is $4,100,000 ($4,000,000 × 1.025).

The next year's interest payments = $4,100,000 \times 1.5\% = \$61,500$

Example 10–10

A company's CFO calculates that labor costs and .associated fringe benefits for this year will total $28,000,000.

If inflation averages 2 percent per year, what amount will the same labor and fringe costs be?

Solution

Future price = Present value $\times (1 + \text{Inflation rate})^n$

Labor and fringe costs in 10 years = $\$28,000,000 \times 1.02^{10} = \$34,131,844$

04 Strategy

1 Introduction

기업은 미래의 불확실성에 대처하기 위하여 사전에 계획(planning)을 수립한다. 이때 기업의 계획을 화폐가치로 표현한 것을 예산편성(budgeting)이라고 한다. 예산편성은 기업의 전략(strategy)와 통합하여야 유용하다. 전략, 계획 및 예산편성의 관계를 그림으로 나타내면 다음과 같다.

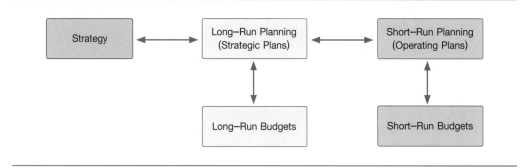

[Figure 10-9] Strategy, Planning, and Budgets

2 Strategy

전략이란 경쟁우위 확보를 위한 체계적인 경영활동으로 환경적응능력을 촉진하고 전사적인 관점에서 경영자원을 통합하는 이론이다. 경영전략은 다음과 같은 절차로 이루어진다.

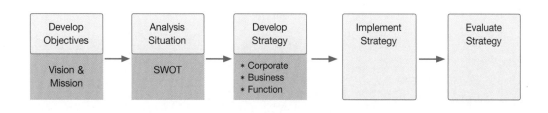

[Figure 10-10]

(1) SWOT analysis

SWOT분석은 기업의 내부환경을 분석하여 강점과 약점을 발견하고 외부환경을 분석하여 기회와 위협을 찾아내어 전략적 대안을 개발하는 기법을 말한다.

Internal abilities	Strength	경쟁우위요인
	Weakness	제약요인
External situations	Opportunity	기술개발, 정부지원
	Threat	경쟁자, 정부규제

SWOT분석은 일반적으로 다음과 같은 SWOT Matrix를 이용한다.

	Strength	Weakness
Opportunity	강점을 이용하여 기회를 이용	기회를 이용하여 약점을 보완
Threat	강점을 이용하여 위기를 극복	위기극복을 위하여 약점 보완

(2) Types of strategy

전략은 위계에 따라 다음 3가지 유형으로 구분된다.

1) Corporate level

전사적 수준의 전략이란 여러 개의 사업부를 가지고 있는 기업의 본부에서 수립하는 전략으로 주로 기업이 어떤 사업을 해야 하는지를 결정하는 것을 추구하는 전략이다.

2) Business level

사업부 수준의 전략이란 전략적 사업단위(SBU : strategic business unit)수준의 전략으로 기업의 각 사업 영역에서 어떻게 경쟁해야 하는지 결정하는 전략이다. 이 전략은 주로 제품시장을 놓고 경쟁자와 실제로 경쟁하기 위한 전략을 의미하기 때문에 '경쟁전략(competitive strategy)'이라고 한다.

3) Functional level

기능 수준의 전략이란 사업부 수준의 전략을 지원하는 전략으로 사업부에 속해있는 기능부서들의 전략을 의미한다.

(3) Corporate strategy

전사적 수준의 전략은 수직적 통합, 수평적 통합, 다각화 등으로 구분된다.

1) Vertical integration

수직적 통합은 기업이 전후방의 가치사슬(value chain)중에 어디까지를 내부 활동의 범위로 통합할 것인가를 결정하는 전략으로 전방통합과 후방통합의 두 가지로 구분할 수 있다.

전방통합(forward integration)은 원료를 공급하는 기업이 생산기업을 통합하거나, 제품을 생산하는 기업이 유통채널을 가진 기업을 통합하는 것을 말한다. 후방통합(backward integration)은 유통기업이 생산기업을 통합하거나, 생산기업이 원재료 공급기업을 통합하는 것을 말한다.

2) Horizontal integration

수평적 통합은 경쟁력을 강화하거나 또는 경쟁의 정도를 줄이기 위하여 같은 산업내의 기업을 통합하는 것을 말한다.

3) Diversification

다각화 전략이란 기존의 사업과는 다른 새로운 사업 영역에 진출하여 기업의 성장을 꾀하는 방법이다.

(4) Business strategy

마이클 포터(M. Porter)는 경쟁전략(competitive strategy)으로 원가우위전략, 차별화 전략, 집중화 전략을 제시하였다.

1) Cost leadership strategy

원가우위전략은 경쟁기업보다 더 낮은 원가로 재화 또는 서비스를 생산함으로써 경쟁자들을 능가하는 전략이다. 원가 우위를 확보하기 위해서는 대규모의 자본투자로 생산 공정을 자동화하여 인건비를 절감하거나 규모의 경제를 활용하여 원가를 인하한다.

2) Differentiation strategy

차별화 전략은 비싼 가격에도 불구하고 구입을 유도하는 독특한 요인으로 경쟁우위를 확보하려는 전략이다. 브랜드 파워, 혁신적 기술, 마케팅 능력, 기초연구 능력, 관리 능력 등으로 차별화한다.

3) Focus strategy

집중화 전략은 특정 고객, 특정 제품, 특정 지역 등 한정된 영역에 기업 경영자원을 집중하는 전략이다. 이 전략은 세분화된 고객 중 어느 특정 층을 겨냥하여 비용우위나 차별화를 통해 집중적으로 공략한다.

(5) Five competitive forces

마이클 포터(M. Porter)는 기업의 경쟁적 환경 및 경쟁적 우위를 결정하는 요인을 다음과 같이 5가지로 제시하였다.

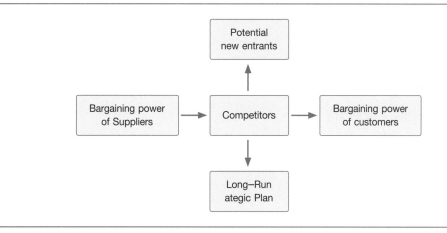

[Figure 10-11]

1) Competition in the industry : 산업 내 경쟁기업과의 경쟁강도

2) Potential of new entrants into the industry : 신규 진입자의 위협

3) Power of suppliers : 공급자와의 교섭력

4) Power of customers : 구매자와의 교섭력

5) Threat of substitute products : 대체제의 위협

05 ⟩ Multiple Choice

01. The local video store's business increased by 12% after the movie theater raised its prices from $6.50 to $7.00. Thus, relative to movie theater admissions, videos are

A. Substitute goods.

B. Superior goods.

C. Complementary goods.

D. Public goods.

02. All of the following are complementary gods except

A. Margarine and butter.

B. Cameras and rolls of film.

C. VCRs and video cassettes.

D. Razors and razor blades.

03. A decrease in the price of a complementary good will

A. Shift the demand curve of the joint commodity to the left.

B. Increase the price paid for a substitute good.

C. Shift the supply curve of the joint commodity to the left.

D. Shift the demand curve of the joint commodity to the right.

04. The movement along the demand curve from one price-quantity combination to another is called a(n)

A. Change in demand.

B. Shift in the demand curve.

C. Change in the quantity demanded.

D. Increase in demand.

05. If a group of consumers decide to boycott a particular product, the expected result would be

   A. An increase in the product price to make up lost revenue.

   B. A decrease in the demand for the product.

   C. An increase in product supply because of increased availability.

   D. That demand for the product would become completely inelastic.

06. In a competitive market for labor in which demand is stable, if workers try to increase their wage,

   A. Employment must fall.

   B. Government bust set a maximum wage blow the equilibrium wage.

   C. Firms in the industry must become smaller.

   D. Product supply must decrease.

07. Price ceilings

   A. Are illustrated by government price support programs in agriculture.

   B. Create prices greater than equilibrium prices.

   C. Create prices below equilibrium prices.

   D. Result in persistent surpluses.

08. The competitive model of supply and demand predicts that a surplus can arise only if there is a

   A. Maximum price above the equilibrium price.

   B. Minimum price below the equilibrium price.

   C. Maximum price below the equilibrium price.

   D. Minimum price above the equilibrium price.

09. In any competitive market, an equal increase in both demand and supply can be expected to always

A. Increase both price and market-clearing quantity.

B. Decrease both price and market-clearing quantity.

C. Increase market-clearing quantity.

D. Increase price.

10. If both the supply and the demand for a good increase, the market price will

A. Rise only in the case of an inelastic supply function.

B. Fall only in the case of an inelastic supply function.

C. Not be predictable with only these facts.

D. Rise only in the case of an inelastic demand function.

Solution

1	2	3	4	5	6	7	8	9	10
A	A	D	C	B	A	C	D	C	C

1. 대체재의 가격 상승 → 원래 재화의 수요 증가
   극장 가격 상승 → 비디오 수요 증가

2. 마가린과 버터는 대체재

3. 보완재의 가격 하락 → 원래 재화의 수요 증가 → 수요곡선 오른쪽 이동

4. ※ 가격 → 수요곡선상의 이동(movement) (changes in quantity demanded)
   ※ 소득, 연관재의 가격 등 → 수요곡선의 이동(shift) (changes in demand)

5. boycott → 재화의 선호도 감소 → 수요의 감소 → 수요곡선 왼쪽 이동

6. 가격(wage)이 상승하면 수요량(employment)은 감소

7. 가격상한제(price ceiling) :
   시장가격 < 가격상한 → 실효성 없음
   시장가격 > 가격상한 → 실효성 있음

8. 가격하한제(price floor)
   시장가격 > 가격하한 → 실효성 없음
   시장가격 < 가격하한 → 공급과잉(surplus)

9. 수요의 증가 & 공급의 증가 → 균형가격 불분명, 균형거래량 증가

10. 수요의 증가 & 공급의 증가 → 균형가격 불분명, 균형거래량 증가

06 Tasked-Based Simulation

Problem-1

Long Lake Golf Course has raised greens fees for a nine-hole game due to an increase in demand.

	Previous Rate	New Rate	Average Games Played at Previous Rate	Average Games Played at New Rate
Regular weekday	$10	$11	80	70
Senior citizen	6	8	159	82
Weekend	15	20	221	223

Required

1. Is the regular weekday and weekend demand inelastic or elastic?
2. Is the senior citizen demand inelastic or elastic?
3. Is the weekend demand inelastic or elastic?

Problem-2

As the price for a particular product changes, the quantity of the product demanded changes according to the following schedule.

Total Quantity Demanded	Price per Unit
100	$50
150	45
200	40
225	35
230	30
232	25

Required

1. Using the arc method, the price elasticity of demand for this product when the price decreases from $50 to $45 is ?

2. Using the simple or point method, the price elasticity of demand for this product when the price decreases from $50 to $45 is ?

Problem-3

The table below presents data about six sets of goods. Each set contains two items: A and B.

Set	Change in Price of A	Change in Quantity Demanded of B
1	+5%	+4%
2	−10%	+5%
3	+8%	−6%
4	−4%	−2%
5	−20%	−15%
6	+18%	−10%

Required

1. Which sets of items demonstrate the greatest substitutability?
2. Which sets of items demonstrate the greatest complementarity?

Problem-4

Consumer income for a given market segment is expected to increase by 4% in the next year. The following are the expected changes in the quantities demanded of certain goods for the same period

Canned soup	-1%
Golf clubs	3%
Sport utility vehicles	2%
Used cars	-2%

Required

What is the income elasticity of demand and classification of the good?

Problem-5

Suppose that business travelers and vacationers have the following demand for airline tickets from New York to Boston:

Price	Quantity Demanded (business travelers)	Quantity Demanded (vacationers)
$150	2,100 tickets	1,000 tickets
200	2,000	800
250	1,900	600
300	1,800	400

Required

1. As the price of tickets rises from $200 to $250, what is the price elasticity of demand for (i) business travelers and (ii) vacationers? (Use the midpoint method in your calculations.)
2. Why might vacationers have a different elasticity from business travelers?

Problem-6

A price change causes the quantity demanded of a good to decrease by 30 percent while the total revenue of that good increases by 15 percent. Is the demand curve elastic or inelastic? Explain.

Problem-7

Cups of coffee and donuts are complements. Both have inelastic demand. A hurricane destroys half the coffee bean crop. Use appropriately labeled diagrams to answer the following questions.

a. What happens to the price of coffee beans?
b. What happens to the price of a cup of coffee? What happens to total expenditure on cups of coffee?
c. What happens to the price of donuts? What happens to total expenditure on donuts?

Problem-8

Suppose that your demand schedule for pizza is as follows:

Price	Quantity Demanded (income = $20,000)	Quantity Demanded (income = $24,000)
$8	40 pizza	50 pizza
10	32	45
12	24	30
14	16	20
16	8	12

Required

1. Use the midpoint method to calculate your price elasticity of demand as the price of pizza increases from $8 to $10 if (i) your income is $20,000 and (ii) your income is $24,000.

2. Calculate your income elasticity of demand as your income increases from $20,000 to $24,000 if (i) the price is $12 and (ii) the price is $16.

Problem-9

The New York Times reported (Feb. 17, 20X2) that subway ridership declined after a fare increase: "There were nearly four million fewer riders in December 20X1, the first full month after the price of a token increased 25 cents to $1.50, than in the previous December, a 4.3 percent decline."

a. Use these data to estimate the price elasticity of demand for subway rides.
b. According to your estimate, what happens to the Transit Authority's revenue when the fare rises?
c. Why might your estimate of the elasticity be unreliable?

Problem-10

Consider public policy aimed at smoking.

a. Studies indicate that the price elasticity of demand for cigarettes is about 0.4. If a pack of cigarettes currently costs $5 and the government wants to reduce smoking by 20 percent, by how much should it increase the price?
b. If the government permanently increases the price of cigarettes, will the policy have a larger effect on smoking 1 year from now or 5 years from now?
c. Studies also find that teenagers have a higher price elasticity of demand than adults. Why might this be true?

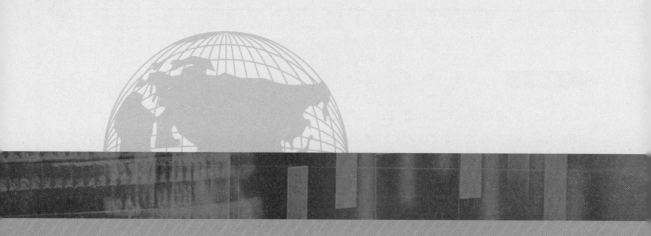

Financial Management For the **US CPA** Exam

Chapter 11

Enterprise Risk Management Frameworks

Volume
8

11 Enterprise Risk Management Frameworks

---

01 ⟩⟩ Introduction to Enterprise Risk Management

---

1 Introduction

(1) COSO

The Committee of Sponsoring Organizations of the Treadway Commission (COSO) is an organization that develops guidelines for businesses to evaluate internal controls, risk management, and fraud deterrence.

Regarding ERM, in 2004, COSO issued Enterprise Risk Management(ERM)— Integrated Framework. This framework was updated with the release in 2017 of "Enterprise Risk Management–Integrating with Strategy and Performance," which highlights the importance of considering risk in both the strategy-setting process and in driving performance.

(2) Risk

The possibility that events will occur and affect the achievement of strategy and business objectives.

(3) Enterprise Risk Management (ERM)

The culture, capabilities, and practices, integrated with strategy-setting and performance, that organizations rely on to manage risk in creating, preserving, and realizing value.

2 The concepts of value

(1) Value is defined by the type of entity

1) For-Profit Commercial Entities

Value is usually shaped by strategies that balance market opportunities against the risks of pursuing those opportunities.

2) Not-for-Profit and Governmental Entities

Value may be shaped by delivering goods and services that balance the opportunity to serve the broader community against any associated risk.

(2) Management decisions

1) Creation

Value is created when benefits of value exceed the cost of resources used. Resources may include people, financial capital, technology, process, and brand.

2) Preservation

Value is preserved when ongoing operations efficiently and effectively sustain created benefits. High customer satisfaction with profitable product lines is evidence of value preservation.

3) Erosion

Value is eroded when faulty strategy and inefficient/ineffective operations cause value to decline.

4) Realization

Value is realized when benefits created by the organization are received by stakeholders in either monetary or non monetary form.

(3) ERM

Organizations encounter risks of falling to provide or optimize value to stakeholders. ERM provides a framework to manage risks to provide a reasonable expectation of achieving value objectives.

3 Enterprise Risk Management and Strategy

(1) Mission, Vision and Core Values

ERM recognizes that attitudes toward risk shape the development of mission, vision, and core values.

1) Mission

represents the core purpose of the entity, including why it exists and what it hopes to accomplish.

2) Vision

represents the aspirations of the entity and what it hopes to achieve over time.

3) Core values

represent an organization's beliefs and ideals about what is good or bad, and acceptable or unacceptable; they influence the behavior of the organization.

(2) Culture, Capabilities, and Practices

1) Culture

Culture represents the collective thinking of the people within an organization. Individuals have unique points of reference that influence how they identify, assess, and respond to risk. Core values correlate with culture.

2) Capabilities

Understanding that managing risk is associated with a company's willingness and capability to navigate change and respond strategically gives an entity a competitive advantage. Competitive advantage produces value for an entity.

3) Practices

A company's practices include the methods and approaches deployed within an entity to manage risk. ERM is an organizational practice continually applied to the entire scope of activities of the business. It is part of management decisions at all levels of the entity.

(3) Integration With Strategy–Setting and Performance

Strategy is set in a manner that aligns with mission and vision. Business objectives flow from strategy. Business objectives drive the activities of all business units and functions. ERM integrates with strategy-setting and operating activities to promote an understanding of how risk potentially affects the entity overall and promote decision making consistent with risk attitudes. Mission and vision correlate with strategy and business objectives.

(4) Managing Risk Linked to Value

1) Risk Appetite

Risk appetite represents the types and amounts of risk, on a broad level, that an organization is willing to accept in pursuit of value. Risk appetite is a range rather than a specific limit and provides guidance on the practices an organization is encouraged to pursue or not pursue.

Risk appetite is expressed first in mission and vision.

Risk appetite varies between products, business units, or over time in line with changing capabilities for managing risk and must be flexible enough to adapt to changing business conditions.

2) Relationship of Value and Risk Appetite

Managing risk within risk appetite enhances an organization's ability to create, preserve, and realize value. ERM seeks to align anticipated value creation with risk appetite and capabilities for managing risk over time.

02 》 ERM Framework

1 Enterprise Risk Management

1) Mission, vision & core values

2) Strategy development

3) Business objective formulation

4) Implementation and performance

5) Enhanced value

2 Five interrelated components

(1) Governance and Culture

Governance sets the organization's tone, reinforcing the importance of, and establishing oversight responsibilities for, enterprise risk management. Culture pertains to ethical values, desired behaviors, and understanding of risk in the entity.

(2) Strategy and Objective

Setting: Enterprise risk management, strategy, and objective-setting work together in the strategic-planning process. A risk appetite is established and aligned with strategy; business objectives put strategy into practice while serving as a basis for identifying, assessing, and responding to risk.

(3) Performance

Risks that may impact the achievement of strategy and business objectives need to be identified and assessed. Risks are prioritized by severity in the context of risk appetite. The organization then selects risk responses and takes a portfolio view of the amount of risk it has assumed. The results of this process are reported to key risk stakeholders.

(4) Review and Revision

By reviewing entity performance, an organization can consider how well the enterprise risk management components are functioning over time and in light of substantial changes, and what revisions are needed.

(5) Information, Communication, and Reporting

Enterprise risk management requires a continual process of obtaining and sharing necessary information, from both internal and external sources, which flows up, down, and across the organization.

3 A set of principles

1) Exercises Board Risk Oversight

The board of directors provides oversight of the strategy and carries out governance responsibilities to support management in achieving strategy and business objectives.

2) Establishes Operating Structures

The organization establishes operating structures in the pursuit of strategy and business objectives.

3) Defines Desired Culture

The organization defines the desired behaviors that characterize the entity's desired culture.

4) Demonstrates Commitment to Core Values

The organization demonstrates a commitment to the entity's core values.

5) Attracts, Develops, and Retains Capable Individuals

The organization is committed to building human capital in alignment with the strategy and business objectives.

6) Analyzes Business Context

The organization considers potential effects of business context on risk profile.

7) Defines Risk Appetite

The organization defines risk appetite in the context of creating, preserving, and realizing value.

8) Evaluates Alternative Strategies

The organization evaluates alternative strategies and potential impact on risk profile.

9) Formulates Business Objectives

The organization considers risk while establishing the business objectives at various levels that align and support strategy.

10) Identifies Risk

The organization identifies risk that impacts the performance of strategy and business objectives.

11) Assesses Severity of Risk

The organization assesses the severity of risk.

12) Prioritizes Risks

The organization prioritizes risks as a basis for selecting responses to risks.

13) Implements Risk Responses

The organization identifies and selects risk responses.

14) Develops Portfolio View

The organization develops and evaluates a portfolio view of risk.

15) Assesses Substantial Change

The organization identifies and assesses changes that may substantially affect strategy and business objectives.

16) Reviews Risk and Performance

The organization reviews entity performance and considers risk.

17) Pursues Improvement in Enterprise Risk Management

The organization pursues improvement of enterprise risk management.

18) Leverages Information Systems

The organization leverages the entity's information and technology systems to support enterprise risk management.

19) Communicates Risk Information

The organization uses communication channels to support enterprise risk management.

20) Reports on Risk, Culture, and Performance

The organization reports on risk, culture, and performance at multiple levels and across the entity.

Governance and Culture	1. Exercises Board Risk Oversight 2. Establishes Operating Structures 3. Defines Desired Culture 4. Demonstrates Commitment to Core Values 5. Attracts, Develops, and Retains Capable Individual
Strategy and Objective	6. Analyzes Business Context 7. Defines Risk Appetite 8. Evaluates Alternative Strategies 9. Formulates Business Objectives
Performance	10. Identifies Risk 11. Assesses Severity of Risk 12. Prioritizes Risks 13. Implements Risk Responses 14. Develops Portfolio View
Review & Revision	15. Assesses Substantial Change 16. Reviews Risk and Performance 17. Pursues Improvement in Enterprise Risk Management
Information, Communication, & Reporting	18. Leverages Information and Technology 19. Communicates Risk Information 20. Reports on Risk, Culture, and Performance

4 Implements Risk Responses

1) Accept

No action is taken to change the severity of the risk. Acceptance is most appropriate as a risk response when risk to strategy and business objectives is within the entity's risk appetite.

2) Avoid

Action is taken to remove the risk (leaving a line of business, etc.). Avoidance is appropriate when an entity cannot devise a risk response that will mitigate the risk to objectives.

3) Pursue

Action is taken that accepts increased risk to achieve improved performance. Pursuit of risk is appropriate when management understands the nature and extent of any changes required to achieve desired performance while not exceeding the boundaries of acceptable tolerance.

4) Reduce

Action is taken to reduce the severity of the risk. Management designs risk mitigation techniques to reduce risk to an amount of severity aligned with the target risk profile and risk appetite.

5) Share

Action is taken to reduce the severity of the risk. Sharing risk with such techniques as outsourcing and insurance lower residual risk in alignment with risk appetite.

03 ❯❯ Application of ERM to ESG Risks

1 ESG-Related Risks

(1) Environmental Issues

Include broad aggregate matters such as pollution, deforestation, and climate change. ESG values include positive efforts contributing to environmental protection.

(2) Social Issues

Include such legal and social matters as occupational health and safety, customer relations, employee relations, and human rights. ESG values include positive efforts contributing to socially responsible behavior and outcomes.

(3) Governance Issues

Include proactive board membership and succession planning, promoting fair compensation, promoting diversity and inclusion, establishing strong data security, preventing bribery and fraud, preventing culturally and politically insensitive remarks, and preventing discrimination. ESG values include positive efforts within an entity's governance to produce sustainable outcomes.

2 Application of ERM to ESG-Related Risks

(1) Governance and Culture for ESG-Related Risks

This component of the ERM framework focuses on the oversight and culture of an entity and how that is applied to the entity's approach to risk management. For ESG-related risks, it is important that management is aware and understands applicable ESG-related risks.

(2) Strategy and Objective-Setting for ESG-Related Risks

When applying to ESG-related risks, management must consider the impact of the strategy and business objectives on nature and society and ensure that these impacts are considered in the short, medium, and long term. An entity must build

upon the foundational knowledge discussed in the previous component and begin to gain a deeper understanding of the potential impacts through an analysis of existing and emerging ESG-related risks.

(3) Performance for ESG-Related Risks

1) Identification

Entities may use many different approaches for identifying ESG-related risks, including megatrend analysis, SWOT analysis, impacts and dependency mapping, and stakeholder engagement. A stakeholder workshop may include discussions in which risk events are identified, likelihood and impact of events are reviewed, root causes of the event are identified, and prevention and detection approaches are evaluated for potential effectiveness. Ensuring collaboration between risk management and sustainability practitioners is key to the proper identification of ESG-related risks.

2) Assessment and Prioritization

It is necessary to appropriately assess and prioritize risks to ensure that the entity's response is appropriate given the nature and severity of the risk. Leveraging ESG expertise is important to ensure that risk severity is appropriately assessed and communicated to management in a way that they understand.

3) Response

Responding to identified risks is critical to an effective ERM framework. An entity considers the source of the risk, the cost and benefit of responses, and the overall risk appetite. A thorough understanding of the short-, medium-, and long-term impacts of ESG related risks is important to ensure an appropriate response.

(4) Review and Revision for ESG-Related Risks

Ongoing review and revision of the risk management approaches are an important component of ensuring that the approaches remain effective. For ESG-related risks, entities must continuously assess internal and external changes to ensure risks are appropriately identified and prioritized and seek improvements to ESG-related risk responses.

(5) Information, Communication, and Reporting for ESG-Related Risks

The key objective of the ERM framework related to effective communication and reporting is that management and other stakeholders remain informed of risks so they are able to make informed decisions. Reporting may be to internal or external stakeholders and may be mandatory or voluntary. Because ESG issues can be complex, it is critical that data reported is accurate.

Financial Management For the **US CPA** Exam

부록

- 현가표(Present Value Interest Factor : PVIF)

- 연금의 현가표(Present Value of Interest Factor for Annuity : PVIFA)

- 종가표(Future Value of Interest Factor : FVIF)

- 연금의 종가표(Future Value of Interest Factor for Annuity : FVIFA)

1 현가표(Present Value Interest Factor : PVIF)

$$PVIF = \frac{1}{(1+i)^n} \ (n=기간, \ i=기간당 \ 할인율)$$

n/i	1.0	2.0	3.0	4.0	5.0	6.0	7.0	8.0	9.0	10.0
1	0.99010	0.98039	0.97087	0.96154	0.95238	0.94340	0.93458	0.92593	0.91743	0.90909
2	0.98030	0.96117	0.94260	0.92456	0.90703	0.89000	0.87344	0.85734	0.84168	0.82645
3	0.97059	0.94232	0.91514	0.88900	0.86384	0.83962	0.81630	0.79383	0.77218	0.75131
4	0.96098	0.92385	0.88849	0.85480	0.82270	0.79209	0.76290	0.73503	0.70843	0.68301
5	0.95147	0.90573	0.86261	0.82193	0.78353	0.74726	0.71299	0.68058	0.64993	0.62092
6	0.94205	0.88797	0.83748	0.79031	0.74622	0.70496	0.66634	0.63017	0.59627	0.56447
7	0.93272	0.87056	0.81309	0.75992	0.71068	0.66506	0.62275	0.58349	0.54703	0.51316
8	0.92348	0.85349	0.78941	0.73069	0.67684	0.62741	0.58201	0.54027	0.50187	0.46651
9	0.91434	0.83676	0.76642	0.70259	0.64461	0.59190	0.54393	0.50025	0.46043	0.42410
10	0.90529	0.82035	0.74409	0.67556	0.61391	0.55839	0.50835	0.46319	0.42241	0.38554
11	0.89632	0.80426	0.72242	0.64958	0.58468	0.52679	0.47509	0.42888	0.38753	0.35049
12	0.88745	0.78849	0.70138	0.62460	0.55684	0.49697	0.44401	0.39711	0.35553	0.31863
13	0.87866	0.77303	0.68095	0.60057	0.53032	0.46884	0.41496	0.36770	0.32618	0.28966
14	0.86996	0.75788	0.66112	0.57748	0.50507	0.44230	0.38782	0.34046	0.29925	0.26333
15	0.86135	0.74301	0.64186	0.55526	0.48102	0.41727	0.36245	0.31524	0.27454	0.23939
16	0.85282	0.72845	0.62317	0.53391	0.45811	0.39365	0.33873	0.29189	0.25187	0.21763
17	0.84438	0.71416	0.60502	0.51337	0.43630	0.37136	0.31657	0.27027	0.23107	0.19784
18	0.83602	0.70016	0.58739	0.49363	0.41552	0.35034	0.29586	0.25025	0.21199	0.17986
19	0.82774	0.68643	0.57029	0.47464	0.39573	0.33051	0.27651	0.23171	0.19449	0.16351
20	0.81954	0.67297	0.55368	0.45639	0.37689	0.31180	0.25842	0.21455	0.17843	0.14864

n/i	11.0	12.0	13.0	14.0	15.0	16.0	17.0	18.0	19.0	20.0
1	0.90090	0.89286	0.88496	0.87719	0.86957	0.86207	0.85470	0.84746	0.84034	0.83333
2	0.81162	0.79719	0.78315	0.76947	0.75614	0.74316	0.73051	0.71818	0.70616	0.69444
3	0.73119	0.71178	0.69305	0.67497	0.65752	0.64066	0.62437	0.60863	0.59342	0.57870
4	0.65873	0.63552	0.61332	0.59208	0.57175	0.55229	0.53365	0.51579	0.49867	0.48225
5	0.59345	0.56743	0.54276	0.51937	0.49718	0.47611	0.45611	0.43711	0.41905	0.40188
6	0.53464	0.50663	0.48032	0.45559	0.43233	0.41044	0.38984	0.37043	0.35214	0.33490
7	0.48166	0.45235	0.42506	0.39964	0.37594	0.35383	0.33320	0.31393	0.29592	0.27908
8	0.43393	0.40388	0.37616	0.35056	0.32690	0.30503	0.28478	0.26604	0.24867	0.23257
9	0.39092	0.36061	0.33288	0.30751	0.28426	0.26295	0.24340	0.22546	0.20897	0.19381
10	0.35218	0.32197	0.29459	0.26974	0.24718	0.22668	0.20804	0.19106	0.17560	0.16151
11	0.31728	0.28748	0.26070	0.23662	0.21494	0.19542	0.17781	0.16192	0.14757	0.13459
12	0.28584	0.25668	0.23071	0.20756	0.18691	0.16846	0.15197	0.13722	0.12400	0.11216
13	0.25751	0.22917	0.20416	0.18207	0.16253	0.14523	0.12989	0.11629	0.10421	0.09346
14	0.23199	0.20462	0.18068	0.15971	0.14133	0.12520	0.11102	0.09855	0.08757	0.07789
15	0.20900	0.18270	0.15989	0.14010	0.12289	0.10793	0.09489	0.08352	0.07359	0.06491
16	0.18829	0.16312	0.14150	0.12289	0.10686	0.09304	0.08110	0.07078	0.06184	0.05409
17	0.16963	0.14564	0.12522	0.10780	0.09293	0.08021	0.06932	0.05998	0.05196	0.04507
18	0.15282	0.13004	0.11081	0.09456	0.08081	0.06914	0.05925	0.05083	0.04367	0.03756
19	0.13768	0.11611	0.09806	0.08295	0.07027	0.05961	0.05064	0.04308	0.03670	0.03130
20	0.12403	0.10367	0.08678	0.07276	0.06110	0.05139	0.04328	0.03651	0.03084	0.02608

2 연금의 현가표(Present Value of Interest Factor for Annuity : PVIFA)

$$PVIFA = \frac{1 - \dfrac{1}{(1+i)^n}}{i}$$

n/i	1.0	2.0	3.0	4.0	5.0	6.0	7.0	8.0	9.0	10.0
1	0.99010	0.98039	0.97087	0.96154	0.95238	0.94340	0.93458	0.92593	0.91743	0.90909
2	1.97039	1.94156	1.91347	1.88609	1.85941	1.83339	1.80802	1.78326	1.75911	1.73554
3	2.94098	2.88388	2.82861	2.77509	2.72325	2.67301	2.62432	2.57710	2.53129	2.48685
4	3.90197	3.80773	3.71710	3.62990	3.54595	3.46511	3.38721	3.31213	3.23972	3.16987
5	4.85343	4.71346	4.57971	4.45182	4.32948	4.21236	4.10020	3.99271	3.88965	3.79079
6	5.79548	5.60143	5.41719	5.24214	5.07569	4.91732	4.76654	4.62288	4.48592	4.35526
7	6.72819	6.47199	6.23028	6.00206	5.78637	5.58238	5.38929	5.20637	5.03295	4.86842
8	7.65168	7.32548	7.01969	6.73275	6.46321	6.20979	5.97130	5.74664	5.53482	5.33493
9	8.56602	8.16224	7.78611	7.43533	7.10782	6.80169	6.51523	6.24689	5.99525	5.75902
10	9.47130	8.98259	8.53020	8.11090	7.72174	7.36009	7.02358	6.71008	6.41766	6.14457
11	10.36763	9.78685	9.25262	8.76048	8.30642	7.88687	7.49867	7.13896	6.80519	6.49506
12	11.25508	10.57534	9.95400	9.38507	8.86325	8.38384	7.94269	7.53608	7.16073	6.81369
13	12.13374	11.34837	10.63495	9.98565	9.39357	8.85268	8.35765	7.90378	7.48690	7.10336
14	13.00370	12.10625	11.29607	10.56312	9.89864	9.29498	8.74547	8.24424	7.78615	7.36669
15	13.86505	12.84926	11.93793	11.11839	10.37966	9.71225	9.10791	8.55948	8.06069	7.60608
16	14.71787	13.57771	12.56110	11.65230	10.83777	10.10590	9.44665	8.85137	8.31256	7.82371
17	15.56225	14.29187	13.16612	12.16567	11.27407	10.47726	9.76322	9.12164	8.54363	8.02155
18	16.39827	14.99203	13.75351	12.65930	11.68959	10.82760	10.05909	9.37189	8.75563	8.20141
19	17.22601	15.67846	14.32380	13.13394	12.08532	11.15812	10.33560	9.60360	8.95011	8.36492
20	18.04555	16.35143	14.87747	13.59033	12.46221	11.46992	10.59401	9.81815	9.12855	8.51356

n/i	11.0	12.0	13.0	14.0	15.0	16.0	17.0	18.0	19.0	20.0
1	0.90090	0.89286	0.88496	0.87719	0.86957	0.86207	0.85470	0.84746	0.84034	0.83333
2	1.71252	1.69005	1.66810	1.64666	1.62571	1.60523	1.58521	1.56564	1.54650	1.52778
3	2.44371	2.40183	2.36115	2.32163	2.28323	2.24589	2.20959	2.17427	2.13992	2.10648
4	3.10245	3.03735	2.97447	2.91371	2.85498	2.79818	2.74324	2.69006	2.63859	2.58873
5	3.69590	3.60478	3.51723	3.43308	3.35216	3.27429	3.19935	3.12717	3.05764	2.99061
6	4.23054	4.11141	3.99755	3.88867	3.78448	3.68474	3.58918	3.49760	3.40978	3.32551
7	4.71220	4.56376	4.42261	4.28830	4.16042	4.03857	3.92238	3.81153	3.70570	3.60459
8	5.14612	4.96764	4.79877	4.63886	4.48732	4.34359	4.20716	4.07757	3.95437	3.83716
9	5.53705	5.32825	5.13166	4.94637	4.77158	4.60654	4.45057	4.30302	4.16333	4.03097
10	5.88923	5.65022	5.42624	5.21612	5.01877	4.83323	4.65860	4.49409	4.33894	4.19247
11	6.20652	5.93770	5.68694	5.45273	5.23371	5.02864	4.83641	4.65601	4.48650	4.32706
12	6.49236	6.19437	5.91765	5.66029	5.42062	5.19711	4.98839	4.79323	4.61050	4.43922
13	6.74987	6.42355	6.12181	5.84236	5.58315	5.34233	5.11828	4.90951	4.71471	4.53268
14	6.98187	6.62817	6.30249	6.00207	5.72448	5.46753	5.22930	5.00806	4.80228	4.61057
15	7.19087	6.81086	6.46238	6.14217	5.84737	5.57546	5.32419	5.09158	4.87586	4.67547
16	7.37916	6.97399	6.60388	6.26506	5.95424	5.66850	5.40529	5.16235	4.93770	4.72956
17	7.54879	7.11963	6.72909	6.37286	6.04716	5.74870	5.47461	5.22233	4.98966	4.77463
18	7.70162	7.24967	6.83991	6.46742	6.12797	5.81785	5.53385	5.27316	5.03333	4.81220
19	7.83929	7.36578	6.93797	6.55037	6.19823	5.87746	5.58449	5.31624	5.07003	4.84350
20	7.96333	7.46944	7.02475	6.62313	6.25933	5.92884	5.62777	5.35275	5.10086	4.86958

3 종가표(Future Value of Interest Factor : FVIF)

$$\text{FVIF} = (1+i)^n \ (n=\text{기간}, \ i=\text{기간당 할인율})$$

n/i	1.0	2.0	3.0	4.0	5.0	6.0	7.0	8.0	9.0	10.0
1	1.01000	1.02000	1.03000	1.04000	1.05000	1.06000	1.07000	1.08000	1.09000	1.10000
2	1.02010	1.04040	1.06090	1.08160	1.10250	1.12360	1.14490	1.16640	1.18810	1.21000
3	1.03030	1.06121	1.09273	1.12486	1.15762	1.19102	1.22504	1.25971	1.29503	1.33100
4	1.04060	1.08243	1.12551	1.16986	1.21551	1.26248	1.31080	1.36049	1.41158	1.46410
5	1.05101	1.10408	1.15927	1.21665	1.27628	1.33823	1.40255	1.46933	1.53862	1.61051
6	1.06152	1.12616	1.19405	1.26532	1.34010	1.41852	1.50073	1.58687	1.67710	1.77156
7	1.07214	1.14869	1.22987	1.31593	1.40710	1.50363	1.60578	1.71382	1.82804	1.94872
8	1.08286	1.17166	1.26677	1.36857	1.47746	1.59385	1.71819	1.85093	1.99256	2.14359
9	1.09369	1.19509	1.30477	1.42331	1.55133	1.68948	1.83846	1.99900	2.17189	2.35795
10	1.10462	1.21899	1.34392	1.48024	1.62889	1.79085	1.96715	2.15892	2.36736	2.59374
11	1.11567	1.24337	1.38423	1.53945	1.71034	1.89830	2.10485	2.33164	2.58043	2.85312
12	1.12682	1.26824	1.42576	1.60103	1.79586	2.01220	2.25219	2.51817	2.81266	3.13843
13	1.13809	1.29361	1.46853	1.66507	1.88565	2.13293	2.40984	2.71962	3.06580	3.45227
14	1.14947	1.31948	1.51259	1.73168	1.97993	2.26090	2.57853	2.93719	3.34173	3.79750
15	1.16097	1.34587	1.55797	1.80094	2.07893	2.39656	2.75903	3.17217	3.64248	4.17725
16	1.17258	1.37279	1.60471	1.87298	2.18287	2.54035	2.95216	3.42594	3.97030	4.59497
17	1.18430	1.40024	1.65285	1.94790	2.29202	2.69277	3.15881	3.70002	4.32763	5.05447
18	1.19615	1.42825	1.70243	2.02582	2.40662	2.85434	3.37993	3.99602	4.71712	5.55992
19	1.20811	1.45681	1.75351	2.10685	2.52695	3.02560	3.61653	4.31570	5.14166	6.11591
20	1.22019	1.48595	1.80611	2.19112	2.65330	3.20713	3.86968	4.66096	5.60441	6.72750

n/i	11.0	12.0	13.0	14.0	15.0	16.0	17.0	18.0	19.0	20.0
1	1.11000	1.12000	1.13000	1.14000	1.15000	1.16000	1.17000	1.18000	1.19000	1.20000
2	1.23210	1.25440	1.27690	1.29960	1.32250	1.34560	1.36890	1.39240	1.41610	1.44000
3	1.36763	1.40493	1.44290	1.48154	1.52087	1.56090	1.60161	1.64303	1.68516	1.72800
4	1.51807	1.57352	1.63047	1.68896	1.74901	1.81064	1.87389	1.93878	2.00534	2.07360
5	1.68506	1.76234	1.84244	1.92541	2.01136	2.10034	2.19245	2.28776	2.38635	2.48832
6	1.87041	1.97382	2.08195	2.19497	2.31306	2.43640	2.56516	2.69955	2.83976	2.98598
7	2.07616	2.21068	2.35261	2.50227	2.66002	2.82622	3.00124	3.18547	3.37931	3.58318
8	2.30454	2.47596	2.65844	2.85259	3.05902	3.27841	3.51145	3.75886	4.02138	4.29982
9	2.55804	2.77308	3.00404	3.25195	3.51788	3.80296	4.10840	4.43545	4.78545	5.15978
10	2.83942	3.10585	3.39457	3.70722	4.04556	4.41143	4.80683	5.23383	5.69468	6.19173
11	3.15176	3.47855	3.83586	4.22623	4.65239	5.11726	5.62399	6.17592	6.77667	7.43008
12	3.49845	3.89598	4.33452	4.81790	5.35025	5.93603	6.58007	7.28759	8.06424	8.91610
13	3.88328	4.36349	4.89801	5.49241	6.15279	6.88579	7.69868	8.59936	9.59645	10.69932
14	4.31044	4.88711	5.53475	6.26135	7.07570	7.98752	9.00745	10.14724	11.41977	12.83918
15	4.78459	5.47356	6.25427	7.13794	8.13706	9.26552	10.53872	11.97374	13.58953	15.40701
16	5.31089	6.13039	7.06732	8.13725	9.35762	10.74800	12.33030	14.12902	16.17154	18.48842
17	5.89509	6.86604	7.98608	9.27646	10.76126	12.46768	14.42645	16.67224	19.24413	22.18610
18	6.54355	7.68996	9.02427	10.57517	12.37545	14.46251	16.87895	19.67324	22.90051	26.62332
19	7.26334	8.61276	10.19742	12.05569	14.23177	16.77651	19.74837	23.21443	27.25161	31.94798
20	8.06231	9.64629	11.52309	13.74348	16.36653	19.46075	23.10559	27.39302	32.42941	38.33758

4 연금의 종가표(Future Value of Interest Factor for Annuity : FVIFA)

$$FVIFA = \frac{(1+i)^n - 1}{i}$$

n/i	1.0	2.0	3.0	4.0	5.0	6.0	7.0	8.0	9.0	10.0
1	1.00000	1.00000	1.00000	1.00000	1.00000	1.00000	1.00000	1.00000	1.00000	1.00000
2	2.01000	2.02000	2.03000	2.04000	2.04500	2.06000	2.07000	2.08000	2.09000	2.10000
3	3.03010	3.06040	3.09090	3.12160	3.13702	3.18360	3.21490	3.24640	3.27810	3.31000
4	4.06040	4.12161	4.18363	4.24646	4.27819	4.37462	4.43994	4.50611	4.57313	4.64100
5	5.10100	5.20404	5.30914	5.41632	5.47071	5.63709	5.75074	5.86660	5.98471	6.10510
6	6.15201	6.30812	6.46841	6.63298	6.71689	6.97532	7.15329	7.33593	7.52333	7.71561
7	7.21353	7.43428	7.66246	7.89829	8.01915	8.39384	8.65402	8.92280	9.20043	9.48717
8	8.28567	8.58297	8.89234	9.21423	9.38001	9.89747	10.25980	10.63663	11.02847	11.43589
9	9.36853	9.75463	10.15911	10.58279	10.80211	11.49132	11.97799	12.48756	13.02104	13.57948
10	10.46221	10.94972	11.46388	12.00611	12.28821	13.18079	13.81645	14.48656	15.19293	15.93742
11	11.56683	12.16871	12.80779	13.48635	13.84118	14.97164	15.78360	16.64549	17.56029	18.53117
12	12.68250	13.41209	14.19203	15.02580	15.46403	16.86994	17.88845	18.97713	20.14072	21.38428
13	13.80933	14.68033	15.61779	16.62684	17.15991	18.88214	20.14064	21.49530	22.95338	24.52271
14	14.94742	15.97394	17.08632	18.29191	18.93211	21.01506	22.55049	24.21492	26.01919	27.97498
15	16.09689	17.29342	18.59891	20.02359	20.78405	23.27597	25.12902	27.15211	29.36091	31.77248
16	17.25786	18.63928	20.15688	21.82453	22.71933	25.67252	27.88805	30.32428	33.00339	35.94973
17	18.43044	20.01207	21.76158	23.69751	24.74170	28.21287	30.84021	33.75022	36.97370	40.54470
18	19.61474	21.41231	23.41443	25.64541	26.85508	30.90565	33.99903	37.45024	41.30133	45.59917
19	20.81089	22.84056	25.11686	27.67123	29.06356	33.75998	37.37896	41.44626	46.01845	51.15908
20	22.01900	24.29737	26.87037	29.77807	31.37142	36.78558	40.99549	45.76196	51.16011	57.27499

n/i	11.0	12.0	13.0	14.0	15.0	16.0	17.0	18.0	19.0	20.0
1	1.00000	1.00000	1.00000	1.00000	1.00000	1.00000	1.00000	1.00000	1.00000	1.00000
2	2.11000	2.12000	2.13000	2.14000	2.15000	2.16000	2.17000	2.18000	2.19000	2.20000
3	3.34210	3.37440	3.40690	3.43960	3.47250	3.50560	3.53890	3.57240	3.60610	3.64000
4	4.70973	4.77933	4.84980	4.92114	4.99337	5.06650	5.14051	5.21543	5.29126	5.36800
5	6.22780	6.35285	6.48027	6.61010	6.74238	6.87714	7.01440	7.15421	7.29660	7.44160
6	7.91286	8.11519	8.32271	8.53552	8.75374	8.97748	9.20685	9.44197	9.68295	9.92992
7	9.78327	10.08901	10.40466	10.73049	11.06680	11.41387	11.77201	12.14152	12.52271	12.91590
8	11.85943	12.29969	12.75726	13.23276	13.72682	14.24009	14.77325	15.32699	15.90203	16.49908
9	14.16397	14.77566	15.41571	16.08535	16.78584	17.51851	18.28471	19.08585	19.92341	20.79890
10	16.72201	17.54873	18.41975	19.33729	20.30372	21.32147	22.39311	23.52131	24.70886	25.95868
11	19.56143	20.65458	21.81432	23.04451	24.34927	25.73290	27.19993	28.75514	30.40354	32.15041
12	22.71318	24.13313	25.65018	27.27074	29.00166	30.85016	32.82392	34.93106	37.18021	39.58049
13	26.21163	28.02911	29.98470	32.08865	34.35191	36.78619	39.40399	42.21865	45.24445	48.49659
14	30.09491	32.39260	34.88271	37.58106	40.50470	43.67198	47.10266	50.81801	54.84090	59.19591
15	34.40535	37.27971	40.41746	43.84241	47.58041	51.65949	56.11012	60.96525	66.26067	72.03509
16	39.18994	42.75327	46.67173	50.98034	55.71747	60.92501	66.64883	72.93899	79.85019	87.44210
17	44.50083	48.88367	53.73906	59.11759	65.07508	71.67301	78.97913	87.06801	96.02173	105.93052
18	50.39592	55.74971	61.72513	68.39405	75.83635	84.14069	93.40559	103.74025	115.26585	128.11662
19	56.93947	63.43967	70.74940	78.96922	88.21180	98.60320	110.28453	123.41349	138.16636	154.73994
20	64.20282	72.05243	80.94682	91.02491	102.44357	115.37971	130.03290	146.62792	165.41797	186.68792

8th
Financial
Management

2023년 11월 01일 8판 1쇄 발행

저 자 | 김용석
편집·디자인 | 유진강(아르케 디자인)
인쇄·제본 | 천광 인쇄

펴낸이 | 김용석
펴낸곳 | (주) 이러닝코리아
출판등록 | 제 2016-000021
주 소 | 서울시 금천구 가산동 60-5번지 갑을그레이트밸리 A동 503호
전 화 | 02)2106-8992
팩 스 | 02)2106-8990

ISBN 979-11-89168-32-2 93320